UNTIMELY AFFECTS
Gilles Deleuze and an Ethics of Cinema

Nadine Boljkovac

EDINBURGH
University Press

© Nadine Boljkovac, 2013, 2015

Edinburgh University Press Ltd
The Tun – Holyrood Road
12 (2f) Jackson's Entry
Edinburgh EH8 8PJ

www.euppublishing.com

First published in hardback by Edinburgh University Press 2013

This paperback edition 2015

Typeset in Sabon by
Servis Filmsetting Ltd, Stockport, Cheshire,
and printed and bound in Great Britain by
CPI Group (UK) Ltd, Croydon CR0 4YY

A CIP record for this book is available from the British Library

ISBN 978 0 7486 4644 9 (hardback)
ISBN 978 1 4744 0474 4 (paperback)
ISBN 978 0 7486 6970 7 (webready PDF)
ISBN 978 0 7486 8360 4 (epub)

The right of Nadine Boljkovac
to be identified as author of this work
has been asserted in accordance with the
Copyright, Designs and Patents Act 1988,
and the Copyright and Related Rights
Regulations 2003 (SI No. 2498).

Contents

Acknowledgements

I would like to thank the publishers for permission to reprint material from the following articles and chapters:

'From depths and ashes, love's eternal return' in *Open Letter: A Canadian Journal of Writing and Theory*, Fourteenth Series, Number 6, 'Remembering Barbara Godard', ed. Ray Ellenwood, Jennifer Henderson, Eva Karpinski and Ian Sowton (July 2011): 144–61. With *Open Letter*'s kind permission.

'Mad Love' in *Gilles Deleuze: Image and Text*, ed. Eugene W. Holland, Daniel W. Smith and Charles J. Stivale (London: Continuum, 2009), 124–42. By kind permission of Bloomsbury Publishing Plc.

'Signs without name' in *Deleuze Studies*, Volume 5, Number 2, *Schizoanalysis and Visual Culture*, ed. Phillip Roberts and Richard Rushton (July 2011), 209–40. Reprinted with the kind permission of Edinburgh University Press.

'Intimacy and Prophecy: Marker and Resnais's Memories' in *Anamnesia: Private and Public Memory in Modern French Culture*, ed. Peter Collier, Anna Magdalena Elsner and Olga Smith (Oxford: Peter Lang, 2009), 257–69. Reproduced with the kind permission of Peter Lang Ltd.

❧

I remain grateful to Edinburgh University Press, and particularly to Philosophy Commissioning Editor, Carol Macdonald, truly the loveliest and most thoughtful editor with whom one could work. I also thank Naomi Farmer for the pleasure of working with her, and James Dale for his assistance.

Acknowledgements

I thank Emma Wilson for enabling this project in the first instance as my PhD Supervisor at the University of Cambridge. Emma, I will be forever grateful. With gratitude always for years of mentorship and inspiration, I deeply thank Tom Conley (Harvard University) and James Williams (University of Dundee). I also thank Ian James (University of Cambridge) and Janine Marchessault (York University Canada).

With this paperback re-release of *Untimely Affects: Gilles Deleuze and an Ethics of Cinema*, I reaffirm my gratitude to those acknowledged in the hardcover edition of 2013, including many mentors, colleagues and students with whom I worked at the University of Cambridge (Department of French, Faculty of Modern and Medieval Languages); Brown University (Pembroke Center for Teaching and Research on Women and the members of the 2012–13 'Economies of Perception' Seminar, and my wonderful students of 'Sensing Time: Affect and the Moving Image' in the Department of Modern Culture and Media, and Pembroke Center); University of Edinburgh (Institute for Advanced Studies in the Humanities); University of Aberdeen (School of Language and Literature); York University Canada (Graduate Program of Film; Graduate Program in Social and Political Thought); and University of Toronto (Cinema Studies Program; Department of English). I warmly thank the Centre for Modernism Studies in Australia at the University of New South Wales, especially Julian Murphet, Sean Pryor, Tom Apperley, Angelos Koutsourakis, Mark Steven, Sigi Jöttkandt.

And I extend special thanks to Adrian Martin, Alina Cherry, Amber Musser, Anna Hickey-Moody, Anne Bottomley, Brad Evans, Charlie Blake, Charles Stivale, Christopher Fynsk, Colin Gardner, Craig Lundy, Dana Gooley, Daniel Potter, Dan Smith, David Martin-Jones, Debbie Spikins, Dennis Rothermel, Donna Goodnow, Ed Keller, Eleanor Kaufman, Eric Cazdyn, Faith Wilding, Felicity Colman, Fiona McCahey, Frederick Young, Gavin Keeney, Hanjo Berressem, Helen J. Bullard, Joe Hughes, Jussi Parikka, Kass Banning, Lennard Davis, Levi Bryant, Leyla Haferkamp, Livia Monnet, Loreta Gandolfi, Malini Guha, Melanie Doherty, Meredith Bak, Michael Zryd, Nathan Moore, Nicholas Rombes, Nigel Rothfels, Nikolaj Lübecker, Pauline Phemister, Philip Hoffman, Rachel White, Robin Curtis, Ronald Bogue, Ron Broglio, Sandra Danilovic, Scott Forsyth, Sha Xin Wei, Siobhán Carew, Susan McHugh, Suzie Young – and

ACKNOWLEDGEMENTS

all friends from Cambridge, Aberdeen, Edinburgh, Providence, Paris, Toronto, Sydney, and places in between.

In memory and with gratitude always, Barbara Godard, and Susan Manning.

Many thanks as ever to Ian Buchanan and Claire Colebrook, Co-Series Editors of the Plateaus – New Directions in Deleuze Studies Series.

Finally, I thank family members who have most supported me. I thank my big brother, and little nephews for the joy of being their aunt, and my grandmother, Rose, in memory and with love.

For my parents.

Abbreviations

Abbreviations used throughout the text correspond with the key below that refers to English versions, if available, of Marker and Resnais's respective films, and English editions of Deleuze and Deleuze and Guattari's texts. Please consult the References for distribution and French and English publication details.

Works by Chris Marker

LJ   *La Jetée* (1962)
SS   *Sans Soleil* (1983)
LSA   *Le Souvenir d'un Avenir* (2001, with Yannick Bellon)
CP   *Chats Perchés* (2004)

Works by Alain Resnais

NB   *Nuit et Brouillard* (1955)
HMA   *Hiroshima mon amour* (1959)

Works by Gilles Deleuze

B   *Bergsonism* (1991)
C2   *Cinema 2: The Time-Image* (1989)
D   *Dialogues II* (2002, with Claire Parnet)
DI   *Desert Islands and Other Texts 1953–1974* (2004)
DR   *Difference and Repetition* (1994)
ECC   *Essays Critical and Clinical* (1997)
EPS   *Expressionism in Philosophy: Spinoza* (1990)
FB   *Francis Bacon: The Logic of Sensation* (2003)
FLB   *The Fold: Leibniz and the Baroque* (1993)
K   *Kafka: Toward a Minor Literature* (1986)
LS   *Logic of Sense* (1990)
N   *Negotiations 1972–1990* (1995)
NP   *Nietzsche and Philosophy* (1983)

PS   *Proust and Signs* (2000)
PI   *Pure Immanence: Essays on A Life* (2001)
SPP   *Spinoza: Practical Philosophy* (1988)
TR   *Two Regimes of Madness: Texts and Interviews 1975–1995*
      (2006)

Works by Gilles Deleuze and Félix Guattari

AO   *Anti-Oedipus* (1983)
ATP   *A Thousand Plateaus* (1987)
WIP   *What is Philosophy?* (1994)

Images

Love always Mom
In memory Dad

and immemory

Chris Marker (29 July 1921 – 29 July 2012)
and
Alain Resnais (3 June 1922 – 1 March 2014)

A more modest and perhaps more fruitful approach would be to consider the fragments of memory in terms of geography. In every life, we would find continents, islands, deserts, swamps, overpopulated territories and terrae incognitae. From this memory we can draw the map, extract images with more ease (and truth) than do stories and legends. That the subject of this memory is found to be a photographer or a filmmaker does not imply that his memory is more interesting than that of any passing gentleman (or moreover, than that of the lady), but simply that he has left traces with which one can work, and contours to help draw up the map.

Chris Marker, Selected notes from the CD-ROM booklet,
Immemory, Éditions du Centre Pompidou, 1998

Introduction

> To think is to reach a non-stratified material, somewhere between the layers, in the interstices. Thinking has an essential relation to history, but it is no more historical than it is eternal. It is closer to what Nietzsche calls the Untimely: to think the past *against* the present – which would be nothing more than a common place, pure nostalgia, some kind of return, if he did not immediately add: '*in favor*, I hope, of a time to come'. (TR: 241)

To identify and defend the argument, strategies and contributions of this film-philosophy study, which emerge against the proliferating field of 'Deleuze studies' and the works of French film artists Chris Marker and Alain Resnais, it is crucial to first consider the actual events that gave rise to this book's selection of films and writings. This book's impetus derives from its cine-philosophical interrogations of war, suffering, affliction and, significantly, humanity's complicity and shame in these means of its own ruin from which it must yet become and survive. These actual experiences that History has identified, compartmentalised and assessed – the Holocaust, Hiroshima, the peril and prognostics of nuclear devastation, further injustices of fascism, colonialism and capitalism – compel this exploration of a select number of Marker and Resnais films in relation to Gilles Deleuze's writings, interviews and lectures.

Always in conjunction with these actual real expressions of events, this book simultaneously strives to experience the virtual real events, *intensities, sensations, affects* and *becomings* that coexist alongside the actual. This book attempts, that is, to engage with the dual actual and virtual, tangible and intangible depth and surface, expression and sense series that comprise reality and life.[1] Repeatedly Deleuze declares that 'if we want to grasp an event, we must not show it, we must not pass along the event, but plunge into it, go through all the geological layers that are its internal history' (C2: 254–5); this is to explain and consider an event, as James Williams writes, in relation to its always two-sided virtual and actual structure, 'the ways in which actual events touch on virtual events' (Williams 2003: 9).

1

This book then delves within the historical events it confronts to encounter and extract their past-future implications and persistence, singularities and forces from which Marker and Resnais have forged *something new*. The untimely singularity of Marker and Resnais' cinematic responses to certain monumental events of twentieth- and twenty-first-century history, the following chapters insist, counter circular interpretations and limitations of various discourses of traumatic commemoration. The performative engagements of these chapters further maintain that – through their capacity to perceive past and future *at once*, to embrace, that is, the 'mobile instant' between the ever yet to come *and* always already past – the films of this study discover means to negotiate history, memory and death through possibilities for difference, thought and life.

By way of this study, I thus propose a method of film-philosophy that sensorily thinks through virtual experiential processes and domains of memory and past in relation to actual bodies and states of affairs. The select Marker and Resnais films of this book leap among ages of the past to grasp and expose moments of a pure past, the whole of the virtual past that was never present and that differs eternally, impersonally. Through filmic realisations of a pure past, 'we' come to experience a past in our contracted present that exceeds the individual via a reflexive doubling, or 'counter-actualisation'.

This 'splendour' of the event, which is its impersonal perpetual split or crack into past-future that shatters the limits of the individual and time of Chronos, embraces the '"they" of pre-individual singularities'; which is why, as Deleuze claims:

> there are no private or collective events, no more than there are individuals and universals ... Everything is singular, and thus both collective and private, particular and general, neither individual nor universal. Which war ... is not a private affair? Conversely, which wound is not inflicted by war and derived from society as a whole? (LS: 152)

As Marker and Resnais' films unleash the personal through the universal and universal through personal by way of affects and sensations that persist through ever-new 'differenciations', the films' ever-new actualisations of the virtual past affirm the future. In this way, the films of Marker and Resnais enable us to discern that exchange between actual and virtual, present and past-future through dynamic, novel actualisations of the real.

For as the cinema captures its 'self' and time's duration through its own lens it manifests a crystal-image. This auto-perceptibility or reflexivity glimpses that 'paradoxical instance', 'aleatory' mobile point, instant or crack upon the line of the Aion where every concentrated present splits and launches eternally into past-future. These images, the following chapters contend, reveal and advance the power and potential of the cinematic medium to confront, reactivate and replay – and thus express, transform, *sense*, *think* and *live through* or counter-actualise – certain catastrophic and delimiting events of existence that have, in the face of life's ceaseless series of flux and variation, permanently scarred humanity's constructions of its 'self' and 'other'. While they break open the double actual-virtual structure of life to explore interactions and events that are both corporeal and incorporeal, Marker and Resnais' films most profoundly glimpse that relation between mortal personal death and life's impersonal immanent becoming.

As seen through the cinemas of Marker and Resnais, humanity continually discovers innovative means of repression and destruction that are counter-actualised and expressed by these filmmakers' revelations of the same. Marker and Resnais' productions of life through their cinematic excursions, in other words, extrapolate the emergences and becomings of systems that effectively subvert productivity for despotic uses and end. Yet, how does humanity turn against itself? In the face of mass sufferings and graves, what hope has life for new becomings? The means through which we must, as Williams suggests, 'act in such a way as to allow the ["irresolvable"] problem, and how we shall follow on from it, to appear or to become expressed in us' (Williams 2003: 156), the ways through which survival is yet possible, follow on in this book from the urgently ethical principles of Deleuze (and Félix Guattari)'s philosophy, and Marker and Resnais' films.

Through our physical events, wounds and sufferings, that is, we must discover new becomings, ideas and sensations if we are to transform or redouble the events that have befallen us. To thereby become 'worthy of our events' as Deleuze urges, to embrace the *event* through an ethics of *Amor fati*, is to 'tap into but never stand independent of', as Williams writes, the asymmetrical virtual-actual series of life. '*Freedom comes with the generation of sense within determined actual and virtual circuits*'; we can 'select within events that have nonetheless selected us' (Williams 2008a: 157); we can newly express the catastrophic through the generation and expression of 'sense', that 'splendor and magnificence of the event' that Deleuze describes which is 'inside what occurs, the purely expressed'

(LS: 149), the forces, sensations, *thisnesses* that our, Marker and Resnais' experimental acts express and exude. We can, in other words, live through and along the edge of that which at once empowers and defeats us.

Destructive force or violence is thereby conceived in this book as apocalyptic *and* affirmative, as fatal with respect to instances of degradation and mortal death, and emancipative through creative lines of film and philosophy. 'The difference between the two poles [of the "war machine"] is great', assert Deleuze and Guattari, 'even, and especially, from the point of view of death: the line of flight that creates, *or* turns into a line of destruction' (ATP: 423). Inasmuch as a 'war machine' can turn a 'line of flight into a line of death' (ATP: 229), it can also and must then become a creative line of flight. While my analyses probe the provocative, poignant, graceful movements and means through which their films reveal reality, Marker and Resnais' cinemas are, in this sense, conceived by this book as 'machines', as moving assemblages of interacting past-future images, perceptions or 'bodies' and audio-visual relations that do not replicate, reproduce or represent as they effect something new.

א

Now they have hit the bull's-eye. (LJ)

Who among us keeps watch . . . to warn of the arrival of our new executioners? (NB)

It is this element which rises from the scene, shoots out of it like an arrow, and pierces me. (Barthes 1981: 26–7)

The conjunction of Marker and Resnais in this book parallels the artists' early associations[2] and later instances of intertextual homage, as through the affective replaying of Resnais' *Hiroshima mon amour* by way of Marker's *Chats Perchés*. Since the 1950s, both artists' cinemas have profoundly contributed to a sociopolitical movement of intellectual and artistic thought in modern cinema and art while their works have singularly defied generic classification, incorporation or entrenchment. As Emma Wilson observes:

the directors whose work and whose cinematic trajectory . . . bear closest comparison to Resnais are his early collaborators Chris Marker and Agnès Varda, whose relation to the Nouvelle Vague was, like Resnais', tangential, and whose very different works over subsequent decades are yet equally marked by attention to memory, virtuality and mourning on the one hand, and to the textures, shapes and surfaces of the material world on the other. (Wilson 2006: 195)

While Marker's prolific multi-media practice pursues the hauntingly intangible across faces, places and times, and as Resnais' recent films foray into more conventional narratives ever yet resonant with traces of his earlier works, it is yet essential to assert, à propos Wilson's vital perception, that the trajectories of both artists' careers will not be charted by these pages.

This book is not committed to a comprehensive study of either Marker or Resnais' oeuvre as it seeks rather to experience and affectively respond to dual virtual-actual relations actualised through the films, relations and forces towards which Wilson intimates, and that this Introduction has thus far attempted to evoke. With respect to both Marker and Resnais' careers, illuminating, thorough discussions exist, to which the rapidly emergent 'Marker field' of study bears witness through such significant texts on Marker's practice as Nora Alter, Sarah Cooper and Catherine Lupton's. Against less contemporary, auteurist Resnais studies, Wilson's 2006 *Alain Resnais* powerfully reinvigorates Resnais scholarship. As it delicately discerns experiences and events across decades of Resnais' career, from his earliest to more recent films, Wilson's writing offers nuanced, sensory explorations of the ephemeral yet interminable via contemplations of fleetingness and permanence, pain and memory, death, decay and loss.

These ever variable, fluctuating, oft seeming paradoxical sensations, mixtures and singular differences of image, sound, score and *affect* in the films of both Marker and Resnais passionately inspire this study of a select series of films. Each film, this book contends, uniquely, creatively responds to certain historic, 'traumatic' events of history through manifestations of living, lingering spectres of past and their edifices, monuments, museums, graves and ruins of 'present' that also demand significance in time. Less premised then upon the entirety of Marker and Resnais' practices than upon select evocations of 'diverse degrees and levels' of past that speak to circuits between personal-impersonal, intimate-universal, present and past-future as well as to viewer-character-film, this book expressly confronts limits of linear time and its 'upright', dogmatic or transcendent image of thought and life. As the films of this study challenge and expand the cinema's potential to directly reveal time's perpetual duration, they at once indelibly affect and are affected by variations between states and affective degrees of intensities including horror, shock, sadness, peace, wonder or amusement that are aroused or diminished with each collision of screen and viewer.

This book emerges from these encounters and is itself deeply affected by its commitment and attention to 'memory, virtuality and mourning on the one hand, and to the textures, shapes and surfaces of the material world on the other', to repeat Wilson's observations. As it continuously unfolds and refolds questions of cinema and life, thought, time and death, this book then layers various responses and perceptions as expressed through Marker, Resnais, Deleuze, Guattari, Barthes, Blanchot, Nietzsche, Spinoza, myself, among others. As a performative enquiry that experiences and interacts with the works of Marker, Resnais and Deleuze, it acknowledges certain strategies and techniques, including Marker's metatextual commentaries, Resnais' tracking movements, and Deleuze's novel repetitions, while it searches to reveal the depths of its engagements with the films and writings.

In other words, this book is a product of tangible affect, the 'feeling' of events as provoked via pure, impersonal affects that pierce – pure sadness, joy, or love, if to love is to fully experience the bliss of impersonal freedom. 'Feelings are ages of the world', writes Deleuze, 'thought is the non-chronological time which corresponds to them' (C2: 125). This is as much to say, with reference to Marker and Resnais' cinematic 'membranes', that the incorporeal intensities, the fluctuating sorrows, pains and loves, that are in continual exchange, or perpetual duration, might find bodily release 'around', 'behind' and 'even inside the image' (C2: 125). For sensations resist finite definition, possession, subjectification or periodisation, and any film might exceed the limitations of its sensory-motor movement-image schema through time-images that interrogate diverse, coexistent ages and affects of an impersonal open whole or 'univocal' world.

This making perceptible of the imperceptible is a challenge that obsesses this book. While these pages cannot claim to 'do philosophy', they do ceaselessly question, through the 'tools' or concepts of Deleuze's philosophy, the visionary possibilities of Marker and Resnais' realisations as world- or life-creations that open to an indiscernibility of actual and virtual around, behind, inside and beyond the screen. To experience the cinema as an intensive, living 'body' or series of images through which we might perceive actual and virtual at its most minute point, or crystal-image, is to move towards a 'becoming-imperceptible' through an immanent awareness of self and other. Can Marker and Resnais' cinemas extend towards or even realise that mobile point? How to touch and express the ineffable? Through the unknown, uncertain, infinitesimal and seemingly unattainable, this book enacts, as a means of response, its own interminable pursuit of a becoming-imperceptible.

ﻉ

Here we catch a glimpse of a future in which all mysteries are resolved . . . this will come about because these readers, each working on his slice of universal memory, will lay the fragments of a single secret end to end, a secret with a beautiful name, a secret called happiness. (Resnais with 'Chris and Magic Marker' et al. 1956)

If philosophy has abdicated the classical image of reason, then it can only resort to other planes of expression in an effort to escape from its impasse, which is somehow equal to the impasse of the 'world' itself after the events of 'Auschwitz' and 'Hiroshima'. Henceforth, philosophy itself must become a philosophy of the 'event'. (Lambert 2002: 18)

Why then a study of Marker and Resnais through Deleuze, and how? The decision to limit this study to considerations of these filmmakers' works in relation to questions of affect, sensation and violence through explorations of real time and pure difference affords a unique association of the two artists. For despite several existent studies of their respective works, as well as numerous texts devoted to the Nouvelle Vague that include discussion of Marker and Resnais, an extensive twofold examination of both artists' practices remains hitherto absent. Yet, in light of the intersections between their works, the oft observed similarities of narrative theme and cinematic style, as well as the artists' own near lifelong friendship, an alliance of the two filmmakers through a dedicated study seems a matter of course.

An association then of Marker and Resnais' films through an academic study may seem appropriate given these obvious linkages throughout conventional filmic history, theory and textual analysis. However, inasmuch as Marker and Resnais' cinemas do not pursue a predetermined course but rather open to re-*production* and a repeating of 'difference in itself'; inasmuch as Marker and Resnais' productions of difference defy reductive thematic appraisal as they challenge the very notion of canonisation and their affixed 'Art Cinema Classic' status, this book strives not to review or recapitulate recognised resemblances, either throughout each respective career or between the two. Indeed, the select films of this book resist codification and formulisation as they endlessly reactivate and replay the untimeliness of events, and by so doing transform filmic genre and practice.

This study seeks then to suggest techniques and means through which Marker and Resnais' films inventively repeat problems and questions so that their works continually transform themselves. These movements towards the new profoundly correspond with Deleuze's designation through Nietzsche of an eternal return of difference via the third synthesis of time: 'Repetition in the eternal return', writes Deleuze, 'excludes both the becoming-equal or the becoming-similar' (DR: 115). With each repetition, with each searching tracking movement, multi-layered voiceover or evocative series of image superimpositions, the films freshly layer new thoughts, affects and sensations so that each film creatively replays interactions of virtual and actual. The challenge of this book is not the obvious, expected, recognised or historicised but its fascination with the untranslatable differing, affecting and becoming as expressed through Resnais' *Nuit et Brouillard* (1955) and *Hiroshima mon amour* (1959), and Marker's *La Jetée* (1962), *Sans Soleil* (1983), *Le Souvenir d'un avenir* (2001, with Yannick Bellon) and *Chats Perchés* (2004).

Of all Marker and Resnais' films, these particular films most affect 'me', hence their selection for this study and my endless encounters with their image series and revelations of coexistences in time and virtual memory by way of actual bodies, relics or fragments. Even so, this book remains entirely aware of the effects of transcribing affect to word, an act that inevitably arrests transitory movements of increasing or decreasing, active or reactive affective forces, becomings and variations that the process of this book aspires to touch and reveal. The act of translating my processual experiences through the films is thus processual itself and performative in that through evocative quotation, close analysis and creative repetition of Marker, Resnais and Deleuze's thoughts, these pages attempt not to copy or apply 'Deleuzian philosophy' to the films but rather to participate in an open-ended process between book, film and text. Through this method of film-philosophy that explores potentials for thought and life via cinema and its provocations of sensation, this book discovers Marker and Resnais' works anew.

The following chapters embrace not only the intertextuality of Marker, Resnais and Deleuze's works as produced through serial repetitions and layers within and across their own and each other's works,[3] as well as the works of other thinkers and artists across disciplinary domains and temporal ages, but these chapters also generate a series of repetitions themselves. These interact with the films and texts to expose an irreducible difference between each repetition, film, text and book chapter. Which is to say, this book provides as much of a definitive Marker, Resnais or Deleuze interpretation or reading as the works themselves offer with respect to the virtual-actual events they explore.

'There I was', ruminates Barthes, 'alone in the apartment where she had died, . . . looking for the truth of the face I had loved. And I found it' (Barthes 1981: 67). The *difference* towards which each chapter, film and text attempts to think, the pure difference or 'difference in itself' that strikes and pierces when we at last find it and perceive the possibility of a virtual world and the pre-individual singularities that comprise us, is articulated throughout these pages as *thisness*, *haecceity*, *punctum*, madness, love, happiness – indefinable singularities and vibrations that shatter a self and 'move the soul'. Deleuze writes:

> The more our daily life appears standardised, stereotyped and subject to an accelerated reproduction of objects of consumption, the more art must be injected into it in order to extract from it *that little difference* which plays simultaneously between other levels of repetition, and even in order to make the two extremes resonate – namely, the habitual series of consumption and the instinctual series of destruction and death. (DR: 293; emphasis mine)

There is always, that is, the possibility of discerning and discovering *that little difference* throughout each film of this book. Through the banality of a ferry's journey, a billboard's advertisement, shopping departments, city parks, museum exhibits, train stations, historic sites and photo albums we might always sense a woman's face, a cat, a past, and the threat of an impending future that might also always be made different. 'Thrown at the right moment, he may stay there and move without trouble', *La Jetée*'s narrator explains. Perhaps, if inexplicably 'freed from the accidents of internal and external life . . . from the subjectivity and objectivity of what happens' (PI: 28), we too might obtain an imperceptibility through time.

As Marker and Resnais' films glimpse this freedom, they gesture towards that imperceptible crack between the two extremes of actual and virtual, a crack whose shattering reverberates and resonates through the bodies of the films, this book and my self. At the heart of these chapters is then an open sensitivity to profound, intense differences through film and through which we might counter the threats of cruelty, stupidity and the 'most ignoble destructions of war' (DR: 293), and it to these chapters this book now turns.

It is never the beginning or the end which are interesting ... What is interesting is the middle. (D: 39)

Notes

1. '*What is a series, then?*' writes James Williams. '*It is a disjunctive synthesis running in different ways across two interdependent but irreducible sides of reality.*' 'They are processes to be observed, or better, lived through' (Williams 2008a: 27, 26).
2. Whether or not formally credited, for Marker's extensive contributions to Resnais' films (among these their co-authored 1953 *Les Statues meurent aussi*), the films of others, and even his own works are often credited to playful Marker personas. The opening credits of Resnais' 1956 *Toute la mémoire du monde*, for example, identify collaborator Marker as 'Chris and Magic Marker', while Marker's 1983 *Sans Soleil* credits its photography to 'Sandor Krasna', Marker's fictional double throughout the film, the never-seen traveller whose letters the film's narrator reads. These are glimpses of the ever resistant, differing, multiplying 'Marker' persona. Moreover, Marker's cartoon cat, Guillaume-en-Egypte, also appeared repeatedly as a stand-in for elusive Marker on DVD sleeves, throughout online blogs, installation communiqués, and wherever else Marker and Cat prowled.
3. As Chapter 4 notes, Marker's works interestingly do not figure in Deleuze's cinematic analyses despite this book's contention that remarkable reverberations exist between Marker and Deleuze's expressions and creations via film and philosophy.

Art's Resistance

André Malraux develops a beautiful concept; he says something very simple about art; he says it is the only thing that resists death. (Deleuze 1998b: 18)

Deleuze and Art: An Introduction

As scarred by horrors that shame the notion of humanity, the twentieth century and first moments of the twenty-first encompass years and decades during which, as Giorgio Agamben argues, death becomes inaccessible and 'men do not die, but are instead produced as corpses' (Agamben 1999: 75). Art's relation, and more specifically photographic and cinematographic relations to such violence, suffering and its survival remain enigmatic as proliferating debates persist pertaining to the possibilities and effects of art in the duration and aftermath of devastating events. Of the competing discourses, contemporary literary trauma theory has become a foremost perspective; such theorists address a 'crisis' that paradoxically 'defies and demands' verbalisation and witness (Caruth 1996: 5). However, the resultant fetishisation of traumatic event and subject through circular considerations of wars, destruction and traumas both private and universal arguably stupefies thought, pre-empting opportunities for productive life practices.

In contrast to the 'absolutely accurate and precise' traumatic flashback or re-enactment as sustained by theories of identity and representation (Caruth 1995: 151–3), the philosophy of Deleuze promotes difference and its affirmation in thought. Whereas the notion of an experiencing human subject and her traumatic repetitions fortify several theoretical discourses as spawned from Freudian psychoanalysis, Deleuze and Guattari propose a *schizoanalysis*. Such an active, inherently ethical and affirmative approach counters death with life and art as it discovers possibilities for survival and creation beyond inertia's threat via victimisation and its potential propensity towards infectious impotence.

Through Nietzsche and Spinoza, Deleuze insists that thought and art must do violence to reactive forces that beget violence through a power of *ressentiment*, what Deleuze and Guattari describe as 'double suicide' and 'a way out that turns the line of flight into a line of death', a line of pure destruction and abolition (ATP: 229–30). When questioned in interview regarding the violence of which he writes, Deleuze responded:

> You say there's a certain tragic or melancholic tone in all this. I think I can see why. I was very struck by all the passages in Primo Levi where he explains that Nazi camps have given us 'a shame at being human.' Not, he says, that we're all responsible for Nazism, as some would have us believe, but that we've all been tainted by it: even the survivors of the camps had to make compromises with it, if only to survive. There's the shame of there being men who became Nazis; the shame of being unable, not seeing how, to stop it; the shame of having compromised with it; there's the whole of what Primo Levi call this 'gray area.' . . . This is one of the most powerful incentives toward philosophy, and it's what makes all philosophy political . . . There's no democratic state that's not compromised to the very core by its part in generating human misery. What's so shameful is that we've no sure way of maintaining becomings, or still more of arousing them, even within ourselves. (N: 171–2)

The ability to unsettle the preconceived and overcoded, to discover life through direct images of time and affect that expose the matter-movement flow of perceptions and images of which Deleuze and Bergson write, is to create anew. This is, as Deleuze claims, 'the power of modern cinema (when it stops being bad)' (C2: 172). Elsewhere Deleuze writes, 'the less human the world is, the more it is the artist's duty to believe and produce belief in a relation between man and the world' (C2: 171). If damage has been done to our illusionary world of eternal truths, what remains? Deleuze responds: 'bodies, which are forces, nothing but forces . . . Power (what Nietzsche calls "will to power" . . .) is this power to affect and be affected, this relation between one force and others . . . the shock of forces, in the image or of the images between themselves' (C2: 139).

In *War and Cinema: The Logistics of Perception*, Paul Virilio suggests that 'in cinema there is no longer such a thing as an "accurate" reflection'. He continues:

> 'Everything', [actor Paul] Wegener said in 1916, 'depends on *a certain flow in which the fantastic world of the past rejoins the world of the present*' . . . Cinema is war because, as Dr Gustave Le Bon wrote in 1916, 'War touches not only the material life but also the thinking of nations . . .

it is not the rational which manages the world but forces of affective, mystical or collective origin which guide men ... immaterial forces are the true steerers of combat.' (Virilio 1989: 30; citing Le Bon, *Enseignements psychologiques de la guerre européenne*)

By this, Virilio acknowledges the 'immaterial' forces that constitute thought and life. Of these forces both active and reactive, it is from the latter, those negative, resentful and destructive, that the violence of war emerges. It is this line of destruction, as Deleuze and Guattari write, that produces the 'most catastrophic charge' (ATP: 230). They continue:

> Paul Virilio's analysis strikes us as entirely correct in defining fascism not by the notion of the totalitarian State but by the notion of the suicidal State: so-called total war seems less a State undertaking than an undertaking of a war machine that appropriates the State and channels into it a flow of absolute war whose only possible outcome is the suicide of the State itself. (ATP: 231)

Indeed, the 'war machine' Deleuze and Guattari identify has 'nothing to do with war' but with 'revolutionary movements': a war-machine, Deleuze contends, refers even to 'artistic movements' and ways of 'inventing new space-times' (N: 172). Such creative becoming vitally contrasts the ever-ominous threat of a line of flight's suicidal *reterritorialisation*, which finds illustration through the example Deleuze and Guattari provide of the State incited by Hitler wherein the '*war machine ... no longer had anything but war as its object*'. As thus appropriated, a war machine 'would rather annihilate its own servants than stop the destruction'; all other dangers to life, Deleuze and Guattari admit, 'pale by comparison' (ATP: 231).

These pages encounter dangers of their own as the notion of a derivative 'Deleuzian approach' cancels the primacy of *difference* with sameness and inertia – any attempt to explicate or replicate dynamic layers of thought and 'lines of flight' would prove impossible and paradoxical. Yet, given their challenge to prevalent representational means of rational expression and comprehension, entirely new sensory practices and 'styles' of thinking may seem equally as difficult to communicate or grasp. Such creative ways of mutation and further difference – as through cinema, art, music or literature – evoke the associative processes of Deleuze's geo-philosophy. How then to read art and its signs through the tools of Deleuze's creative practice? How to discern a work's signs, its movements, worlds and affects without reverting to quests for meaning, reproduction and authenticity that would eradicate potentials for new experience and creation? In response, Deleuze advocates a method of experimentation and creative 'stuttering' free from the constraints of our selves, order words and dogmas, a stuttering to which this book will return, and that Deleuze describes as he writes:

> To make one's language stutter ... it is a matter of digging under the stories, cracking open the opinions, and reaching regions without memories, when the self must be destroyed ... Style becomes nonstyle, and one's language lets an unknown foreign language escape from it [Proust], so that one can reach the limits of language itself and become something other than a writer, conquering fragmented visions that pass through the words of a poet, the colors of a painter, or the sounds of a musician. (ECC: 113–14)

To communicate or grasp accepted interpretation or established 'knowledge' is to participate in what Deleuze terms a 'society of control' and its integration of the same. For thought's regulation according to dictates of authorised information and 'public knowledge' negates the power of difference as it arrests life and creation through definitive meanings and subtle control. Of such delimitations of thought Bergson suggests that:

> millions of phenomena succeed each other while we hardly succeed in counting a few ... To conceive of durations of different tensions [e.g., animal, plant life, etc.] is perhaps both difficult and strange to our mind, because we have acquired the useful habit of substituting for the true duration, lived by consciousness, an homogenous and independent Time ... In short, ... to perceive consists in condensing enormous periods of an infinitely diluted existence into a few more differentiated moments of an intenser life, and in thus summing up a very long history. To perceive means to *immobilize*. (Bergson 1991: 207–8; emphasis mine)

By this, Bergson proposes that there is not a single rhythm of duration but several different rhythms whose various speeds or flows comprise life's eternal virtual-actual series of coexisting circuits while their multiple speeds attest to their respective places in the scale of being (Bergson 1991: 207). The contraction and dilation of these diverse flows, their different speeds, indicate a body or organism's complexity; as Bergson states, the 'greater or lesser tension of their duration ... their greater or lesser intensity of life' (1991: 210).

Human perception, as derived from life's flow of matter-movement, delays this flow of difference and becoming through its consciousness of alternative durations. By way of such perception via cinema's virtual domains, the actualised 'present' gives way to what Bergson defines as a coexistence of disparate layers, sheets, continuums, planes or ages of past, 'a continuum with fragments of different ages', as writes Deleuze (C2: 123), through which time becomes both past and always to come.[1] As will be explored throughout the following chapters, Deleuze discerns potentials within post-Second World War cinema to reveal durations beyond that of any character, family or group as certain films open to a virtual world-memory. An eternal 'sort of immediate, consecutive or even simultaneous double' of the actual through its virtual counterpart in 'perpetual exchange' persists whereby the virtual eternally coexists alongside the actual so that time, as Deleuze claims following Bergson, is always a 'passing of the present' and 'preservation of the past' (Deleuze 2002: 150–1).

Deleuze often terms the virtual-actual, actual-virtual exchange a *crystal*, and the 'tightest' or most indiscernible moment of the virtual-actual oscillation a *crystallisation*. Significantly, while Deleuze regards the practices of science, art and philosophy as fundamentally creative and correlated through a limit common to all the disciplines, which communicate together 'on the level of . . . the constitution of space-times' (1998b: 16), he underscores a 'fundamental affinity between the work of art and the act of resistance' (1998b: 18) and focuses earnestly in this respect upon the cinema. Through the cinema's revelation of space-times and crystalline virtual-actual coalescences 'between the immediate past which is already no longer and the immediate future which is not yet' (C2: 81), cinematic time-images open to non-hierarchical, virtual becomings, affects and percepts of worlds other than those that can be recognised, a time of *difference* in-itself, an *untimely* time that brings only the new, the eternal repetition of the different. Whereas the movement-image of pre-Second World War cinema finds narrative cohesion and chronological organisation through the sensory-motor schema that Bergson identifies of habitual movement and response, the postwar time-image that Deleuze discerns encounters the very splitting or crack of time towards past and future. 'Time consists of this split, and it is this, it is time', Deleuze via Bergson contends 'that we *see in the crystal* . . . the perpetual foundation of time, non-chronological time, Cronos and not Chronos . . . The visionary, the seer, is the one who sees in the crystal, and what he sees is the gushing of time as dividing in two, as splitting' (C2: 81).

The contemporaneous virtual past actualises in the present; this actualisation of pure memory or recollection, the paramnesia or déjà-vu to which Deleuze and Bergson refer, gives way to a cinematic autonomous consciousness of time. Such consciousness corresponds to the apprehension of a self's instantaneous, paradoxical dissolution as a subject, a fracturing the following chapters will further examine through film, and the pure memory of a world directly exploring time, sensation and the remnants of regimes that have sought to regulate, control and 'cleanse' difference and its flows. Deleuze paraphrases Bergson as he explains:

> Every moment of our life presents the two aspects, it is actual and virtual, perception on the one side and recollection on the other ... Whoever becomes conscious of the continual duplication of his present into perception and recollection ... will compare himself to an actor playing his part automatically, listening to himself and beholding himself playing. (C2: 79)

As the cinema discovers non-communicable means to think and create through the freeing of affect and time from the foundations of identity, representation and redundancy, it affirms the resistance of which Deleuze writes that radically counters conventional interpretations of freedom. Through virtual worlds, that is, the cinema manifests a 'veritable transformation' or 'great circulation of elements' (Deleuze 1998b: 16) that, via disjunctions of image, sound, score, speed, light and intensity, affect the sensory body of the spectator, a subjectivity produced by the doubling of crystalline time, a becoming of consciousness enabled through virtual memory. The emergence of the cinematic time-image in the post-Second World War period fundamentally derives not only from 'the most ordinary states of sleep, dream, or a disturbance of attention' but also from limit-situations that break with the mundane quotidian as a 'cinema of seeing' replaces that of action (C2: 55; 9). Deleuze distinguishes the time-image then as a means

> of reaching a mystery of time, of uniting image, thought and camera in a single 'automatic subjectivity' ... a character finds himself prey to visual and sound sensations (or tactile ones, cutaneous or coenaesthetic) which have lost their motor extension. This may be a limit-situation, the imminent arrival or consequence of an accident, the nearness of death. (C2: 55)

Freedom or resistance surfaces from the interstices and disparate audio-visual layers of modern cinema's time-images that affect, via a virtual perception or intervention, a *violence* or 'inhuman' power that overwhelms habitual response as might a traumatic experience.

Urged to impossibly think life's immanent flow of becoming, time or *immanence* itself, the processes and connections of this thought rupture the screen. What remains in the place of any authoritative authentic or accurate cinematic representation[2] are forces that fracture character and viewer through affective singular experiences.

While writing on the 'adaptation of the real to the interests of practice' through empiricism and dogmatism, Bergson proposes an alternative method that would 'seek experience at its source, or rather above that decisive *turn* where, taking a bias in the direction of our utility, it becomes properly *human* experience' (Bergson 1991: 183–4). This third course through 'pure intuition' would place us in

> pure duration, of which the flow is continuous and in which we pass insensibly from one state to another: a continuity which is really lived, but artificially decomposed for the greater convenience of customary knowledge ... The duration *wherein we see ourselves acting*, and in which it is useful that we should see ourselves, is duration whose elements are dissociated and juxtaposed. The duration *wherein we act* is a duration wherein our states melt into each other. (1991: 186)

Deleuze identifies the signs of the cinematic movement- and time-images through Bergson's distinction between extensive and intensive duration, or 'automatic subjectivity' and grounded duration on the one hand and, on the other, imperceptible fluid duration or pure difference, whose subordination to human homogenised time again begets extensive disjointed spatialised duration. While linear quotidian time indirectly experiences and perceives time, crystal time-images directly expose time in its pure intensive state as they make perceptible the imperceptible.

The question always remains: how to free ourselves, to think difference itself, attain absolute deterritorialisation, the plane of immanence? In other words, the challenge is always to become *imperceptible*, to attain the line or flight of greatest creativity and speed through the elimination of despair, death and *ressentiment*. This liberating possibility surfaces through time-images that release a free flow of images or creative becomings. One may wonder, as Deleuze and Guattari acknowledge, 'what are they all rushing toward', these becoming-others or lines of flight. 'Without a doubt', Deleuze and Guattari insist once more, they rush 'toward becoming-imperceptible. The imperceptible is the immanent end of becoming, its cosmic formula' (ATP: 279).

The time-image's revelation of time's virtual-actual doubling corresponds then to the formation of subjectivity. As Deleuze suggests, 'subjectification is about . . . bringing a curve into the line, making it turn back on itself, or making force impinge on itself. So we get ways of living with what would otherwise be unendurable' (N: 113). Through Bergson, Deleuze espouses a method of intuition whereby the reflexive awareness described, the 'duration wherein we see ourselves acting', would simultaneously coincide with the 'duration wherein we act' so that our actions and actualisations would be discerned at each moment within their context of interactions and connections.

This difficult act or *counter-actualisation* is also a *becoming-other*, a *becoming-imperceptible*. Memory makes possible the image of a self, as Deleuze argues. Which is to say, as it opens to a realm of the virtual, perception perceives itself and time's duality with its two heterogeneous directions launched towards both future and past. The actualisation of this consciousness 'always still in the future and already in the past' suggests again 'an actor's paradox' and the actor or self's possible redoubling or enactment of counter-actualisation (LS: 150). In relation to a self's emergence or actualisation through the intuition of time, memory, pure past and its consequent fragmentation through the same process of recollection, the violence of which Deleuze writes with and without Guattari in *Cinema 2: The Time-Image, Difference and Repetition, What is Philosophy?, A Thousand Plateaus, Logic of Sense* and elsewhere suggests that this dissolution of a unified self becomes 'traumatic' in itself. Deleuze and Guattari muse:

> what violence must be exerted on thought for us to become capable of thinking; what violence of an infinite movement that, at the same time, takes from us our power to say 'I'? . . . a set of ambiguous signs arise . . . thought as such begins to exhibit snarls, squeals, stammers; it talks in tongues and screams, which leads it to create, or to try to. (WIP: 55)

Among factors that give rise to the time-image, an image that reveals the cinema's perception of itself as it experiments at the limits of what it can do, Deleuze cites the Second World War as a violent encounter to thought. This shattering of stable constructions by force enables intensive perception and new approaches to life, seeing and being. Such affective experience generates the spectator/character and its reflexivity, a reflexivity embodied within the crystal time-image and that generates new becomings, relations and engagements with the world. From this 'cinema of the seer' and these visionary sleepwalkers who lose themselves to the violence and intensity they witness, who have 'learnt to see' because they have been 'struck to the core by the simple unfolding of images ... [and] something unbearable, beyond the limit', Deleuze evokes a character who has become viewer himself, whose situation 'outstrips his motor capacities on all sides' (C2: 2–3).

From this rarely perceived virtual image of time that ceaselessly splits and persists, Virilio suggests that cinema and war have developed their inhuman, machinic perception in tandem, through which militaristic surveillance doubles the all-seeing cinematic world while societies of control come into dominance (Virilio 1989: 2). This perpetuation of information and communication at the 'speed of electronic circuitry' and light provokes Deleuze's intervention: 'let us at least say that there is counterinformation' (Deleuze 1998b: 18). People may move '"freely" without being at all confined yet while still being perfectly controlled' through communication and information (1998b: 18). Communication, Deleuze continues, is the 'transmission and the propagation of a piece of information' which 'we are supposed to be ready or able to ... believe'. Ominously he claims, 'this is our future' (1998b: 18).

But counterinformation, which may be produced through the time-image's act of creative resistance, counters the subtle control enforced through instruments of communication and information. Cinema, Deleuze argues, possesses the potential to free thought and life from confinement, if only temporarily, through the liberation of affects and the 'creation of a people'. 'The people, who "are still missing" and yet already there' (C2: 255), as Deleuze repeats Paul Klee, are the bodies who will experience a *becoming with the screen*. In the wake of the collapse of the sensory-motor schema and its action-image, this paradoxical reflexivity of nonhuman subjectivity or identity in cinema thus enables resistance through dissociations, layerings and series of visual and sound that generate creativity via difference. Such *folding* of the world into the self then distinguishes human duration as a flow of greater complexity or perceptual intensity among other flows. As Deleuze suggests, art does not represent the world; rather, the world becomes, worlds become, through the foldings and unfoldings of diverse subjectivities and flows so that these folds of the world reshape and rethink the present for future possibilities.

Yet, as Deleuze also observes, 'wherever we turn, everything seems dismal' (LS: 158), for dangers which threaten new becomings and life remain pervasive. Deleuze's examinations of beliefs and structures that diminish life and give way to catastrophic horror and war for war's sake, *where death in and of itself becomes a goal,* open to discussions of a fold, an effect that shatters and counteracts 'healthy' faith in moral, eternal categories as it creates 'revolutionary means of exploration' (LS: 189). 'Is there some other health', Deleuze asks, 'like a body surviving as long as possible its scar, . . . and never giving up the idea of a new vital conquest'? (LS: 160–1). By way of response, Deleuze again insists upon an act of replaying or redoubling, upon foldings, unfoldings and refoldings that expose not only the actual events of our lives but also their underlying virtual intensities and affective significances.

To counter-actualise, then, is to refold, break open and recombine thought, not to sense a totalising, homogeneous world but to strive to explore fragmentary, imperceptible relationships, to become imperceptible, neither actual nor virtual, this nor that, but always becoming, differing. In this way, an individual forsakes determined classification for an active individuation. To truly 'have faith in this world' is to believe in the world at hand rather than an illusionary transcendence, and to discover a new 'health', one that might explode and refold damaging illusions that inhibit creativity, life and thought.

The persisting actual-virtual, virtual-actual exchange then also corresponds to the double structure of every event. Following Maurice Blanchot, Deleuze negotiates the disintegration of the self in relation to life's creative flow and the painful incarnation of destruction and death at the level of the corporeal body. One might ask how we are to think life's immanent flow in relation to death itself, that most personal mortal event. Yet if death exists in all feeling, if life, that is, is always a series of affective increases or decreases in power, the means to thinking life through empowering repetition and the eternal return lies through art or, more specifically, modern cinema's production of sensation and singular essences. For through its potential to expose virtual essences, affects, percepts and time's flow as becoming and pure duration itself, through its revelations of impersonal singularities that negate one's personal present death with an impersonal dying that opens to past-future becomings, modern cinema responds anew to forces both active and reactive at play in the modern world.

Towards Marker and Resnais

Ever at risk of the hazard hitherto described, of attempting to specify the always *indefinite* and thereby 'inevitably reintroducing transcendence', this exploration will strive to suggest new connections and lines of flight that emerge from within and between the films of Marker and Resnais. The movements to be traced are paradoxical: at the same time as creations come into existence and *being*, they simultaneously open and connect further in *becoming-other*. 'Becoming [like time and movement] is always double, that which one becomes becomes no less than the one that becomes – block is formed, essentially mobile, never in equilibrium', Deleuze and Guattari insist (ATP: 305). Hence, the power of modern cinema to perceive the individual-universal/universal-individual as it reveals the makings and unmakings of a devastated world ever at mend and at war. The 'sheets of internal life and the layers of external world plunge, extend and intersect with increasing speed' writes Deleuze. 'Death does not fix an actual present, so numerous are the dead who haunt the sheets of past' (C2: 209, 116).

While the perceiving mind may attune itself to the 'needs of practical life' so that our memory, as Bergson argues, 'solidifies the continuous flow of things' (Bergson 1991: 210), that which exceeds human perception, that flow whose qualities travel in every direction 'like shivers (through an immense body)' (1991: 208), is of particular importance to this book. The following chapters will therefore 'seek experience at its source' (1991: 184) as they negotiate collective and personal singular experiences of war and violence. In other words, despite the immobilising effects of this very chapter, subsequent pages of this book will interrogate sensation through filmic encounters that defy reductive recognition and rationalisation and that shatter common notions of experience, subjectivity, time, memory, art and the cinema itself.

As Deleuze and Guattari repeatedly insist, destructive forces double each possibility for flight; caution must be taken to pursue the line of greatest resistance and creativity. If again, as Deleuze writes, 'every event is like death, double and impersonal in its double', then potentials for new life emerge from each event; life, which is becoming, ceaselessly continues through pre-individual singularities that comprise the 'I'. 'In it *I* do not die' (LS: 152), Deleuze maintains after Blanchot. By its mortal end, the actual present and a human body gives way to 'the impersonality of dying' that no longer 'indicates only the moment when I disappear outside my self, but rather the moment when death loses itself in itself, and also the figure which the most singular life takes on in order to substitute itself for me' (LS: 153). Should we attain a duration wherein we both act and perceive the very duration from which we derive, we would thus achieve the freedom Deleuze describes.

Yet, and even as Gregg Lambert writes that the 'very existence of a book that claims to clarify and explain another writer already makes the first (so-called "primary") writer redundant to his or her own efforts' (Lambert 2002: ix), the act of replacing networks of audio-visual images and the possibilities they afford with prosaic analysis seems a most perilous threat, especially if the intent is to engage with experience at its most unique and deeply affective. In fact, Deleuze and Guattari suggest two planes, a transcendent and an immanent, the plane of composition. Inevitably, these chapters develop from the former, 'a teleological plan(e), a design, a mental principle . . . a plan(e) of transcendence', a sort of 'metalanguage' that 'exists alongside' the films and plane of composition as these words remain unable to present the films' flows themselves. But as Deleuze and Guattari question, 'is not Stockhausen also obliged to describe the structure of his sound forms as existing "alongside" them since he is unable to make it audible?' (ATP: 265–6).

And so, while these pages certainly fragment the speeds and movements of the films they consider, they variously ally cinema's vital, floating time and affects that move and reveal movement, that affect and are affected, with *difference, desire, ecstasy, epiphany, love, pathos – the indelible effect, a madness, that becomes the very ineluctable yet contingent essence, charm, thisness of an encounter with art, which also constitutes a friendship and the condition for thought.* Art in this vital and virtual sense is, again, an act of resistance inasmuch as the cinematic medium, which possesses the potential to directly expose time as *difference* as it forever produces new differences and other worlds, is 'capable of restoring our belief in the world' (C2: 181). Deleuze writes:

> Resnais' [*and Marker's?*] characters do not just return from Auschwitz or Hiroshima, they are philosophers, thinkers, beings of thought in another way too. For philosophers are beings who have passed through a death, who are born from it, and go towards another death, perhaps the same one . . . The great post-war philosophers and writers demonstrated that thought has something to do with Auschwitz, with Hiroshima, but this was also demonstrated by the great cinema authors . . . this time in the

22

most serious way. This is the opposite of a cult of death ... The sheets of past come down and the layers of reality go up, in mutual embraces which are flashes of life: what Resnais calls 'feeling' or 'love', as mental function. (C2: 208–9)

When 'carried to its nth power', cinema directly manifests time, from which human duration abstracts itself in a solidification of time's eternal flow and 'simultaneity of fluxes' (B: 81). However, through its multiple discordant sonic and visual layers, what Deleuze terms a 'free indirect discourse' whereby the 'marks of an indirect origin', 'the power of the free indirect', cannot be affixed to any subjectivity (C2: 242), the cinema further overturns transcendent thought and any single authorial perspective. Deleuze further clarifies:

Whenever we write, we speak as someone else ... we are uncovering a world of pre-individual, impersonal singularities. They are not reducible to individuals or persons, nor to a sea without difference. These singularities are mobile, they break in, thieving and stealing away, alternating back and forth, like anarchy crowned, inhabiting a nomad space ... The poet Ferlinghetti[3] talks about the fourth person singular; it is that to which we try to give voice. (DI: 143)

Beyond predetermined identity constructions and formulaic thought, Marker and Resnais' cinemas effect this creative, open space of the *fourth person singular* that breaks from classic convention and emulations of religious, moral and judgemental values that threaten eventual nihilism. The *something* thought and cinema 'have to do with' Auschwitz, Hiroshima, prior, subsequent and future horrors is, once more, *resistance* through creative lines that diverge from socially determined binaries of good/evil, true/false. As it reveals virtual processes free from tendencies and beliefs that delimit and solidify life and its edicts, 'art alone', Deleuze claims, 'succeeds entirely in what life has merely sketched out' (PS: 55).

As the following chapters seek to creatively and productively encounter cinema, to become sensitive to its signs through Marker and Resnais, this book will attempt to avoid film criticism's 'twin dangers' of simple description and forced interpretation based upon concepts 'taken from outside film', from psychoanalysis or linguistics, for example (N: 57; see also C2: 280). If 'what is enveloped in the sign is more profound than all the explicit significations' (PS: 30), the *signs* of Marker and Resnais' films and the affective, sensory violence they do are integral to the following investigations.

Deleuze and Guattari state that art is '*a bloc of sensations*' comprised of percepts and affects (WIP: 164), while the cinema, according to Deleuze, is an art of 'auto-temporalization' and 'self-movement' (N: 58), a phenomenon more radically revelatory of time and space than any other art. In lieu of conventional accounts of cinema based upon textual analysis, mimesis and representation, Deleuze then proposes that cinema is an intensive, creative system of signs that discovers a non-hierarchical means of 'stammering' through a 'method of BETWEEN, "between two images", which does away with all cinema of the One' (C2: 180). To engage with cinema in this way is to create concepts, to practice philosophy not as an application of existent terms or as a reflection upon notions of authenticity and truth but as a practice enabled and engendered by cinema itself. This is a working cinematic philosophy that experiences the affects and signs emitted by cinema. The question, as Deleuze concludes, is no longer '"What is cinema?" but indeed "What is philosophy?"' (C2: 280). For as the cinema becomes eternally new through experimental means, the practices of philosophy and film ever converge and interpenetrate; through images, signs and concepts, film and philosophy encounter limits of thought that effectively open to affirmative new means of life and production.

Yet again, is it possible to commit to discourse what cannot be restricted? How can this investigation evade its inherent danger of stabilising and diminishing an art's intensities and singularities? Deleuze repeats Nietzsche when he urges that language, cinema and thought be pushed to their *limits* where thought might 'take flight' and 'free life from what imprisons it'. If 'creating isn't communicating but resisting' (N: 143), then the translation of Marker and Resnais' films to prose risks, once more, repressing their resistances to hegemonic structure through the very same. If the works of Marker and Resnais attain pure visions through sensory signs that defy concretion and reduction, this exploration seeks means to translate their untranslatable modes as it questions what it means to think their cinemas through the signs of difference and repetition that Deleuze discerns.

But what possibilities exist when disintegration and violence surface in the world we recognise, when destruction and death disrupt the reality we extract and synthesise from duration's flow, when thought's violation through horror disables automatic mechanisms? As when, from 'the second day, certain species of animals crawled again from the depths of the earth, and from the ashes' of a Hiroshima Resnais and Marguerite Duras affectively preserve (HMA), life must persist in discovering new becomings through violent encounters of thought and experience both affirmative and destructive. The always new fragments the human, shattering her subjective haven to expose time for itself in its pure state, a duration that always already eludes human perception.

Forced into thinking, thought perceives the 'unthought', unknown and untimely, duration and perception's flow, the 'outside' beyond the self, so that the world becomes and becomes cinematic through an immanent perception of time and movement. Images, each a system of temporal relations among elements, reveal thought itself as a power born from the furthest outside and deepest inside so that the process of imaging or perception returns the concept of becoming-imperceptible. This power of becoming everybody or everything makes of the world a becoming where 'to reduce oneself to an abstract line, a trait, in order to find one's zone of indiscernibility' is to thus to be present 'at the dawn of the world' (ATP: 280).

Such is also to attain the photographic or cinematic threshold. The significant distinction Deleuze and Guattari proceed to identify between photography and cinema becomes vital in what follows to a consideration of cinematic affect in relation to Roland Barthes' *punctum*. The photograph's halting of time, what Barthes considers to be 'the very essence, the *noeme*', the 'That-has-been' or 'Intractable' of photography (Barthes 1981: 76–7), disables a photograph from exposing the flow of duration and time, a potential embodied by modern cinema's time-images. To this Barthes refers when he writes of the photograph as that which is '*without future*', hence 'its pathos' and 'melancholy'. In photography, Barthes finds 'no protensity, whereas the cinema is protensive, hence in no way melancholic (what is it, then? – It is, then, simply "normal," like life)' (1981: 89–90).

As Deleuze suggests, the cinema indeed launches towards a future as it liberates movement and directly reveals time. But as it also delves beneath ashes, 'geological sections' and 'archaeological layers' to unearth regions and stratums of harrowing pasts (C2: 254), the cinema's images and character-spectators or *spectres* also 'return from the dead' to live in full consciousness of the whole past and the deaths buried among its layers. The chapters to follow will argue that Marker and Resnais' time-images enter within ages of the past as their assemblages of voice, sound and visual image become percepts of nonhuman vision, of Auschwitz, Hiroshima, Paris and 'any-space-whatever', fractured, haunting, unknown places with names at once familiar. 'Deserted ground is the only thing that can be seen', Deleuze observes, 'but this deserted ground is heavy with what lies beneath . . . the voice speaks to us of corpses, of the whole lineage of corpses that come to reside underground' (Deleuze 1998b: 16–17).

Barthes' assertion of cinema's 'normalcy' and lack of the melancholic will then be countered with possibilities of piercing singular intensities or *punctum* that empower the motionless photograph but that realise exceptional force in the affective experiences and becomings of the cinematic screen-spectator-character. Barthes describes 'a blind field' which, he argues, the cinema creates by right: 'the cinema has a power which at first glance the Photograph does not have: the screen (as Bazin has remarked) is not a frame but a hideout; the man or woman who emerges from it continues living: a "blind field" constantly doubles our partial vision' (Barthes 1981: 55–7). While tracing this duration of life through limits of life and death, Barthes' remarks in 'The Photographic Message' regarding the 'traumatic photograph' prefigure his later *Camera Lucida*. In the former, Barthes writes:

> trauma is just what suspends language and blocks signification . . . the traumatic photograph . . . is the one about which there is nothing to say: the shock photo is by structure non-signifying: no value, no knowledge, at the limit no verbal categorisation can have any hold over the process instituting its signification. (Barthes 1977: 19)

However, as this book will maintain, while *punctum* is indeed that which defies signification and meaning, its virtual value or sense seems a corollary of the pure affect Deleuze and Guattari describe. As an intensive power that affects the viewer's receptive body, which in turn affects the photo or screen beyond the limits of the frame, *punctum*, like the *affects* of which Deleuze and Guattari write that 'transpierce the body like arrows' (ATP: 356), rises freely from the work itself. As 'we' are drawn into the work through a pure impersonal awareness, the affective violent encounter, the *punctum*, launches us towards immanent becoming.

This production of sensation does not extend to redundant mainstream spectacles and re-presentations of 'arbitrary violence' (N: 60).[4] As Deleuze and Guattari insist, we search in vain for sensation 'if we go no farther than reactions and the excitations that they prolong, than actions and the perceptions that they reflect' (WIP: 211–12). In lieu of that which preserves as it strives for authenticity and replication, art and cinema might free the affects created within a work that 'draw us into its compound' and make us become with it (WIP: 175). To discover true experience through art, to seek an imperceptible becoming in the affective spaces between the work and its perception, is to create artistic events which renew the past. Certain historic events then, as encountered through cinema, are not re-presentations but ever-new events of becoming that surface once more through the release of the event's singular affects, percepts and emotions. In this respect, Deleuze writes of a 'pure element' of emotion which precedes all representation, 'itself generating new ideas' (B: 110–11).

To think, will or grasp the event is to pass through it, beyond the finite realm of our beings towards the infinite; through its 'finite', actual forms, art seeks the same. As Deleuze and Guattari write, 'art wants to create the finite that restores the infinite' (WIP: 197). The notion of a finite traumatic event might, in this sense, relate to Deleuze's concept of event as a momentary effect of an encounter of forces without beginning or end that never returns the same. For when confronted by tragedy, horror and death, grounding human perspective and a static interpretation of time's flow become lost as experience opens to 'true experience'. Through such violent encounters, life and an apprehension of its eternal return may be met without illusion. Perhaps we may then become 'worthy of events' as we act on and against our present. Of this endless process that may discover a freer future through negotiations of past-present sufferings and ordeals, Deleuze remarks:

> The eternal return is indeed the category of the ordeal, and we must understand, as such, of events, of everything that happens. Misfortune, sickness, madness, even the approach of death have two aspects: in one sense, they separate me from my power, in another sense, they endow me with a strange power, as though I possessed a dangerous means of exploration, which is also a terrifying realm to explore. The function of the eternal return, in every case, is to separate the superior from the moderate means ... The words 'separate' or 'extract' are not even adequate, since the eternal return *creates* the superior forms. It is in this sense that the eternal return is the instrument of the expression of the will to power: it raises each thing to its superior form, that is, its *nth* power. (DI: 125)

The implications of Marker and Resnais' immanent ethics for creative resistance and life, for thinking 'what moves us' in terms of the 'three virtues' of 'imperceptibility, indiscernibility, and impersonality', re-conceptualise resistance as an affirmative process (ATP: 280). If life persists through becomings, its survival lies through difference and creation inasmuch as modern cinema's time-images discover new life beneath the ruins of the Second World War so that the 'creation of a new people' is no less than the task of modern cinematic resistance. The following pages will explore the creative folds and new assemblages of Marker and Resnais' cinemas, as well as the seeming paradox of affectivity without subjectivity in relation to a micropolitics at the level of the molecular.

Like memory itself, the films' dimensions expand or shrink as does the plane of composition from which they give rise; each viewing produces differences; each assemblage and composition of affects, colours, movements, sounds, textures, tones and lights circulates and exchanges newly. Again, Bergson's principle of reality as a coexistence of different '"durations," superior or inferior to "ours," all of them in communication', informs becoming that 'lacks a subject distinct from itself' (ATP: 238). The non-personal feeling released through Marker and Resnais' films is a ceaselessly changing assemblage of affects and durations. But what is it then to 'be moved'? If Deleuze's is a philosophy of joy, its most profound expression may be discovered in passages wherein some being is moved, saddened or shamed. Can feeling and emotion thus be reconciled with a philosophy of non-subjectivity?

As their thoughts circulate about children, friendship and the pure sensations of affects both active and passive, Deleuze and Guattari consider *haecceities*, or relations of speeds and slownesses, in lieu of subjective emotion. Yet, as they often repeat, much caution is needed to prevent the plane of consistency, composition or creation from becoming a pure plane of death. As this introductory chapter suggests, in its defiance of dogmatic, habitual ways of thought, traumatic experience assails the senses so that sensations and affects of shock and violence pass between cinema's time-images. However, whereas the shock necessarily encounters new experience, its contemporary psychoanalytic or psychotherapeutic treatments deny progressive courses.

In response to an immanent ethics such as Deleuze's, psychoanalysis and other forms of self-therapy might wonder what alternatives remain for survival and life if they are to reject strategies of healing that commence with a subject's memories and feelings. But could a state of circular victimisation, as engendered through ideologies of God(s) and self that long for resurrection and salvation, infect as would a contagion with inescapable suffering and loss? If life through sorrowful human experience begets moral and religious rationalisations, is life yet alive? What can an immanent ethics do through cinema, what can a cinema of resistance impart to a grieving world, whose grief is all too real and inevitable? By way of response, the chapters to come turn towards Marker and Resnais' films that ever explore a body's affective power and perceptions, responses and interactions.

As it extracts from life that which exceeds semantic or semiotic meaning, art endures through affects and percepts, through that something that can only be specified as sensation, speeds, rhythms, 'blocs' of sensations, all that does visceral violence to thought and convention. That 'most mysterious' empowering relation between resistance and art to which Deleuze refers (1998b: 19) thereby haunts the succeeding pages which seek to discover the emergence of a people yet to come in the encounter between human struggle and the work of art.

Notes

1. Deleuze refers to Bergson's famous cone whereby the actual present and its past, the virtual image that always doubles the actual, exist at the cone's point. Virtual sections or circuits comprise the cone as it widens, 'each of which contains all our past as this is preserved in itself (pure recollection)' (C2: 294, n. 22). For further reading see, among others, Rodowick 1997.
2. With respect to any 'representation of reality' and André Bazin's contributions to film theory, Deleuze's thought moves beyond binaries of real/false, world/copy or source/representation to consider how idealised illusions of accuracy and resemblance, reality and truth emerge. Yet, as Dudley Andrew discerns, both Bazin and Deleuze 'track the crucial shift' from classic to modern cinema by their regard for the cinema as an evolutionary becoming whose 'power lies in the extremes of life and death' (see Andrew 1997: 88, 89, 84).
3. Excerpt from 'To the Oracle at Delphi', by Lawrence Ferlinghetti (2001: 79):

   > the voice of the fourth person singular
   > the voice of the inscrutable future
   > the voice of the people mixed
   > with a wild soft laughter –
   > And give us new dreams to dream,
   > Give us new myths to live by!

29

4. Deleuze speaks freely with regard to 'most cinematic production, with its arbitrary violence and feeble eroticism' that 'reflects', in his view, 'mental deficiency rather than any invention of new cerebral circuits' (N: 60).

2

Figures of Life

The artist is a seer, a becomer. (WIP: 171)

War nods off to sleep, but keeps one eye always open. (NB)

Consciousness is only a dream with one's eyes open. (SPP: 20)

First sight of the camp: it is another planet. (NB)

'NACHT, "nuit", disaient-ils, c'est l'oubli. NEBEL, "brouillard", c'est la fumée dans laquelle vous vous volatiserez tous – ihr werdet krepieren, "vous crèverez tous!"' (Raskin 1987: 16). Against 'night' and 'fog', against the threat of forgetting humanity's capacity for mass extermination and dehumanisation, Resnais' 1955 *Nuit et Brouillard* forges. In search of life through the imperceptible, impossible sight of 'another planet' bent on shame and annihilation, *Nuit et Brouillard* confronts actual and virtual remains of the Holocaust as the film's audio-visual assemblages of relentless, painstaking movements, plaintive score and dispassionate voiceover profoundly violate our sight and means for sensory release from the affective violence, the 'endless, uninterrupted fear . . .' (NB). If, as Deleuze contends, 'Resnais succeeds in showing, by means of things and victims, not only the functioning of the camp but also the mental functions, which are cold, diabolical, almost impossible to understand which preside over its organization' (C2: 121), *Nuit et Brouillard* also undercuts these efficient murderous operations through piercing revelations of horrors that at once resist and disavow their very exposure: 'no description, no image can reveal their true dimension' (NB).

Even 'a peaceful landscape', 'a meadow in harvest', 'a road where cars and peasants and couples pass', 'even a resort village with a steeple and country fair' can all 'lead to a concentration camp', the film's voiceover persists. As it reveals the horrifically surreal through these actual forms and beings of a rational world, *Nuit et Brouillard* effectively exposes and confronts forces of death and self-immolation. This 'ethics of self-creation' and resistance through art strives to initiate life-affirming movement even and especially in the face of

1 'A peaceful landscape', Nuit et Brouillard *(Resnais 1955)*

death for, as in 'all creative activities', writes Ronald Bogue, 'the goal is to instigate movement, to make something happen' (Bogue 2004: 6).

As this chapter will argue, *Nuit et Brouillard* creates and even profoundly affirms life and movement, it makes something happen, through series of audio-visual images that testify not only to the Event of the Holocaust and its crumbling camp remains in pastoral countrysides but also to the *virtual remains*, the lingering affects and events of fear, sadness and hope that pervade each image, archive, stone and artefact.[1] 'Whether it be a philosophy, an artwork, or a self', Bogue concludes, 'that which is shaped engages a passage from chaos to chaosmos,[2] a mutative *form-in-formation* that inaugurates something new' (Bogue 2004: 6; emphasis mine).

If the actual, present, personal death of a self may result from its destructive encounters with other bodies that decompose its powers and capacities for entering into more empowering, affirming relations, as Deleuze contends following Spinoza, it is perhaps this aspect of actual-virtual existence, this fragility and intimate susceptibility to the 'illnesses of the lived' (WIP: 173), that the 'Lazarean' artist goes beyond. He who has confronted death in life, writes Deleuze, 'returns from death, from the land of the dead', to pass through death, be born from it, and 'go towards another death, perhaps the same one' (C2: 208). 'Through having reached the percept as "the sacred source"', Deleuze and Guattari continue, 'through having seen Life in the living or the Living in the lived', artists and philosophers return 'breathless and with bloodshot eyes ... they have seen *something* in life that is too much for anyone, too much for themselves, and that has put on them the quiet mark of death' (WIP: 172; emphasis mine).

Even then as life turns to destruction, and personal death most shameful and humiliating, even as productivity and efficiency effect new series of genocides and weaponry so that we might never escape our shame at being human (see N: 172), this very *something* in life that is too much for anyone is still 'also the source or breath that supports [artist-philosophers] through the illnesses of the lived' (WIP: 172–3). For this *something* released through impossible pain, suffering and sight is a nonhuman becoming, a powerful force that may forge new life and affects through art in the face of horror and ruin.

Through this 'purely transitive' *something* that can only be specified as sensation – through *affects* that go beyond the *affec-tions* or 'corporeal traces' and existing states of an affected body towards the variations, transitions, passages and lived durations that are experienced *between* actualised states and affecting bodies (SPP: 48–9) – art might provide new sights or percepts as its becom-ings make us become with them while 'we' are drawn 'into the com-pound' (WIP: 175). In this sense, we might then also approach *Nuit et Brouillard* as a *form-in-formation* in the manner Bogue suggests, and that Deleuze and Guattari propose when identifying a 'monu-ment' that 'does not commemorate ... but confides to the ear of the future the persistent sensations that embody the event: the constantly renewed suffering of men and women ... their constantly renewed struggle' (WIP: 176–7).

Such a practical cine-philosophy and ethics of living resides, as Deleuze and Guattari claim, 'in the vibrations, clinches, and openings it gave to men and women at the moment of its making'. As 'a monu-ment that is always in the process of becoming' (WIP: 177), a cin-ematic living monument or series of images and percepts freed from any fixed temporal or transcendent, omnipotent perspective, *Nuit et Brouillard*, these pages fundamentally contend, passes through death ... but is yet reborn by it.

For through its embodiment and replaying of the Holocaust as an event of endless dying and suffering, as a confluence of dynamic affective forces without beginning or end, as a 'never-ending cry' (NB) whose resonances the film expresses in relation to death's two virtual-actual aspects, *Nuit et Brouillard* ceaselessly questions *how*. Hence the film's pursuit of the roots and emergences of despotic repression that reveal the Holocaust as an effect of a destructive life ethic that denounces, categorises and hierarchises life as it affixes terms of sin and redemption. *Nuit et Brouillard*'s victims are bodily effects of such systematisation: 'Shaved. Tattooed. Numbered. Caught up in some incomprehensible hierarchy' (NB).

Yet despite this holocaustal contagion and ethic of hatred 'bent on self-destruction' and 'multiplying . . . cults of death' (SPP: 12) through intolerance, subservience and shame, the film as a formative, affective body grasps the sense and persistence of the historic event, and so life in the process. For the sensory encounters between film and viewer that expose reactive forces of death incite not 'a cult of death', as Deleuze writes with regard to Resnais' works and that of other postwar philosophers, writers and cinema authors (C2: 209). Rather, alongside its depictions of life and hope beyond death, *Nuit et Brouillard* eventually encounters a life free from subjectivity and objectivity as singularly embodied by the dying figure of the skeletal *Muselmann* who lingers precariously, inhumanly, at the interstice between personal death and impersonal, immanent life. Through its cuts and edits between still and moving images, the film explores this edge between lived and living, actual death and immanent life, a crack the film intensely expresses through these living spectres or *Muselmänner* that haunt and exceed its frames.

As it focuses then upon the persistent effects and affects of the actual event of the Holocaust, *Nuit et Brouillard* embraces futural possibilities of movement via extensive tracking movements that traverse layers of pasts. Such movement at once also exposes the tangible effects of stasis, of judgement and condemnation, as the camera tracks along barbed enclosures to peer within clawed gas chambers and ovens . . . As ever, death lines each possibility for life. Yet, as we are drawn into the affective time-spaces of *Nuit et Brouillard* through our encounters with the screen and its affects, movements and intensities, these glimpses of various 'sheets of past' reveal the persisting remnants of the Holocaust event that subsist beneath official, oft tampered with record. Through these imperceptible sensations and singularities of past made tangible through the film, these affects of madness, fear or cold that evoke a hollowed and inhumane existence beyond historic fact and authorised account, *Nuit et Brouillard* defies not only threats of forgetting and denial but also the hierarchical primacy of literal translation or 'authentic' representation, and so challenges death with life.

Through its 'active forgetting' and expression of the intensity, impact and import of the event that strikes via the film as if for a first time, *Nuit et Brouillard* embodies an ethics of joy and affirmation of life and existence. Such an ethics eschews attempts at recognition, empathy or understanding as it exposes, through 'silent layers of earth' (C2: 255), indefinable sensations that empower a body's capacity to 'be' and act. In lieu of any quest for truth or meaning then, this singular encounter with the past and the event through layers of earth, bones and ashes affirms life's incessant movements and possibilities.

As it then passes into scarred landscapes and ruins, the film's non-human 'eye' scours material traces that open to the film's moments of virtual intensity, pure experience or sensation that resist description or rationalisation. As liberated from any fixed subject's perspective and notion of morality, like the sensations that the film releases, this impersonal pure consciousness surveys the decaying camps in the 'present-day' while fragments of archival footage and photographs reveal a more distant past. Through this new, ethical consciousness comprised of sensory presences beneath actual historical detail, *Nuit et Brouillard* breaks from human 'molar' or fixed perception. As the camera tracks along barbed wires and through time to expose this becoming consciousness, the movements evoke Brian Massumi's description of a movement from 'continuous, nonconscious *self-perception*', the 'background perception that accompanies every event, however quotidian', to the perception or making conscious of such commonly nonconscious self-perception (Massumi 1996: 229).

This making perceptible of the imperceptible, this revelation and exposure of open time and its duration through the film by way of time-images that relinquish chronological and narrative causal determinations, permits the impossible sight of the Holocaust to surface through affective intensities never yet realised. Massumi's identification of this surfacing, perceiving or making conscious of autonomous affect as a movement towards the asubjective consciousness described above 'allows', as he writes, 'affect to be effectively analysed – as long as a vocabulary can be found for that which is imperceptible but whose escape from perception cannot but be perceived' (1996: 229).

By way of its asubjective virtual perception or percepts, *Nuit et Brouillard* then forges a 'subterranean *Ethics*' (SPP: 29), an apersonal seeing that plunges into the image's 'archaeological', 'geological' ages, layers, sections and 'buryings' in interrogative testimony to, as Deleuze writes à propos the postwar time-image, 'the victims slaughtered . . . to fertilize a field, the struggles that took place and the corpses thrown out' (C2: 244). We are yet always also reminded of the virtual excess or forever unknown, or, as Massumi remarks, of 'that something [that] has always and again escaped', that 'remains unactualized, inseparable from but unassimilable to any *particular*, functionally anchored perspective' (Massumi 1996: 228).

As these pages have thus far proposed, this unactualised tension *Nuit et Brouillard* evokes between actual-virtual, personal-impersonal, decomposition-composition, death and life makes visible the most terrifying interstice of life at its limit between the shameful impotence of this world and the potentials of worlds and life yet to come. 'Nine million dead haunt this countryside', bodies of 'indeterminate ages' that died with their 'eyes wide open' . . . (NB). Death fixes no actual present, Deleuze writes, 'so numerous are the dead who haunt the sheets of past' (C2: 116). Once more, the question repeats: how to live and truly see? Can life persist through endless humiliations as life itself breaks life? Of this 'betrayal of the universe and of mankind', we might again return to Deleuze's thoughts through Spinoza as he writes of a 'humanity bent on self-destruction . . . always busy running life into the ground, mutilating it, killing it outright or by degrees, overlaying it or suffocating it with laws, properties, duties, empires' (SPP: 12).

Nuit et Brouillard's response to this problem of how yet to live is, again, its 'revolutionary becoming' (N: 171); the means through which it thereby 'makes something happen' affect and inspire these pages. From the depths of wounds and memories *Nuit et Brouillard*'s form-in-formation then gives rise, this chapter contends, to a new living monument and movement that boldly testifies to a vital 'new consciousness', 'vision' and 'appetite for living' (SPP: 13).

We turn a blind eye to what surrounds us. (NB)

There's no democratic state that's not compromised to the very core by its part in generating human misery . . . There's no longer any image of proletarians around of which it's just a matter of becoming conscious. (N: 173)

Every representation of death concerns its inadequate aspect, whereas the unconscious discovers and seizes upon the other side, the other face. (DR: 114)

What remains to be seen of an abandoned concentration camp; what of the unseen remains? From the image of a vast field and open sky, *Nuit et Brouillard*'s camera slowly descends into the 'stratigraphic thicknesses' of the image (C2: 254). It tracks along wire enclosures and remnants of abandoned concentration camps in 'present' day[3] as we peer between the thorny veins or wires of the barbed barriers. Names of a strange collectivity punctuate the dispassionate voiceover, 'Strüthof, Oranienburg, Auschwitz, Neuengamme, Belsen, Ravensbruck, Dachau' (NB), while the camera's eye, the 'only visitor' to which the voiceover refers, releases pure affects of emptiness, barrenness, coldness and harshness. The film does not explicitly label its visual images and, as Jean Cayrol's desolate commentary and Hanns Eisler's occasionally gentle yet always also foreboding soundtrack layer an oft nightmarish visual track, the filmic elements remain surreally, jarringly autonomous. By way of these filmic affronts to comprehension and conventional filmic composition, *Nuit et Brouillard* confronts the incommensurable wretchedness of the camps.

Despite the horrors the film then exhumes, through its singular audio-visual elements and the incongruity of their disjunctive relations, *Nuit et Brouillard* seemingly paradoxically engenders a sense of 'univocity' or interconnectedness. For through its interrelating albeit disjunctive elements the film releases a power of difference and variation that does not attempt to repeat the Holocaust as it actually was, as might a closed attempt at definitive representation or resemblance. Rather, via the whole of its relations that sense and reveal infinite virtual life or potential, time's perpetual duration, *Nuit et Brouillard* repeats anew the event of the Holocaust as it makes 'readable' or perceptible its 'stratigraphic thicknesses' (C2: 254) and past singular layers.

This imaging of the event is, again, not founded upon notions of duplication and authenticity as the film's explorations problematise the seemingly separate worlds of reality and art or representation. *Nuit et Brouillard*'s images, in other words, do not exist distinctly from 'real life', and the inmate's 'body' might be recognised in a manner Bergson describes, as another expression of existence's one substance or immanence, as an 'aggregate of the material world, an image which acts like other images, receiving and giving back movement' (Bergson 1991: 19). Memories, imaginings, perceptions and fictions are as 'real', *Nuit et Brouillard* suggests, as the Histories, Truths and Universals the film dissects.

As enabled through the productive force of an unconscious[4] that endlessly questions and micro-analyses how life emerges and changes dimension in a single, 'univocal' world, the film's asubjective seeing or vision exposes the event's horrors through startling singularities of unrecognisable affects and striking sensations. And so, while *Nuit et Brouillard* evaluates without judgement, as its title evokes the ageless cries engendered through Hitler's decree,[5] we are potentially deeply affected.

For through the film's assemblages of shocking sights and lyrical compositions that give sight to this surreal other 'planet', *Nuit et Brouillard* ruptures habitual perception and any sense of the familiar. Resonances of certain actual things and places that might commonly imply happiness or freedom – a country village, train stop, suitcase or child's toy – morph throughout the film. Yet *Nuit et Brouillard*'s strangeness lies not only in these transformations and collisions between terrifying visuals and nimble woodwinds, in the film's editorial and musical 'beauty' and intricacy,[6] in the grace and gentility of its ironic juxtapositions and compositions, but also and most profoundly in its affront to a self's elemental capacity to be both moved and 'freed' through a violent process of defamiliarisation.

The film's terrifying encounter with the concentration camps, with certain states of existence that catapult self-assured identity into new worlds of unrecognisable difference, involves a violence that indeed creates new affects and experiences. This becoming and newness as generated through the actual production of the camps is, however, a *reactive becoming* that reverses and horrifically turns life-affirming active force and activity against itself. As these pages have suggested, *Nuit et Brouillard* subverts this reactive power through its creative force that surfaces via images and encounters with the camps' actual and incorporeal traces and ruins.

The film's genealogical critique then, as advanced through an asubjective consciousness, perceives a collective consciousness or 'soul' that resists the notion of a rational consciousness that might offer explicit condemnations of evilness and fascism in the manner of an authoritative, informational documentary. Alternatively, *Nuit et Brouillard* presents a tactile version of the horror and its endless cry, for which there can be no veracity, description or meaning. 'The blood has dried, the tongues have fallen silent . . . A strange grass covers the paths once trod by inmates . . . No footstep is heard but our own' (NB).

ٮ٭

> Here is the setting: buildings that could pass for stables, garages or workshops. (NB)

A picturesque sequence of images nearly halfway through *Nuit et Brouillard* underscores the film's exploration of the surreal and mundane, imaginary and real, poles that frequently tend throughout the film 'towards a point of indiscernibility', as Deleuze also observes with regard to the time-image in general (C2: 9). From within a camp's barbed wires and against the film's plaintive score, the camera peers at serene landscapes. It glimpses an open, wide field of swaying grass with village, homes and steeple beyond, the frame delimited by the camp's barrier posts. The film then cuts to a still shot taken from behind another wired barrier. From behind these wires, a magnificent castle can be seen in the near distance, while a tree frames the uppermost left corner of the still frame. This shift from moving to still image repeats several other instances throughout the film that manifest this fissure between movement and stasis and that progressively come to realise a point of virtual-actual indiscernibility. For as *Nuit et Brouillard* cuts across coexistent times, rhythms and speeds, their relations become increasingly indiscernible through exchanges and conversions that approach the interstice between life and death, corporeality and incorporeality. Against these encounters through layers of time and a background of absolute real terror conjoined with nostalgia for a world apart from the camps, the detached voiceover remarks: 'At times like these the real world, the world from before, with its peaceful landscapes, could seem not so far off' (NB).

Endlessly, by way of black and white archival stills and colour footage, lighter and more aggressive refrains, the brightness of an 'indifferent' autumn sky and the darkness of a camp at night as glimpsed through an archival still, *Nuit et Brouillard* interleaves distant layers of past within the more recent past or 'present' of the film. As it delves within these pasts to expose the negative, deathly forces of the camps that historical accounts fail to grasp, the film derives its empowering vision, its impersonal virtual perception, through its thrust beyond the limits of common perception. The poles of 'objective and subjective, real and imaginary, physical and mental' (C2: 9), to repeat Deleuze's thoughts on the time-image, can indeed be seen throughout the film to continually interact, convert and converge.

As the camera tracks along camp ruins, its extreme proximity to the wires and barriers facilitates our own nearness to the actual and virtual reality of the horror through space and time. In this way, *Nuit et Brouillard* makes visible both sides, both the actual and virtual of the event, as it produces 'a whole "coalescence" of the perceived with the remembered, the imagined, the known', as Deleuze suggests with respect to 'a perception of perception' via the time-image (C2: 245). Again and repeatedly, the film stresses these limits towards which it strives as it scavenges the camp grounds through time, imagination and memory: 'The reality of these camps, despised by those who built them, and unfathomable to those who endured them – what hope do we have of truly capturing this reality?' (NB).

Forced, humiliated, mutilated to the limit and edges of life, the inmate peers through the wires and forever into the 'crack' between life and death as collisions between 'reality' and fantasy within the camps open in the film to a world of relations and immanence that the *Muselmann* alone perceives. For through this terrifying new vision, through crystal-images that expose time's perpetual founda-tion, and through the impossible sight of the *Muselmann* figure itself, the film delves further into the event and virtual past. The cries, affects and suffering *Nuit et Brouillard* discovers as it nears the point of indiscernibility between life and death correspond to the description Deleuze provides of a 'crystal [that] always lives at the limit . . . itself the "vanishing limit between the immediate past which is already no longer and the immediate future which is not yet"' (C2: 81).

In a most shivering way, the *Muselmann*, again, embodies this limit, precipice or aspect of death Deleuze describes, and through which one attains the 'pure sight' of those who have 'passed through death' and yet 'continue to live . . . in a shivering way, with tired-ness and prudence' (C2: 108–9). Even prior to its sight of the *Muselmänner*, *Nuit et Brouillard* opens to such a self-affection or auto-perception in time via movements that correspond to what Deleuze terms a 'camera-consciousness' (C2: 23), as the film enters into certain mental connections ever yet connected to sensation. Of this, and with regard to Resnais' cinema in general, Deleuze observes that 'feeling, affect, or passion are the principal characters of the brain-world' (C2: 210). As *Nuit et Brouillard*'s camera tracks within and along abandoned camp's barracks, the 'wooden barracks where people sleep three to a bed' (NB), and as the camera turns to seemingly touch the wooden and stone 'beds' as it passes along their edges, this emission of 'feeling' as 'mental function' intensifies (C2: 209).

Further within the barracks the camera continues, its gaze the gaze of an unknown seer that exists between times and the seeming 'worlds' of the surreal and real that fold within each other. As the film exposes ever-greater depths of depravity, it reveals images of various inmates whose faces bear the effects and horrors of fanaticism and intolerance. Reduced to an indefinite, singular life before subjectification, and forced to confront the 'immensity of an empty time where one sees the event yet to come and already happened, in the absolute of an immediate consciousness' (PI: 29), the nameless spectre bears only its designation, 'N.N.', an abbreviation, as survivors testify, for both 'Nacht und Nebel' and 'NOMEN NESCIO – "name unknown"' (Raskin 1987: 16).

This depersonalisation of the inmate, so shockingly shameful, defaces the notion of human as it opens towards a becoming-imperceptible, a non-personal individuation that enables the *Muselmann*'s profound capacity to perceive its own self-dissolution within the entirety of time. The film enacts constant exchanges between the personal and impersonal by way of the *Muselmann* and material relics – mounds of hair, spectacles, a handwritten recipe, a child's doll. These become both profoundly personal and indicative of a specific moment in time, as well as surreally impersonal, incorporeal, 'infinitive' and open to an immense duration wherein past affronts present and future through the film's eye.

The *Muselmann*'s becoming-imperceptible then, this chapter's most shocking claim, proposes the inmate as *a* life, as one who is 'no longer a person, but a becoming' (Smith 1997: xxxiv). However, as the *Muselmann*'s becoming-imperceptible emerges through a *becoming-reactive*, through the emergence and contagion of a highly efficient death machine, subsequent pages of this chapter will consider filmic images through which such a life of absolute desolation yet opens to new sight and *a* life of 'pure immanence', 'beyond good and evil' (PI: 29).

જ

They had kept their eyes open while they slept . . . It is a world without sleep . . . Everything, with a frightening clarity, is clear. (ECC: 206, n. 86)

And where sleep itself presented a threat – no description, no image can reveal their true dimension: endless, uninterrupted fear . . . Of this brick

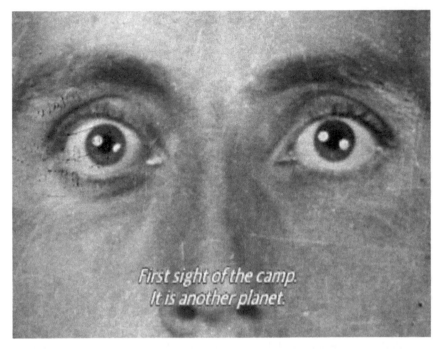

First sight of the camp.
It is another planet.

2 'Endless, uninterrupted fear', Nuit et Brouillard *(Resnais 1955)*

dormitory and these tormented dreams we can but show you the outer shell, the surface . . . These are all we have left to imagine a night of piercing cries . . . Try to get to sleep quickly. (NB)

From within the barracks 'where people slept three to a bed', where 'sleep itself presented a threat', and where the film's camera now slowly tracks in the 'present', *Nuit et Brouillard* pursues its affective course without representation of a general universal humanist or nationalist subject. Instead, as hitherto observed, the film produces a collective assemblage or soul via audio-visual assemblages that resist the finality of closed historical documentation. Through its impersonal, foreign enunciation, through disparate elements which never placate, legitimise, narrativise or authoritatively explicate sensations that emanate freely from the gruesome images, *Nuit et Brouillard* viscerally impinges upon the viewer's body. In the face of the horrors, the film unleashes virtual persistent affects while the soundtrack repeatedly voices endless despair: indeed, 'Who does know anything?' 'What hope do we have of capturing this reality?'

Again, *Nuit et Brouillard* does not endeavour to capture or represent this reality. The film's strategy rather strives to make visible invisible forces and intensities that demand a nonhuman seeing or pure autonomous vision that opens to a moment of world rendered durable through the percepts of a landscape that *sees* (see WIP: 169), in a time open to the outside, the whole of time that quotidian perception and experience cannot perceive. As the film's footage and archival images encounter the actual remnants and remains, the apparatuses, structures and blocks of the camps, it releases the virtual affects, forces and singularities of the actual happening as it actualises the destructive relations that gave rise to the camps. The film reveals these repressive relations through its own perception of perception or absolute consciousness whereby it grasps the singular instant that exists between the 'still-future and already-past' (LS: 151), and as such exposes this perpetual duration in which we exist, whose temporality is that of always already past and eternally yet to come.

Despite the film's somewhat chronological course as it charts the Third Reich's uprising through archival footage, *Nuit et Brouillard* more profoundly performs a geological, untimely quest that interrogates the materialisation of this destructive machine through cuts between colour 'present-day' footage and black and white archival footage. '1933. The machine goes into action' (NB). Through this penetration into the camps, layers and sheets of past, the film increasingly oscillates between mobility and immobility, past and present, relations that intensify the film's sensations of dread, uncertainty, disgust, repulsion and extreme emptiness. It is this ever-reversible exchange between virtual and actual that makes visible the relations of time into which we plunge.

The film's impersonal nonhuman 'third eye' then enters within the horrors of the camps. Through moving and still images, whose speeds of mobility and immobility again suggest the extension and contraction of virtual-actual past-present time, and the intricacy of human perception with its consciousness of alternative durations, the film's encounter with the actual event of the Holocaust reveals itself as a confrontation with the limits of thought itself. In contrast to the deathly war machine that would 'rather annihilate its own servants than stop the destruction' (ATP: 231), *Nuit et Brouillard* effects its own creative 'war machine' or revolutionary movement whose movements interrogate life as they re-counter or counter-actualise, replay or redouble the event and so effect new creation and life through sense of the suffering. This is not to diminish or deny the Holocaust but to embrace its implications and significance through past-present-future time alongside the creative time and act of the film that opens, via impossible sorrow, to past-future survival and becoming.

Through landscapes that 'see' in the absence of humans who, as Deleuze and Guattari write, 'have passed into the landscape and are themselves part of the compound of sensations' (WIP: 169), *Nuit et Brouillard* pursues its excavation of the affects and forces of the actual event. The film cuts from the still black and white photo of a castle in the 'real world beyond' to commence a rightward pan from a perspective high within a former camp observation tower. As the camera continues its pan across land viewed from within the camps in 'present day' colour, the landscape bespeaks the silent voices, their cries and screams of terror. Such, as artist Francis Bacon attests, is to 'paint the scream more than the horror' (FB: 51). There is, that is, 'a relationship between the visibility of the scream . . . and invisible forces, which are nothing other than the forces of the future' (FB: 51).

The inmate's world, continues the film's commentary against the now sombre, weary soundtrack, 'was this closed, self-contained universe, hemmed in by observation posts from which soldiers kept watch, aiming at the prisoners, on occasion killing them out of boredom' (NB). Various ages of coexistent pasts collide as the camera assumes this former soldier's position within the watchtower before the film cuts to yet another black and white photograph. A man of indiscernible age hangs lifeless from a wired barrier; his head falls away from his body, his mouth agape, as he clutches at the wires in this immobile image that effectively mobilises and replays countless ages and terrors that resurface throughout Resnais' oeuvre, as throughout modern time – Algiers as well as Berlin, Bosnia, Guantanamo Bay . . .

The human body, often missing from the film's ceaseless tracks across the landscapes, assumes previously unrealised dimension through its literal and *figural* evocations of absence, elimination and deadness. But 'how can a moment of the world', Deleuze and Guattari demand, 'be rendered durable or made to exist by itself?' By way of response, they quote Virginia Woolf, who advocates an elimination of '"all waste, deadness, superfluity," everything that adheres to our current and lived perceptions' (WIP: 172). As Bogue observes, Deleuze often 'speaks of pure intensities, pure events, pure affects, pure images . . . an extraction of an abstract, vital line' (Bogue 2004: 10) to so 'extract from madness', as Bogue quotes Deleuze, 'the life which it contains, while hating the lunatics who constantly kill life, turn it against itself' (D: 53).

This precisely is *Nuit et Brouillard*'s feat. For, as it extracts from the camps the 'cold, diabolical' mental functions 'which preside over its organization' (C2: 121), the film opens through these liberated intensities and its sight of the *Muselmann* to a 'memory of the world' (C2: 122) that eliminates the personal, 'anecdotal, memory-laden, intentional subject' (Bogue 2004: 10). The 'superimposed ages of Auschwitz', writes Deleuze (C2: 122), open to the immensity of time and thought itself as the film questions the potential for thought and life in the face of those who turn it against itself.

Forces freed from the victims and bodies that once endured them arise in the film through both the unpeopled surreal landscapes, filmed in colour in a more recent past, and the human and once human forms the film sights by way of archival stills and footage. The latter images inscribe a vacancy upon the film, a vacancy further reflected by the infinite glares of the emptied, emaciated figures, the near-corpses or *Muselmänner*, who died with their eyes wide open. Against the ominous tones of a bass clarinet, the film cuts from the black and white still of the man hanging upon the wires to yet another black and white shot taken from a distance further away of a seeming corpse enmeshed by wires. Repeatedly, disturbingly, persistently *Nuit et Brouillard* entreats: what is a human body, a life, death? 'The body', writes Deleuze with particular relevance to the fragile human body,

> is never in the present, it contains the before and the after, tiredness and waiting. Tiredness and waiting, even despair are the attitudes of the body ... This is a time-image, the series of time. The daily attitude is what puts the before and after into the body, time into the body, the body as a revealer of the deadline ... Perhaps tiredness is the first and last attitude, because it simultaneously contains the before and the after ... *not* the drama of communication, but the immense tiredness of the body ... which suggests to thought 'something to incommunicate', the 'unthought', life. (C2: 189)

Shorn of identity and potential for life, the *Muselmann* contains the before and the after as it achieves a becoming-imperceptible. No longer human but a shadow at the crevice between life and death, this shivering stilled life of 'immense tiredness' bears the immensity of time. The making visible of time in the body, the 'mount[ing of] the camera on an everyday body' (C2: 189), opens then once more to what Deleuze through Spinoza identifies as a 'an *unconscious of thought* just as profound as *the unknown of the body*' for, 'as conscious beings, we never apprehend anything but the *effects* of [our] compositions and decompositions' (SPP: 18–19).

Which is to say, once more, by way of landscapes, artefacts and bodies exposed through both still and moving images, *Nuit et Brouillard*'s immanent practical ethics makes visible the relations, sensations and forces that effected the constructions of the camps. Moreover, through discovery of an unconscious of thought and unknown of the body, the film challenges the cinema's potential to truly think beyond given consciousness and knowledge. The means through which *Nuit et Brouillard* offers these new sights, direct sensations and powers of resistance by way of assemblages that express humankind's resiliency will be further examined below. As the film's commentary claims, 'man is resilient. Though the body's worn out with fatigue, the mind works on' (NB).

ン

> The 'Figure' is the form that is connected to a sensation, and that conveys the violence of this sensation directly to the nervous system. (Smith 2003: xiii)
>
> *Figuren*: 'Where death cannot be called death, corpses cannot be called corpses.' (Agamben 1999: 70)
>
> The Germans made us refer to the bodies as *Figuren*, that is, as puppets. (Lanzmann 1985: 13)[7]
>
> In the end, each inmate resembles the next: a body of indeterminate age that dies with its eyes wide open. (NB)

From within the camps, within the barracks where inmates once 'slept', a camera ascends the stacked 'beds' with a steady upward climb. The slight quivering of the rising camera extends *Nuit et Brouillard*'s refutation of any comprehensive history, stable representation or assimilable knowledge as the camera's movement confers an affecting tactility to this moving shot. Such a trembling of the image, as if the camera operator's own hands did shake, becomes even more unexpectedly discernible and poignant throughout the film's still shots. Nearly imperceptible, this subtle unsteadiness of a seemingly handheld camera destabilises any distinction in the film between movement and stasis, life's mobility and death's immobility – binary designations that are undermined by the film's explorations of the ambiguous, indiscernible tensions and extremes

of life that pervade degrees between living and dying, and that perpetually defy description and comprehension.

As the film strives through its sensory relations and minute movements to tangibly, tactilely convey the ephemeral, virtual, always
transient past-future – the affective experiences of an historic event
whose systematic production of death manufactured a macabre
quotidian beyond human thought, comprehension and all life – this
apparent shakiness in the audio-visuals effects a breaking-down or
faltering as voice, image and sound elements each concede a tremulous instability and arbitrariness in representation.

In effect, through its onslaught of historic images, the violently
graphic archival stills that dominate the film's quest to ascertain the
'personal' reality of a monumental deportation and epic wounding of
human dignity, *Nuit et Brouillard* paradoxically evokes a desperate
critical uncertainty. For as it expresses the personal through most
impersonal means of 'seeing', the film's seemingly ceaseless amassing
of horrifying images and autonomous, *'non-corresponding'* sound
(see C2: 240) deepens the overpowering shame of stockpiled human
bodies and fragments, those endless masses of shoes, spectacles,
hair, limbs . . . headless bodies . . . heads with staring eyes . . . The
film's incursion within the camps becomes no less than an endless
ungrounding of life itself through its revelations of coexistent times
and the *Muselmann*, whose precarious life between mortal death and
immanent life profoundly opens, as noted, to the duration of time.

Certain authentic, historic archival images of the 'real' cannot
approach the stench of it all, *Nuit et Brouillard* stresses, as the film
instead seizes upon the images' reality through their real actual
properties and real virtual sensory intensities and sensations. As the
images enter through layers of past into the funereal 'fog' of the event
to scavenge the depths of its carnage, *Nuit et Brouillard* releases sensations that comprise the actual event and sustain its ever-enduring
effects. Such intensities must be sensed and seen with a 'third eye' or
'new clarity', as Deleuze also suggests through Bacon's art, a *'haptic
vision'* (FB: 129) that 'implies', as writes Daniel Smith, 'a type of
seeing distinct from the optical' (Smith 2003: xxvi).

The film's piercing shock, that is, derives from its capacity to
touch through sight, to overwhelm through deeply moving affective
assemblages of horror, sorrow and awe as generated between the
affects of viewer and screen. Between the film's audio-visual connections, disjunctions and montages, and the viewer's own responses
and speeds, *Nuit et Brouillard*'s profound intensity surfaces and

materialises. As an image that embodies and opens to the immensity of time that derives from situations at once both extraordinary and banal, the time-image forms a moving film-viewer assemblage so that both 'bodies' affect and are affected by responsive movements between the two.

Nuit et Brouillard's images of sickening content, which emerge surreally through the mundane and everyday, are further intensi- fied by a sardonically ironic tone that destabilises illusions of truth and representation. With regard to the film, Max Silverman writes of a 'world of horror' created from 'the banal and the everyday' whereby 'horror is ordinary and the ordinary is, or can be, horrific' (Silverman 2006: 6). Again, worlds of 'reality' and fantasy collide in *Nuit et Brouillard* as images of pastoral fields, castles, band musicians, handwritten notes and handmade toys appear against a frenetic staccato of horns and strings and horrific images, the sight of countless naked men observed from long distances, and the film's commentary: 'Under the pretext of hygiene, nudity strips the inmates of all pride in one stroke' (NB).

The film's assault deep within the camps' horrors escalates. Perverse becomings overwhelm the screen as human hair, skin, bone and nail open to unthought new dimensions and infinite nightmarish transformations that the film admits it cannot capture. While Claude Lanzmann famously opposes *Nuit et Brouillard*'s use of archival materials,[8] the film's incorporation of images in fact ironically underscores the film's denial of visibility, completion or certainty as its sensory affective experiences of the actual event counter conven- tional considerations of adequacy and reality in representation. *Nuit et Brouillard* thereby declines moral authority as it repeatedly under- cuts its appointment as an official commissioned record not only through images, sounds and words but also through silences and quivering camera movements that betray the endless virtual affective, subterranean presences beneath the actual reality.

The film's archival images and footage excerpts do not then preserve or illustrate the horror, posit any definitive truth or even affix accusation; rather their affective non-representational force continually opens to questions regarding the formation of camps that so profoundly deformed human body and soul. *Nuit et Brouillard* embodies a powerful creative force, one that facilitates the film's progressive re-appropriation of its title. For through the film's imper- sonal, molecular 'third eye' of new sight or sensation that thrusts into the night and fog, the unknown, unthought, intangible and unseen, values of irrefutable verisimilitude and identity retain no applicability as the images' movements, in degrees and speeds of still and moving image slownesses, wound and permanently affect us. *Nuit et Brouillard* thus fiercely embraces the powers of the night and fog to evince the *imperceptible*, the incorporeal becomings, entities and unlimited always past and yet to come *sense* of the horrors, the ever enduring effects and their virtual relations that persist *between* actual fact and artefact.

As it advances with increasingly violent force and ostensible outrage into the camps' worlds, *Nuit et Brouillard* at once overthrows moral restrictions of representation, as grounded upon models of inadequacy and inability, to release the virtual events, the always transient effects, intensities and virtual sense of the Holocaust's endless dying, its incessant cry. The film questions – 'what hope do we have of truly capturing this reality?' – and through its multiple affects of fear, repulsion, awe, its various editing rhythms that oscillate in degrees between a shuddering tranquillity and rapid anxiety with filmic cuts between living and dying, 'real' and camp worlds as incongruous, acerbic and 'barbed' as the vicious wires and hatreds that suppress the camps, the film issues its own shocking reply. All this as we observe the luxurious, sadistic accoutrements of SS domesticity and militancy against images of lives stripped of all human recognition.

These 'lives' or skeletal 'figures', antitheses of life, unrecognisable sticks or *figuren* and custom products of death factories wherein personal actual death is nullified by an indistinctiveness between living and dying, expose, again, a profound, perpetual achronological time. For as the *Muselmänner* facilitate a continual dying, their sight through the film gives expression to Deleuze and Blanchot's consideration of death and its wound. Can these figures of the *Muselmänner*, effects of utter devastation and genocide, coincide with the progressive, positive aspects of an impersonal death, death's virtual side as Deleuze conceives through Blanchot, whereby the decomposition of a suffering, broken body and self becomes also the production and composition of new, singular relations and life? As the *Muselmann* embodies 'the abyss of the present, the time without present' in which it forfeits its self and the 'power of dying', it effectively 'never cease[s] to die', and 'never succeed[s] in dying' (LS: 152); the *Muselmann* endures as *a* life and as the life, sense and memory of the Holocaust.

The *Muselmänner* are thus stripped of individuality and attachment to an unbearable present, constraints of identity that pre-empt singular expressions of life, as Deleuze argues. Yet again, the *Muselmann*'s becoming-imperceptible through self and bodily dissolution and disintegration cannot be affirmatively conceived in relation to a purely destructive and suicidal will that entirely vanquishes life (see ATP: 231). The endless dying of near corpses, those name-, self- and even life-less that are refused a personal, present death of the self, is an effect of an extermination so shameful that it fundamentally challenges the possibility and potential for new life. What then of the *Muselmann*, of death bereft of the personal, and a film's expression of the tensions, angers, fears and personal-impersonal faces of present and eternal time and death? Can *Nuit et Brouillard* reveal life through death?

If, as Williams observes, 'it is part of the death drive that gives determinacy and energy but also destruction' (Williams 2008a: 180), if, as this chapter will continue to explore, personal death might open to immanent life as well as profound pain, can death be positively conceived through the *Muselmänner* the film glimpses? Can an impersonal dying, such as Deleuze distinguishes through Blanchot, be conceived as a creative destruction and dying that negates death as 'death loses itself in itself' via the emergence of a new and 'most singular life' (LS: 153)? If so, enduring sense of the Holocaust event perhaps persists through the *Muselmann*, whose endless dying at the break between death and life, past and future forcibly questions how the present is to prevent devastation by way of its responses to incessantly morphing and multiplying problems. 'How can we prevent deep life from becoming a demolition job'? (LS: 157). How to live if the 'problem of thought', as Williams writes, is 'not how to arrive at a given end' but 'how to live with the unforeseeable yet structured legacies of thought and the desires accompanying it' (Williams 2008a: 182).

Nuit et Brouillard, then, demands our constant struggle against perpetual and final destruction as the film's virtual perception tends towards limits of unified self, history and cinema. Through this making perceptible of the imperceptible, *Nuit et Brouillard* opens onto an unconscious virtual perception that examines how a war-machine effectively turned a line of flight into one of death, and how we might live on in that knowledge and so replay or counteractualise the sense of the event through movements towards new life. How, in other words, might we survive, connect and disconnect through our infinite series of encounters, relations and variations that are forever inscribed by the deep wounds and actual events that pierce us? If actual, fatal death is our final limit as it destroys a self through the cessation of its actual body in a most personal present, what of the *Muselmänner*, those who linger in an indefinite, singular realm perceptible only by those in that in-between between life and death? Is Deleuze's conception of *a* singular life ultimately realised through the film's encounter with our deepest wounds and fears as embodied through the *Muselmann*, whose life has given way to an impersonal composition of virtualities and affects of pure terror, anguish and hunger?

If 'very small children [who] all resemble one another and have hardly any individuality' are 'infused', as Deleuze writes, 'with an immanent life that is pure power and even bliss' (PI: 30), how might we conceive the fragmented and wasted bodies of the concentration camps who all resemble one another? Can pure horror beget life, as through *Nuit et Brouillard*'s incessantly roaming movements? The two aspects of death, corporeal and incorporeal, personal and impersonal, 'differ in nature' (LS: 156), as Deleuze insists, but are also inevitably closely associated so that there is danger of the incorporeal crack's full actualisation in a fragile body.

Which is to say, inasmuch as we might explore the possibilities inherent along the crack's edge, between personal and impersonal death and dying, there is danger of the actual body's destruction and suffering. There can be no joy then through a 'hardened and faded present which alone subsists and signifies death' (LS: 160). Through what Deleuze might term its 'revolutionary means of exploration', or means of counter-actualisation through past layers of time, *Nuit et Brouillard* liberates the event, 'always for other times' (LS: 161).

Alongside Blanchot's claim that even 'death is never present' (see LS: 348), the filmic time-image also, Deleuze maintains, is not in the present. 'On the contrary', he writes, 'it is necessary to move towards a limit, to make the limit of before the film and after it pass into the film . . . to achieve a before and an after as they coexist with the image . . . to achieve a direct presentation of time' (C2: 38). This is our limit or challenge towards which we strive to perceive and think, and what the cinema and *Nuit et Brouillard* most profoundly exhibit: a direct presentation of time that speaks most significantly to not only an 'emancipation of time' but also of life as we attempt to live and follow a 'deeper memory, a memory of the world directly exploring time, reaching in the past that which conceals itself from memory' (C2: 39).

In Resnais' oeuvre Deleuze, again, perceives such a 'temporalisation of the image' via its tracking images (C2: 39). In addition to these images that 'plunge' into time, the concluding section of this chapter will once more examine *Nuit et Brouillard*'s extraordinary emancipation of time and self through its brief encounter with the *Muselmänner*'s endless dying, the virtual affects and effects of which pervade the film as they summon a critical responsibility towards life and a demand for its release from the horrors we generate. As an indefinite entity suspended between life and death, deprived of self, present, will and a power to become, the *Muselmann* becomes our greatest fear. Paradoxically, this figure embodies both immanent life and a suicidal line of destruction manufactured and fuelled by capitalist production.

'The Nazis may win the war. These new towns are part of their economy', *Nuit et Brouillard*'s commentary claims against the score's antagonising string pizzicato while the non-subjectified 'eye' or visual track reveals archival footage of countless camp barrack rows and factories. These 'towns' dominate the screen and *Muselmann*'s future. Yet again, the *Muselmann*'s wavering between life and death in a time of the before and after seems a strange, unassimilable series of paradoxes: can a weak captive body, strained and broken to the limit of survival and yet compelled to the threshold of incorporeal immanent potential, embody an emancipation of time and the self? Through further discussion of the film's exploration of virtual intensities and actual remains in relation to the *Muselmann*'s precarious living, the concluding section of this chapter will indeed reaffirm *Nuit et Brouillard*'s realisation of life and movement despite and even through an event most deprived and enslaved.

> But they are losing the war. There's no coal for the crematoria, no bread for the inmates ... When the Allies open the doors ... (NB)

The strings of the film's score play abruptly and sharply approximately twenty-seven minutes into the film. The visuals resist all description, the strewn 'bodies', shorn skeletons with skin, bones without mass, entangled, unrecognisable, a network of limbs, decay, dirt, death ... How to go on? With combinations of chaotic cuts, frantic handheld camera movements, fluid tracking shots, disconcerting score, images of brutalism and intimate sensualism, Resnais' later 1959 film *Hiroshima mon amour* also viscerally discharges affects of savagery, the shaving of victims, the desperation of gnawing, clawing nails, the indiscernibility of naked, 'dying' bodies. Yet the life through death, love and madness *Hiroshima mon amour* effects seemingly evades *Nuit et Brouillard* as the latter crosscuts from the bulldozing of once human fragments to the marching troops of strong and able-bodied SS personnel to the amassing of skulls and compiling of 'figures' tossed into graves, to the raw gazes of the remaining 'surviving' inmates observing all.

With a more terrifying 'beauty' than *Hiroshima mon amour*, if beauty might be conceived as a creative, productive force that does not mimic or subjectivise, *Nuit et Brouillard* advances the cinema's potential to directly convey time beyond the stasis of recognition, melancholia, absence, fear or death. The cinema's becoming and transformation must, again, discover means of freeing life and thought from the Holocaust's permanent shadow. If through the cinemas of Resnais and Chris Marker this book performs an analysis of 'beauty' as it explores new ways of seeing and thinking in this world of prolific destruction and extermination, of all the films these chapters experience, it is Resnais' terrifyingly beautiful *Nuit et Brouillard* that most fundamentally challenges this book's affirmation of life through beauty, thought and creation.

Nuit et Brouillard's beauty, its exploratory, experiential assessment of repressive formations and redistributions of reactive powers that destroy life, destabilises certitudes proclaimed in the name of morality, religion, transcendence and 'freedom'. The film's 'art', then, is also an art of the self that fractures rational self and world through a productive force or power that incessantly interrogates problems that plague life. As the film rearticulates Spinoza's demand that Deleuze repeats – 'Why is it so difficult not only to win but to bear freedom?' (SPP: 10) – *Nuit et Brouillard*'s inquest challenges notions of hierarchical 'freedom'. For the freedom Deleuze and Spinoza respectively conceive through a *free indirect discourse* and 'inspired free vision' is expanded and expressed through *Nuit et Brouillard* as the film discloses an impersonal, unconscious seeing that 'turns in on itself' (C2: 243).

With regard to this 'perception of perception' that grasps the double-sided aspect of all things, both actual and virtual, real and imaginary, corporeal and incorporeal, in relation to Spinoza's 'inspired free vision' Deleuze writes of

the third eye, which enables one to see life beyond all false appearances, passions, and deaths. The virtues – humility, poverty, chastity,

*They make spoons,
puppets to be hidden away.*

3 *Puppets,* Nuit et Brouillard *(Resnais 1955)*

frugality – are required for this kind of vision, no longer as virtues that
mutilate life, but as powers that penetrate it and become one with it.
(SPP: 14)

This again refers to a 'sobriety' through life, to an impersonal
freedom, to pure sensations and affects that 'extract from madness
the life which it contains, while hating the lunatics who constantly
kill life, turn it against itself' (D: 53). *Nuit et Brouillard*, in this vital
sense, extracts from the event, from the horror and destruction, the
life which it contains.

For as the film conveys a life, freedom and power that finally, in
the face of 'the murderous appetite of men' (SPP: 13), can only be
mobilised through an *untimeliness* 'acting', as Nietzsche and Deleuze
insist, 'counter to our time and thereby acting on our time and, let us
hope, for the benefit of a time to come' (Nietzsche 1997: 60), *Nuit
et Brouillard* nears, once again more profoundly than any other film
this book examines, that frightening interstice between personal and
impersonal life and death. The power *Nuit et Brouillard* profoundly
explores is, in effect, a power to become.

'Hands wrapped in bandages labor on' (NB). Within this previously noted sequence approximately fifteen minutes into the film, wherein a slightly trembling handheld camera journeys upward along the barracks, layers of past collide as *Nuit et Brouillard* glimpses a toy. A hand-carved puppet lies hidden across a high wooden beam. The image resounds at once with the joys of a child while the puppet's face bears Hitler's own, and as the puppet itself evokes the camps' *figuren*. Could we ever glimpse the actual moments in which the nonentities of 'figure' and 'puppet', *Muselmann* and toy, were produced, or could the moments of the toy's safekeeping and *Muselmänner's* dying ever be 'captured'? In contrast to countless other films and their attempts to present 'authentic' or 'faithful' dramatisations, *Nuit et Brouillard's* invasion within this unimaginable world of horror abandons any truth-seeking aspiration as the film explores novel strategies for releasing affect through unprecedented sensory combinations of aural and visual movements.

As the camera ascends, its slow movement recalling the fluid yet cautious and hesitant descent of the film's first shot that propels us into the depths of the camps' worlds, it discovers the puppet. *Nuit et Brouillard* expressly does not suggest an ability or intent to reveal the actual events or remains. The deliberate yet tremulous movement of the camera, and moreover the sight of the toy itself, may seem like a jarring image of simulation, dramatisation or testimonial representation staged following the camps' liberation in an attempt to document a trace of the 'real', a conventional documentary tactic at odds with this film's tactile, non-representational style.

And yet, once again, the film does not concern itself with hierarchical distinctions between real and unreal, human and nonhuman as *Nuit et Brouillard* more thoroughly explores the always real actual and real virtual beyond human classification. Its 'staged' discovery of the puppet moreover contributes to the film's profound tangibility, as manifested not only through its discords of sonic lyricism and visual depravity but also through strategic, achronological cuts across pasts. From various asubjective perspectives the film's roaming, non-centred eye criss-crosses moving and still, colour and black and white footage to directly access the undying sensations. As this chapter has reiterated, in a film indicted with showing too much, *Nuit et Brouillard's* extraordinary force derives as much from its excess of daunting visuals, its content, as from the deeply affective means it employs to reveal and produce such content. The content as ever, as many have affirmed, effects the means.

'They make spoons, puppets to be hidden away' (NB). Immediately before this shot of the puppet, the film reveals a moving black and white long shot of trucks passing filled with people: 'The "black transports" that leave at night and which no one ever hears of again' (NB). The stationary camera watches as the trucks fade into the distance and vehicle exhaust. As the shot fades, *Nuit et Brouillard* cuts to the sudden close shot of the puppet. 'But man is resilient', as is the film against any sentimentalised account. The film rather intensifies its apersonal seeing through its still and moving images that convey an immediate poignancy via the tangible unsteadiness, a volatility augmented by jagged cuts between sound and visual as well as by disparities within each filmic element or track, as in the collisions between long and close shots, and those between lamenting score and remote voice.

And so, as the camera encounters the toy and as the commentary notes the spirit of resilience and survival the puppet might suggest, the shot's intimation of new life is most intensely expressed through the dynamic assemblage of all its filmic components that collectively create a new material, sensory, affective perception of the Holocaust. The film probes more deeply, affects more profoundly, than any personalised representation or 'authentic' replication. Untimely, ever-new, *Nuit et Brouillard*'s means, as engendered by the utmost limit event of recent history, finally incite life through death.

Unlike the showcasing of additional items of 'survival' that the inmates produced – which the film lists via a series of still shots immediately following that of the puppet, images of monsters, boxes, notes, recipes ('Crawfish à la basquaise') – a literally and affectively moving archival image reveals the puppet. For, as perceived against shadows within the black and white footage, the spirited score, and the searching yet unsteady camera movement, the puppet image discharges affects of intimacy and covertness that distinguish this shot from the static shots that follow, even as the camera's unsteadiness prevails throughout all the film's archival images, still and moving alike.

With regard to 'mistaking live footage for still images', the inevitable indiscernibility between living, dying and dead as embodied through the film's frequent series of undecidedly moving and still shots, Wilson writes of the 'fear [that] insists in the inability to distinguish stillness from movement', 'the indeterminacy of living and dead matter' that effects moments, such as that of the puppet, 'of unknowing and undoing' (Wilson 2005: 102). 'In undoing the "good form" of representation', explains Bogue, 'the artist . . . engages invisible forces that never become directly visible – those of the unconscious, which are fundamentally forces of deformation. The "space of the invisible, of the possible", then, is an invented space traversed by unconscious forces that render visual what Lyotard calls the "figural"' (Bogue 1996: 259).

As it persists in rendering visible the invisible and *figural*, *Nuit et Brouillard* subtly maintains a focus upon the conscious act of seeing itself, a seeing that might open to new possibilities for thought. Any potential for life and a time yet to come, for new sight beyond boundaries of identity, is ours, and our potential emerges through those that forever resist sight, and through whose deaths the film sees. 'First sight of the camp: it is another planet' (NB). As it reveals mounds of confiscated spectacles, and stares at eyes whose chilling glare in extreme close-up recall Marcel Duchamp's startling gaze in Marker's 2001 *Le Souvenir d'un Avenir*, *Nuit et Brouillard* unearths layers of past that see. The 'landscape *sees*', to repeat Deleuze and Guattari's words regarding the percept (WIP: 169). 'The percept is the landscape before man, in the absence of man', they continue, and through Deleuze and Guattari's description we might again claim that the *Muselmänner* 'have passed into the landscape' (WIP: 169).

Approximately sixteen minutes into the film, the first image of a *Muselmann* appears, standing with eyes closed in a still long shot, shrouded by a blanket. The film cuts to a closer still shot of another of the living dead that lies upon the ground with a countenance of death, eyes wide open. Within moments, the film cuts to a moving colour shot that approaches an abandoned camp hospital door. 'The building gave the illusion of a real hospital and hope of finding a real bed, but delivered the real risk of death by syringe' (NB). A cut to black and white footage and the film enters horrors of the 'hospital'. Skeletal bodies with shaven heads, wasted limbs upon the beds. The image at first strikes the viewer as a still – could these bodies actually breathe? – yet flittering eyelids reveal movement and 'life'. A chest struggles for air. Of this sequence's frightful indiscernibility between stasis and movement, life and death, Jay Cantor writes:

> Death enters because we had felt protected, because we had thought we were looking at a still, at history that had already happened. Outside history's narrative, we did not have to participate in its forward motion. But because the man will die, because he has been returned for a moment to life, we try to grasp him at the edge of the precipice; and feel our failure, and await death, again, with him. (Cantor 1996: 29)

The film cuts to a closer shot – a body, of indeterminate sex and age, from the foot of a bed. 'The medicines are make-believe. The dressings are mere paper' (NB). This body too, in this moving image, shows signs of faint breathing and life. And yet, 'in the end', as the film looks upon several inmates, each 'resembl[ing] the next: a body of indeterminate age that dies with its eyes wide open' (NB), the sequence concludes with a still image of another naked skeletal torso, eyes terrifyingly wide open, an image whose stillness finally denies the subtlest of final gasps for breath and life.

Muselmann, nonentity, figure, 'puppet', pawn, shadow of life in a cancerous regime of endless dying. In *Nuit et Brouillard*, this figure of an unlimited dying and time affects us via a form akin to that which Deleuze discerns in Bacon's art, that of the *Figure* which 'functions as the material support or framework that sustains a precise sensation' (Smith 2003: xiii). This form, Smith explains, is 'the form that is connected to a sensation, and that conveys the violence of this sensation directly to the nervous system' (Smith 2003: xiii). Through the *Muselmann*, whose indiscernibility is intensified by the film's own exploratory, singular means that shatter determinations of past and present, life and death, we experience a cinema impelled to its limits as actual and virtual become indiscernible and open to a crystallisation of time, a virtual perception creative of a future, a form-in-formation through which we become conscious of ourselves in time.

Inasmuch as we are internal to time, as Deleuze by way of Bergson insists (see C2: 82), following Spinoza Deleuze maintains that death also is not internal to us, for it 'is death's necessity that makes us believe that it is internal to ourselves. But in fact the destructions and decompositions do not concern either our relations in themselves or our essence. They only concern our extensive parts which belong to us for the time being' (SPP: 42). For the time being, in the now we are doomed to attempt to attain and yet destroy, Deleuze even still writes of an 'active joy, a self-affection of essence' and the 'forms by means of which we become conscious of ourselves'. He concludes that 'the more we attain to these self-affections during our existence, the less we lose in losing existence, in dying or even in suffering' (SPP: 43).

'If during our existence we have been able to compose these parts so as to increase our power of acting' (SPP: 40–1), then we have existed fully and intensely. For those engaged in persecution and slaughter, pawns also of their own destruction, theirs is, as ever, an 'external state [that] involves a diminution' linked only with 'other inadequate and dependent states' of limited happiness and life. 'In reality', Deleuze finally concludes, 'we are never judged except by ourselves and according to our states' (SPP: 40). Elsewhere, Ian Buchanan's thought encounters Deleuze and Spinoza's when he writes of a truly attainable freedom:

> By pursuing adequate ideas and by not being deceived by inadequate ideas in any of their guises – superstition, religious dogma, political doctrine, ideology and so forth – we make ourselves free, where free means living in harmonious relations with others. This sublime vision of collective existence persists in Deleuze's thinking, giving it a historicity too little mentioned. (Buchanan 2000: 6)

'Of this brick dormitory and these tormented dreams, we can but show you the outer shell, the surface' (NB). Of this history and these pasts, we can still only discern the surface, shadows and figures. Yet within and through these, upon the virtual, mobile surface or skin of the film – a skin that 'has at its disposal a vital and properly superficial potential energy' (LS: 103) – *Nuit et Brouillard* enacts its encounters through which we might see beyond the ceaseless, never-ending cry.

> *With our sincere gaze we survey these ruins,*
> *as if the old monster lay crushed forever beneath the rubble.*
> *We pretend to take up hope again*
> *as the image recedes into the past,*
> *as if we were cured once and for all*
> *of the scourge of the camps.*
> *We pretend it all happened only once,*
> *at a given time and place.*
> *We turn a blind eye to what surrounds us*
> *and a deaf ear to humanity's never-ending cry* (NB)

Notes

1. See Emma Wilson's detailed and moving account of the film in 'Material Remains: *Night and Fog*' wherein Wilson writes of the 'material details of Resnais' filmmaking'. 'In *Night and Fog*, as elsewhere', she observes, 'Resnais grapples with remnants, with material remains, with human remains, and with the affective horror and intractability of their presence' (Wilson 2005: 90).
2. 'Art', write Deleuze and Guattari, 'is not chaos but a composition of chaos that yields the vision or sensation, so that it constitutes, as Joyce says, a chaosmos, a composed chaos – neither foreseen nor preconceived' (WIP: 204).

3. The shooting script in Richard Raskin's *Nuit et Brouillard by Alain Resnais* notes that the shots are of Auschwitz and Birkenau as filmed in 1955 (Raskin 1987: 73). Raskin's text also explains that Resnais and his crew travelled to Auschwitz and Maidanek (Majdanek) within the year where new sequences were filmed (1987: 29). Yet, as this chapter reiterates, the film's ethic is less concerned with specifics of locations and names as it examines certain forces and processes that gave rise to the Holocaust's entire destructive reality.

4. 'The unconscious', Deleuze writes, 'is a micro-unconscious, it's molecular, and schizoanalysis is micro-analysis. The only question is how any thing works, with its intensities, flows, processes, partial objects – none of which *mean* anything' (N: 22).

5. 'Nacht und Nebel Erlass' of December 1941 (see Raskin 1987: 15).

6. With regard to the film's 'beauty', François Truffaut famously wrote of 'une douceur terrifiante' while Resnais reflected in interview: 'Je crois que si c'est beau, ce ne peut être que plus efficace' (Raskin 1987: 138; 136).

7. See also Primo Levi: 'One hesitates to call them living: one hesitates to call their death death' (Levi 1986: 90); and Agamben: 'we know from witnesses that under no circumstances were they to be called "corpses" or "cadavers," but rather simply *Figuren*, figures, dolls' (Agamben 1999: 51).

8. See, for instance, Wilson regarding the 'opposition of *Night and Fog* and [Lanzmann's] *Shoah*, and in particular the use of images in the former' (2005: 89).

3

From Depths and Ashes

The skin has at its disposal a vital and properly superficial potential energy. (LS: 103)

A philosophy of the surface and of the event is always caught in a struggle with violent and destructive mixtures of bodies; it is always trying to give sense to a life of violent shocks, invasions and punctures. (Williams 2008a: 84)

It is not the other which is another I, but the I which is an other, a fractured I. There is no love which does not begin with the revelation of a possible world as such, enwound in the other which expresses it. (DR: 261)

SHE   It's extraordinary how beautiful your skin is. (Duras 1961: 25)

Ashes, limbs, a haunting refrain. The pulsating woodwinds, strings and piano of the score commence.[1] As they persist, title credits for Resnais' 1959 *Hiroshima mon amour* appear and fade; an image surfaces. This visual image, a networked matrix of lines with offshoots branching in various directions, as might a stitched scar, evokes a rhizomatic surfacing upon an unknown surface, a mysterious formation perceived against a strangely agitating soundtrack. Image and score finally fade to a momentary black silence. Then, as writes Marguerite Duras, 'we see mutilated bodies – the heads, the hips – moving – in the throes of love or death – and covered successively with the ashes, the dew, of atomic death – and the sweat of love fulfilled' (1961: 8).

Through this opening sequence that bodily explores various disembodied intensities, *Hiroshima mon amour* gracefully opens to the most heinous of horrors. Catalysed by a special love between two lovers, the film's sensual evocation of both corporeal scars and incorporeal sensations distinguishes the film as a moving assemblage of terrifying beauty. For through its exploration of love and experimentation alongside devastation and degradation, through a consideration of affirmative life forces and intensities in relation to the shameful and intolerable, the ashes and deaths of Hiroshima and Nevers, *Hiroshima mon amour* exposes a woman's violent

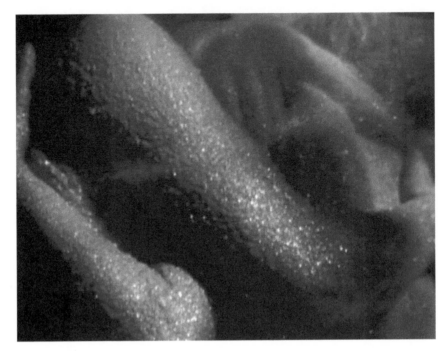

4 *Ashes, limbs, a haunting refrain,* Hiroshima mon amour *(Resnais 1959)*

confrontation with identity, time and death. By way of the woman's becoming-imperceptible or apersonal becoming through this shattering of transcendent illusions, a transformation that realises the woman's counter-actualisation or creative replaying of her wounds, *Hiroshima mon amour* discovers intensities that incite this chapter's questionings of love, eternity and renewal as expressed through the depths of bodies and singular surfaces of skins.

With regard to 'the depth of bodies and the height of ideas', James Williams identifies the surface as a site for *sense* and the *virtual*[2] that embodies also the 'limits or borders of things . . . where identity breaks down and becomes other' (Williams 2008a: 107). 'The surface is', he writes, 'neither ideal nor actual but the condition for the open renewal of the relations between the two', between actual and virtual, depth and height (2008a: 110). In relation to the limits, borders or cracks at which self becomes other, *Hiroshima mon amour* itself pushes to several limits, 'having taken' the woman, as writes Duras, 'to the limit of her refusal to stay at Hiroshima' (1961: 13). On top of her dead German lover, the woman is, again, 'at the extreme limit of pain' (1961: 93). Upon her return home with shaven head following a public humiliation, the woman of *Hiroshima mon amour* 'is at the *exact* limit of her strength'. 'When her mother reaches her', Duras continues, 'she will have exceeded this limit' as she falls into her mother's arms (1961: 99). As it exposes these limits of the woman's self, *Hiroshima mon amour* reveals the sense and affect of agony that the woman and Hiroshima discharge, sufferings which open to life as both woman and city discover a profound becoming-other through the lovers' special love.

Of this creative, apersonal love and desperation for life that manifests itself in the film as a limit or surface between past and future, self and other, we may consider what Todd May describes as 'an event of erotics that arises across and between the surfaces of bodies':

> Love's erotics is a matter between individuals, but it is not only that. It is also a matter between body parts, between surfaces that come in contact. And the individuals to whom those surfaces belong are a product of that contact at least as much as its subject. Our bodies are the actualization of a virtual that love's erotics explores. Erotics explores the virtual on many levels: the individual, the pre-individual, the between-individuals, the between-individual-parts. (May 2005: 169)

Inasmuch as '*there is always something outside our identification as subjects and persons*', writes May, an 'unconscious erotics of bodies' (2005: 168) whereby series of explorations, connections, experimentations and sensations arise without conscious decision or deliberation, the lovers' love in *Hiroshima mon amour* emerges as a productive force and enabling surface that gives rise to sensations that challenge, extend and fragment the vulnerable bodies of the film. Inasmuch, that is, as the lovers of *Hiroshima mon amour* lose themselves through their encounters and sensations, through the intensity of a singular love, the film's body, with that of the lovers', opens to unknown possibilities.

Through its considerations of intensity via the 'actual depth and virtual height' of bodies (see Williams 2008b: 99), their sensations and scars that mark *Hiroshima mon amour* as a moving site of horrors and becomings as released through a love 'necessarily' 'special and "wonderful"', a 'nascent love' (Duras 1961: 9; 10), this chapter examines and touches upon that which defies common reason, sense and consciousness: those virtual processes of love and self-less individuation that vibrate through the movements and encounters between bodies, surfaces and skins. From these depths and 'ashes' of love and death at the limits and cracks of self and identity, *Hiroshima mon amour* emerges, a product of its own series of affective becomings, variations and surface intensities between actual and virtual, body and thought, 'Nevers and love', 'Hiroshima and love' (Duras 1961: 12).

ﻬ

By slow degrees ... from these formless, anonymous bodies their own bodies emerge. (Duras 1961: 8)

We must try to conceive of this world in which a single fixed plane – which we shall call a plane of absolute immobility *or* absolute movement – is traversed by nonformal elements of relative speed that enter this or that individuated assemblage depending on their degrees of speed and slowness. A plane of consistency peopled by anonymous matter, by infinite bits of impalpable matter entering into varying connections. (ATP: 255)

I do not caress your stomach. My hand caresses it. Automatically, and without decision. *There is always something outside our identification as subjects and persons.* (May 2005: 168)

Making love is not just becoming as one, or even two, but becoming as a hundred thousand. Desiring-machines or the nonhuman sex: not one or even two sexes, but *n* sexes. (AO: 296)

As *Hiroshima mon amour*'s exquisitely lyrical opening sequence unfolds, a piano plays, delicately, intimately, tenderly. The ashes on the bodies' surfaces seemingly liquefy as body parts intertwine. To return to May's materialist Spinozian account of bodily affects, encounters and an event of erotics that occurs between the surfaces and tendencies, aspects and *thisnesses*, or haecceities, 'alterations', 'characteristics' and 'inclinations' of one body part *and* another (see Williams 2008: 83), May suggests that love has its 'own erotics' whereby 'there are no longer two individuals': 'There are not fewer beings there, but more ... there is a series of explorations and connections and experimentations that arise not as decisions ... *when individuals lose themselves*' (May 2005: 167; 168; emphasis mine). This chapter will explore this process of emancipatory *depersonalisation* or loss of self through the multiplicity of surfaces and becomings *Hiroshima mon amour* reveals as it probes sensations and events of love and death via the depths of bodies and heights of thought.

Like fresh snow, the ashes fall and cling to arms and limbs that slowly intertwine. As a series of superimposed, extreme close-up images dissolve into one another, and as the strings and woodwinds of the score intervene, *Hiroshima mon amour* continues to explore the ash-covered surfaces. While the film cuts to a shot further permeated by shadow, the ashes gone and skins smoothly bare, light plays upon the fleshly, dewy surfaces and hides in their crevices. With incessant movements of limbs and images, shadows and sounds, the sequence emits a serene agitation that infuses the multiplicity of surfaces, the always two-way or double actual-virtual, corporeal-incorporeal process and series of woman and man, lightness and darkness, suppleness and firmness, surface and depth that *Hiroshima mon amour* explores.

Such is the film's attempt to touch deep actual wounds through sensations and erotics that defy fixed specification as they occupy ever-differing planes, motions and relations of the virtual that can only be sensed. 'Something in the world forces us to think', writes Deleuze, a 'something [that] is an object not of recognition but of a fundamental *encounter* . . . It may be grasped in a range of affective tones: wonder, love, hatred, suffering. In whichever tone, its primary characteristic is that it can only be sensed' (DR: 139). In place of any definable human body or coupling of bodies, this series of images at the film's start reveals a mixture of ashes, skins and joints whose encounters diffuse the notion of a fixed, identifiable, self-possessed and aware self.

Foldings, unfoldings and refoldings of disparate body parts continue to flood the screen. Searching, touching, moving, experimenting, connecting, *becoming thisnesses*, these bodily and intangible presences invoke the senses. Their affective, 'machinic' connections effect dynamic assemblages of unconscious, pre-individual connections *not yet known*. 'Beyond the self and the I', Deleuze argues, 'we find not the impersonal but the individual and its factors, individuation and its fields, individuality and its pre-individual singularities' (DR: 258). Such is to truly explore a body as conceived through Spinoza by Deleuze and Guattari: 'What can a body do?' (ATP: 256). 'We know nothing . . . until we know what it can do, in other words, what its affects are.' 'Not representative but affective' (ATP: 257), the affects that overwhelm *Hiroshima mon amour*'s opening moments, including those of newness, 'eroticism, love, and unhappiness' (Duras 1961: 9–10), speak to relations Deleuze and Guattari identify:

> To the relations composing, decomposing, or modifying an individual there correspond intensities that affect it, augmenting or diminishing its power to act; these intensities come from external parts or from the individual's own parts. Affects are becomings. (ATP: 256)

As the lovers' bodies at last emerge from anonymity, from smoothnesses, barenesses, intertwined interactions and alterations of body parts, aspects and surfaces, his back and shoulders fill the screen. Decisively and calmly, 'as if reciting', he whispers: 'You saw nothing in Hiroshima. Nothing' (Duras 1961: 15). In line with Duras' text, *'all we see are these shoulders'* that the woman 'grips' while she insists: 'I saw *everything. Everything'* (1961: 15). The woman's testimony, expressed as distinctly as the man's refutations, locates the lovers in an irremediably scarred Hiroshima that resists recognition and knowledge, even as she yet avows: 'I saw the hospital – I'm sure of it.'

Upon her words, the film cuts to deep and long corridors of a Hiroshima hospital; patients standing and lying upon beds turn mechanistically, solemnly, resignedly to face the camera's glare as she reiterates: 'How could I not have seen it?' The impersonal filmic eye directly passes into the atmospheric landscape of the woman's sensations to convey a detached, pre-individual seeing or *percept*. This indiscernible and unseen yet tangible and tactile ephemeral presence or nonhuman film-eye haunts and penetrates the buildings and streets of the atomised city whose survivors, premonitory ghostly figures, endure at the 'pace of a dream or a nightmare' (C2: 3), ever in trepidation of the future unknown, into whose depths the woman plunges.

Yet with regard to a past that may only be sensed, the woman's claims and the man's denials of each persist. 'You didn't see the hospital in Hiroshima. You saw nothing in Hiroshima.' As closely interwoven as the lovers themselves, the images of the lovers and city commence a harrowing *pas de deux* of wounding memory as haunting tracking shots of the city are intercut with images of the lovers' bodies. She clutches his shoulder. The score's woodwinds cry.

Four times at the museum. (HMA)

At the same instant birds ignited in midair. Mosquitoes and flies, squirrels, family pets crackled and were gone. The fireball flashed an enormous photograph of the city at the instant of its immolation fixed on the mineral, vegetable and animal surfaces of the city itself. (Rhodes 1986: 715)

Unnatural participations or nuptials are the true Nature spanning the kingdoms of nature ... interkingdoms, unnatural participations ...

there are as many sexes as there are terms in symbiosis . . . We know that many beings pass between a man and a woman; they come from different worlds, are borne on the wind, form rhizomes around roots; they cannot be understood in terms of production, only in terms of becoming. (ATP: 241–2)

Metal . . . as vulnerable as flesh. (HMA)

Once more a piano plays, agitatedly, anxiously, as the film reveals an ostensibly granite-like structure, the Hiroshima Peace Memorial Museum, elevated upon high pillars. Yet, despite the evident effort towards awareness and commemoration, the museum evokes an ironic permanence, officiousness and consequent estrangement or dissociation as a 'modern' albeit dated[3] edifice seemingly removed and remote from the mutilated grounds, wounds and forms of scorched life it documents. 'What museum in Hiroshima?' her Japanese lover demands. As the *'woman's voice'*, writes Duras, *'becomes more . . . more impersonal'*, there are shots of the museum, 'with a return', notes the screenplay, 'at regular intervals, to the bodies' (Duras 1961: 17). The impersonal and surreal commingle as the score assumes a jaunty, jazzy woodwind and piano refrain. The woman's strangely impassive voice perseveres above the animated melody, 'Four times at the museum in Hiroshima . . . the reconstructions, for lack of anything else' (HMA).

Survivor testimonies resonate throughout the film as it stresses the inefficacy of any museum or monument in the face of faceless horrors, and literally faceless victims. 'They [the walking dead] had no faces', reported one survivor, 'Their eyes, noses and mouths had been burned away . . . their ears had melted' (Rhodes 1986: 726). The film's asubjective gaze follows museum visitors whose partially visible bodies appear behind exhibits as walking legs accompanying children entirely visible. 'I saw people walking around' the French woman drones, her words, tone and the film's visuals cast incongruently against the dynamic score. 'People walk around, lost in thought, among the photographs, the reconstructions, for lack of anything else. The photographs, the photographs, the reconstructions, for lack of anything else. The explanations, for lack of anything else . . . I myself, lost in thought, looked at the scorched metal. The twisted metal. Metal made as vulnerable as flesh' (HMA).

Against and through such nameless, faceless horror, *Hiroshima mon amour* discovers means for re-encountering, replaying or counter-actualising the event of Hiroshima's devastation through the woman's becoming-woman, becoming-other and, finally, imperceptible. Which is to say, the woman's becoming-woman and other pertains once more to a limit, crack or threshold. Between fixed designations and their implications that are imposed upon the woman, those of woman, French, daughter, *femme tondue*, mother, lover, wife, and the woman's deterritorialising or destabilising of these distinctions that restrict her capacity to open to an imperceptibility and finally an immanence and power to act free from binary categorisations, is the woman's becoming-woman that enables the film's own impersonal, pure sight.

The woman's becoming-woman breaks, that is, from binary oppositions of sexuality that facilitated her public humiliation, and countless other public humiliations of women in wartime and postwar Europe in the first instance. 'It is', as write Deleuze and Guattari, 'perhaps the special situation of women in relation to the man-standard that accounts for the fact that becomings, being minoritarian, always pass through a becoming-woman' (ATP: 291). Becoming-woman or deterritorialised then 'impl[ies] two simultaneous movements', as they explain, 'one by which a term (the subject) is withdrawn from the majority, and another by which a term (the medium or agent) rises up from the minority'. In this sense, 'even woman must become woman' for 'in a way the subject in a becoming is always "man", but only when he enters a becoming-minoritarian that rends him from his major identity' (ATP: 291).

In other words, the process of the woman's self-dissolution or becoming-other in *Hiroshima mon amour* passes through a becoming-woman that again pushes the woman to and beyond the limits of her identity as woman. Through the woman's becoming-woman and the film's becoming-child, if to see through the eyes of a child is to perceive encounters in this world purely and without distinction between self and other, as does *Hiroshima mon amour* in this immanent sense, both woman and film open to a world free of ego and 'who' she was, to a movement that also witnesses the lovers' becoming with the world: *a becoming-woman of the woman, a becoming-woman of the man, a becoming-Hiroshima of the man, a becoming-Nevers of the woman, a Hiroshima-Nevers, Nevers-Hiroshima.*

Through its singular, dynamic, tactile, exploratory sight that then opens to a child's perspective that symbiotically *becomes with* the world, *Hiroshima mon amour* confronts limits by way of the lovers' love that may also be conceived as the feminine or between, the middle through which the woman's becoming passes. If 'that which will not be pinned down by truth . . . is, in truth, the *feminine*', as Jacques Derrida and Christie V. McDonald propose in an exchange pertaining to improvisation, surprise and dance (Derrida and McDonald 1982: 66), it is through undefined, minor and foreign zones, those limits and cracks between essentialising, hierarchical and transcendent categorisations of sexual and other differences, that life and its forms might become. Again, a line of becoming, as Deleuze and Guattari insist, 'has neither beginning nor end', 'only a middle' (ATP: 293).

With regard to the love, becomings and events that pass between the lovers who pass into the world as they become parts or folds of a post-annihilated assemblage of Hiroshima, with regard to this 'symbiosis' whereby Hiroshima and Nevers, he and she, are uprooted from what they were to 'become "with"' the other, we may consider Deleuze and Guattari's remarks regarding 'a composition of speeds and affects involving entirely different individuals, a symbiosis' that engenders a 'language that is no longer that of words, in a matter that is no longer that of subjects. *Unnatural participation*' (ATP: 258). For the woman's becoming is effected through Hiroshima, the man and Nevers' becomings-other; all relations are forever folded and refolded anew.

One cannot, then, become-other without the other becoming something else as well. This is not merely an encounter among people, as between a woman and a man, but one also encounters, as Deleuze writes, 'movements, ideas, events, entities' (D: 6). As one term encounters the other, a single becoming emerges between the two, 'an effect, a zigzag, something which passes or happens between two', 'a bloc of becoming, an a-parallel evolution' or 'double capture' that 'is between the two, outside the two, and which flows in another direction' (D: 6–7). The relations and compositions of she-he, Nevers-Hiroshima, their surfaces and depths, sounds and visuals, corporeal and incorporeal caresses, touches and movements are chance becomings that discover new life through intensities of wonderful potential and affirmative force. How this 'chance couple' met, Duras corroborates, 'will not be revealed in the picture. For that is not what really matters. Chance meetings occur everywhere in the world. What is important is what these ordinary meetings lead to' (Duras 1961: 8), what proliferates between two, always in the middle, 'neither', as writes Deleuze, 'past nor future' (D: 31).

Via the lovers' chance meeting or encounter and the *becomings* between the two, she of Nevers, he of Hiroshima, a pure immanence arises of a 'qualitative duration of consciousness without a self' (PI: 25). Such a moment 'gives way to an impersonal and yet singular life that releases a pure event freed from ... the subjectivity and objectivity of what happens', a 'haecceity no longer of individuation but of singularization', a 'singular life immanent to a man who no longer has a name' (PI: 28–9). Between the two lovers, she, he, both without name, there then emerges 'an overlapping of Nevers and love, of Hiroshima and love', all 'mixed, without any preconceived principle' (Duras 1961: 12).

And so, as *Hiroshima mon amour* glimpses an improvisational dance of love and chance between the two through which the lovers' selves accede to an endlessly mutating world or assemblage of affects and forces, we cannot 'in the beginning of the film', as Duras states, 'see this chance couple. Neither her nor him' (1961: 8). For this is a couple that emerges only by 'slow degrees' whose relations are such that one body part *becomes with* another as an 'organ' is uprooted 'from its specificity [... to] mak[e] it become "with" the other organ' (ATP: 259). And as the woman speaks of all she has seen and claims to comprehend, children at the museum peer down upon a minute reconstruction of a post-annihilated Hiroshima, their bodies again nearly fully visible in the frame as if to suggest the children's complete permeation with a world they alone can instantaneously and purely perceive. But of the actual destruction, the children and French woman can only imagine. Torn as ever between her various imposed identities, *une femme tondue*, daughter, mother, lover, wife, She of Nevers speaks further of 'agony still fresh': 'Who would have thought?' (HMA)

ร

Human flesh, suspended, as if still alive. (HMA)

The battle itself is an incorporeal event (or sense) with no other reality than that of the expression of my proposition; what we find in the state of affairs are bodies mixing with one another – spears stabbing flesh, bullets flying through the air, cannons firing, bodies being ripped apart – and the battle itself is the effect or the result of this intermingling of bodies ... '[Sense] is exactly the boundary between propositions and things (LS: 22)'. (Smith and Protevi 2008)

The absurdity of war, laid bare, hovers over their blurred bodies. (Duras 1961: 87)

The woman's voice continues. She, once shorn and scorned, speaks of the women of Hiroshima, of the 'anonymous masses of hair that the women of Hiroshima, upon waking in the morning, would find had fallen out' (HMA). The camera tracks along the museum displays, the 'scorched', 'twisted' metal, deformed bicycle, congealed mass of melted bottle caps and formalin specimens of once owned flesh suspended and labelled, the 'shattered stones', all viewed via a new Hiroshima in the process of seeing itself. '*Affects*', write Deleuze and Guattari, '*are precisely these nonhuman becomings of man*, just as percepts . . . are *nonhuman landscapes of nature*' (WIP: 169).

For as it witnesses these layers of its apocalyptic past alongside its gradual reconstruction, this *new Hiroshima* becomes a *pure percept* 'itself', a compound of imperceptible and nonhuman forces that populate the remains of a vanquished city and the French woman herself whose self passes into the charred ruins. Of such skin and flesh freed from once supple and smooth faces and bodies, we may return to Deleuze and Guattari's assertion that 'the being of sensation is not the flesh but the compound of nonhuman forces of the cosmos, of man's nonhuman becomings, and of the ambiguous house that exchanges and adjusts them, makes them whirl like winds' (ATP: 183). As he describes the visual time-image of modern cinema that returns to the past to expose 'the deserted layers of our time which bury our own phantoms' (C2: 244), Deleuze seemingly alludes to these nonhuman forces and becomings, and the lovers they pass between and through.

As the score's whirling woodwinds, strings and piano persist jarringly and erratically while the frantic, frenzied strains, hair and tracking shots relentlessly repeat anew Resnais' *Nuit et Brouillard*, *Hiroshima mon amour* increasingly embodies that 'very definition of the percept' that Deleuze and Guattari propose which 'make[s] perceptible the imperceptible forces that populate the world, affect us, and make us become' (ATP: 182). From within the film's first moments and minutes, its mixtures, movements, surfaces and foldings of living and preserved skins, soundscapes and landscapes evoke the incorporeal, extra and sensory, the 'sense', virtual and very affect of Hiroshima and the woman's devastation and shock, deadness from which both city and woman progressively emerge.

And so, as the score frenetically repeats its cyclical refrain, the anonymous film-eye vigilantly repeats its tracking rounds round the museum. The camera lingers upon photographs within whose glass frames images from across the room rebound as if to reiterate the very limits of secondary photographic or representational 'perception', sensation and commemoration. As the camera passes along the far end of a dual-sided photograph exhibit, the free-standing exhibit divides the film's frame nearly midway so that a woman and three children appear screen left while a man observing photographs appears screen right, both children and adults now fully visible.

With trepidation, the camera tracks past the exhibit, its seemingly apprehensive gaze withheld at the distance of a long shot. Then abruptly, it cuts to a rapid zoom in upon a black and white photograph, 'Victims at Danbara Primary School', as the photograph's reflective glass resists its image's simple capture. Loathsome, shielded by layers of glass and time, the images of human decay implore, *what can be seen, dare you touch*, while the glass surfaces mirror not only the gazes of the wandering visitors but also the Japanese lover's expression that pervades the film's extended opening sequence, 'Nothing. You know *nothing*.'

As the camera pans slowly upward along an extreme close shot of a still that depicts a victim's burned scalp, the man's head bent lowly forward, the gaze upon the surface scar repeats *Hiroshima mon amour*'s opening visual image. That early first image, the rhizomatic matrix of lines that prophetically invokes the series of scars the film's surfacings will exhume, assumes novel significance as a site of monumental real, actual suffering and geography via this latter image of a profound head wound. Both images – the film's first image and this latter shot of a man's wound – relive, reactivate and resituate the atrocities of Hiroshima in both personal and universal dimensions, as both an individual scar and geographical map. 'I was hot in Peace Square', the woman's voice claims against the scar's image and score's agitations; '10,000 degrees in Peace Square'. From the scalp to a track across the Square to the lovers' bodies once more, the camera then returns to the museum. As it tracks along several exhibits with mannequins costumed as victims, the woman's commentary attempts to compensate for the surreal showcases of plastic display. 'The reconstructions were as authentic as possible', she insists.

Yet how can the horrors and sensations of flesh torn and shed, of skins that hung from living lifeless once-human forms, the stench, screams, abhorrent sights of blinded faces be conveyed? 'I saw human bodies in such a state that you couldn't tell whether they were humans' (Rhodes 1986: 723). As if to reiterate the impossibility, the camera at once whips across the museum's space and time, those coexistent 'sheets' of Hiroshima and the woman's pasts that *Hiroshima mon amour* ever singularly and newly encounters, counter-actualises or replays.

For as the museum becomes a site of encounters comprised of various surface and image interactions between glass frames and archival photographs and inquisitive faces, these tangible surfaces probe the dynamics, possibilities, effects and affects of such plays upon sensual perception and becomings. From the sight of the mannequins clad as bomb victims to excerpts of re-enacted footage, the whip pan screen right across the museum in effect enacts *Hiroshima mon amour*'s decisive break from a true-false, factual-fictional dichotomy as it severs perceiver-perceived distinctions.[4] By the camera's rapid pan, that is, the film at once stages an encounter between authenticity and dramatisation that abolishes such binary divisions. This disintegration of the 'border between the logic of facts and the logic of fiction', a severing Jacques Rancière considers with regard to what he terms the 'aesthetic revolution' (Rancière 2004: 38), further extends the film's consideration of all seen and unseen, tangible and intangible.

Layer upon layer, images and times interpenetrate. As photographs are filmed, and films re-filmed within the museum of *Hiroshima mon amour*, what remains to be seen, thought, sensed, made from the remains, the subjectless materials, artefacts, floating senses and incorporeal wounds of the past? Can the singular, virtual, intangible yet ever interminable felt sense of any past forever transform the rest of time and future if, as writes Duras with regard to the event of the German lover's death, 'it is from here that . . . death began, for all eternity' (Duras 1961: 88).

The event is that no one ever dies, but has always just died or is always going to die, in the empty present of the Aion, that is, in eternity. (LS: 63)

When something has actually died it remains as a virtual trace in the relations of 'has died' and 'will die' that it expressed. (Williams 2008a: 146)

I see my life. Your death.
My life that goes on. Your death that goes on. (Duras 1961: 63)

The good or strong individual is the one who exists so fully or so intensely that he has gained eternity in his lifetime, so that death, always extensive, always external, is of little significance to him. (SPP: 41)

A piercing woodwind wails while the Japanese lover's contradictions continue: 'What was there for you to weep over?' 'I saw the newsreels', the French woman counters as the lovers' voices exemplify the autonomous *'literalness'* and 'irreducible dimension' Deleuze describes when he writes of the time-image's 'free indirect' speech act whose voice seemingly 'turns in on itself' (C2: 242–3), a voice akin to the 'calm, colorless, incantatory' voice Duras claims the woman to have (Duras 1961: 15). In archival newsreel footage a camera pans the scalded, barren land as flickering lines and over-exposed shots suggest a certain vulnerability to time and incommensurability between 'objective reality', the idea or representation of Hiroshima, and the horror itself without name, the affect which is, as Deleuze maintains, 'precisely a mode of thought which has no representational character' (Deleuze 1978a).

From the 'depths of the earth, and from the ashes', the woman recites, life crawled: minute becomings *Hiroshima mon amour* captures through the closest of shots. As a worm slips through bloodied earth, and as ants reclaim their territory, the film repeats again Deleuze and Guattari's prescription: 'Always look for the molecular, or even submolecular, particle with which we are allied' (ATP: 11). For among these most miniscule becomings, *Hiroshima mon amour* situates and reveals the woman's own becoming through Hiroshima, a woman-becoming-Hiroshima, Hiroshima-becoming-woman, a gradual blossoming as both city and woman bloom and become through their encounters with each other and the world once more. Yet, within this extended opening sequence of beautiful and horrifying tactility, as she speaks of a Hiroshima that 'was covered in flowers', 'cornflowers and gladioli everywhere, morning glories and day lilies' (HMA), the film alternatively offers newsreel footage of young victims, children with missing hair, gaping, weeping wounds too terrifying and agonising for any person to endure.

Are these children, *Hiroshima mon amour* seemingly pleads, life's only chance of becoming from death? The images nauseate, threaten to overwhelm. Fully visible, too visible, these child victims are not the child visitors to the museum in the film's earlier 'present-day' footage as these images defeat even a child's open or pure perspective, these child victims with half-missing jaws, hair and flesh, 'captured on film for all time' while launched prematurely for death, only to be 'born again from the ashes' (HMA). A once young boy without jaw looks now towards the camera upon this last utterance of the woman's with a wearied, aged gaze we can neither bear nor share. The woman's commentary perseveres as she speaks of 'an extraordinary vitality unheard of in flowers before then' (HMA). Her soft words violently accost the ghastly images of the ghostly, grave children, as their gazes recall the glares of Resnais' *Nuit et Brouillard*, that wide-eyed countenance or spectre of countless timeless victims.

The film's score pierces. Such is the film's struggle through death, decay and desolation as the woman ever slowly strives towards a new capacity for life despite all horror. As an adult hand doctors the fragmented remnants of a child's hand, the woman ruminates: 'Just as the illusion exists in love, the illusion you can never forget, so I was under the illusion I would never forget Hiroshima' (HMA). The affective force of the images and the woman's responses affront as *Hiroshima mon amour* again surges towards a threshold or limit of intensity, 'a *beyond* that [one] cannot manage to render' (Deleuze 1978a; emphasis mine). In effect, if, as Deleuze declares, affects are 'joy or sadness', 'decreases and . . . increases of lived power' whereby 'nothing that exceeds his/her power of being affected is good for a person', then the 'power of being affected' is itself also a 'threshold of intensity' (Deleuze 1978a).

'The most beautiful thing is to live on the edges', Deleuze frequently asserts, on the condition that any intensity will not overwhelm our power of being affected. Such is the limit and crack at which *Hiroshima mon amour* boldly lingers as it challenges: dare look. Doctors probe an empty socket, shifting the victim's head towards our reticent glance, her eye-less gaze turned upon ours. Look no further, the film dares. Against this most heinous image upon which the film tortuously pauses, the woman repeats: 'Just like love.' Then, the film cuts, returning at last to the lovers' embrace, '*the perfect embrace of the bodies*', writes Duras (1961: 21), warm hand upon soft, enfolded flesh. The score nearly halts. 'I saw the survivors too', she affirms, 'and those who were in the wombs of the women of Hiroshima.' A seemingly deformed child turns now towards us; the soothing score augments the horror. Serene agitation.

❧

SHE   Afterward, I don't remember any more.
HE   How long?
SHE   (*still in a trancelike state*) Eternity. (Duras 1961: 59)

I am a degree of power and it is in this sense that I am eternal . . . A quantity of power we have always called an intensity. It is to this and to this alone that Spinoza assigns the term 'eternity'. (Deleuze 1978a)

Eternity is not the same thing as 'duration' and thus it does not mean 'lasting forever'. Minds can understand themselves as partaking of a larger totality ... which is by definition eternal in the enjoyment of its perfection and love. (Braidotti 2006: 148)

I needed a city the size of love itself. (Duras 1961: 89)

Hiroshima mon amour: what to make of a film about a woman making a film about peace in Hiroshima? What of Hiroshima, self-possession and love itself? Via Spinoza, Deleuze invokes a higher form or 'third kind of knowledge, intuition' as enabled by an experimental, empowering process of *auto-affection, autopoiesis* or 'self-affection' (SPP: 43). In so far as we then 'become conscious of ourselves [and] other things', 'from within and eternally' (SPP: 43), the woman of *Hiroshima mon amour* forever newly experiences 'eternity' as she profoundly encounters the nature and limits of her affectivity and its duration. The woman comes to intuit, that is, the lived passages and 'transitions' between her living states, those affects of which she is capable and can sustain at the very threshold of her self as an embodied subject.

Such 'wisdom' facilitated through 'the contemplation of the eternity of the life-forces, not the perennity of death', as Rosi Braidotti illustrates through Deleuze and Spinoza (Braidotti 2006: 148), frees a self for all time as it grasps an interconnectedness among all assemblages of life, human and otherwise. Through this 'nomadic' subjectivity 'suspended between the no longer and not yet' (2006: 156), between the intensive, incorporeal affects and extensive, corporeal effects of her specific, affected body and pains, the woman of the film assumes an 'eternity of the mind' that 'rests on [the mind's] partaking of a larger reflexive totality' (2006: 150; 149), as Braidotti further evinces through Deleuze and Spinoza in her exploration of the ethics of becoming-imperceptible.

If such an awareness of our powers to affect and be affected opens to a 'mode of intrinsic distinction' that speaks to that 'something irreducibly mystical in Spinoza's third kind of knowledge', we are raised, as Deleuze infers, 'to a certain comprehension of causes' (Deleuze 1978a). Through 'relation[s] of affinity', through joyful, pleasing encounters that perfectly combine with our relations to increase our lived power, we enter, that is, into 'another domain' (Deleuze 1978a), as does the woman of *Hiroshima mon amour*. This certain 'knowledge' of which Deleuze and Spinoza write is that which the woman comes to experience, the knowledge of a body's capacity for life, its 'power of being affected' either affirmatively or destructively.

'In a happy love, in a love of joy, what happens?' Deleuze asks. 'You compose a maximum of relations with a maximum of relations of the other, bodily, perceptual, all kinds of natures', he continues, for 'it is always by composing my relations with other relations . . . that I invent this third individual of which the other and myself are no more than parts, sub-individuals' (1978a). If by way of such a 'composition of relations and composition of composed relations' one increases their power, then by their symbiotic encounter, erotics of love and composition of relations, the lovers effect a 'third individual': an apersonal, singular, empowering love that exceeds the lovers as the city of Hiroshima itself becomes a site of improvisation, connection and love that invents and is invented by, affects and is affected by life within and beyond its borders. Inasmuch as the woman's encounter with the city facilitates her movement and becoming towards new sight and immanent knowledge, Hiroshima becomes 'her' love. *Hiroshima mon amour*, a city 'made to the size of love' and the woman's body (see Duras 1961: 25 and 77). As the woman walks a second time through the city's streets towards the film's end, we hear her thoughts:

> We're going to remain alone, my love.
> The night will never end.
> The sun will never rise again on anyone.
> Never. Never more. At last.
> You destroy me.
> You're so good for me. (Duras 1961: 77)

For as the eternally scarred woman, an actress playing the part of an 'eternal nurse of an eternal war' in an eternally scarred city (Duras 1961: 10), becomes increasingly aware through her lover-Hiroshima of the *passages between* the increases and decreases of her power (*puissance*), as she discerns her thresholds, losses and sufferings against a vaster continuum of past-future life beyond her self, she finally confronts her 'best, most beautiful love' (Deleuze 1978a). With regard to the 'power of affect' (ATP: 243), the affective passages and durations of the woman's becoming, we may return to Deleuze's explanation via Bergson and Spinoza of affection and affect whereby an affection, or 'every determinable state at a single moment', always '*envelops an affect*, a passage' (Deleuze 1978a; emphasis mine).

Duration is then this very 'lived passage from one state to another' that is '*irreducible* to any state' (Deleuze 1978a). Which is to say, this 'phenomenon of passage' or 'lived transition' is that which 'happens between two cuts' or successive affections; 'always behind our backs' and 'between two blinks', it is 'something [that] necessarily escape[s]' our spatial decompositions of time, 'so close are . . . two moments of time' (Deleuze 1978a). As ever, moments of pure time, the affective excesses of experience, *thisnesses* and haecceities resist absolute, complete awareness and direct revelation. Sensation, as Deleuze claims, 'is only a break within the flow of absolute consciousness' (PI: 25).

Deleuze, then, describes his philosophy as a 'transcendental empiricism' that refers, 'however close two sensations may be, [to] the passage from one to the other as becoming, as increase or decrease in power (virtual quantity)', movements, transitions and passages that become conscious only through movement towards the immanence of an absolute deterritorialisation (PI: 25). 'It is only when immanence is no longer immanence to anything other than itself that we can speak of a plane of immanence', a 'complete power' and 'bliss' (PI: 27) towards which positive connections and becomings rush, and towards which *Hiroshima mon amour*'s time-images strive through their crystallisations of time.

And so, like an experience of *punctum*, duration resists capture and reproduction as an irreducibility despite the specificity of its transitions that define its affects, those 'constant passages to greater or lesser perfections, continual variations of the existing mode's power of acting' (SPP: 63). 'The affect is what? It is the passage', Deleuze repeats, alongside the *eternity* of essence and *instantaneity* of affections. Through an auto or self-affective consciousness of the *duration* of our lived passages and transitions from state to state, one intensely lives and opens to a fundamental encounter beyond the self, an absolute immanence in itself. In lieu of any staged authenticity or crass commemoration, such as the film derides through shots of a cheap souvenir stand, abandoned gift shop and surrealistic 'atomic tour' bus, as it emits a sensitivity to that which eludes habitual perception and empirical consciousness, *Hiroshima mon amour*, in the manner of Deleuze's thought, examines the conditions and formations of actual experience and consciousness that gave rise to the injustices the film explores.

By way of the affects that comprise the film's 'love story', and which correspond to the duration of a woman-becoming-world, *Hiroshima mon amour* charts the woman's becoming-imperceptible. Such an imperceptibility is, to repeat earlier passages of this chapter, the 'ultimate stage in the becoming-woman, in that it marks the transition to a larger, "natural" cosmic order', as Braidotti writes (2006: 157). As noted, the woman's burgeoning 'knowledge' and experience of eternity in *Hiroshima mon amour* directly pertain once more to a limit, to the limit or crack Deleuze senses between the personal and impersonal which correspond to the time of Chronos and the time of the 'always just died' or 'always going to die, in the empty present of the Aion', or 'eternity' (LS: 63). Whereas the former time of Chronos 'is cyclical, measures the movement of bodies and depends on the matter which limits and fills it out; the other is a pure straight line at the surface, incorporeal, unlimited, an empty form of time, independent of all matter' (LS: 62).

With regard to these two times, a time of depth and of the surface, we may return to the film's series of depths and surfaces which expose the actual bodies and virtual intensities that respectively correspond to these times of Chronos and Aion. Through the ephemeral gaps between *Hiroshima mon amour*'s frequently caustic cuts; through the film's evocations of virtual memory and actual decay, incorporeal life and corporeal death; through affects and *punctum* of persistent loss, suffering and even new hope which endure long after the material remains of depths and ashes, the following sections of this chapter will examine a positive force and power of forgetting through an eternal return of difference.

'The world of the dead', reports Rhodes, 'is a different place from the world of the living and it is hardly possible to visit there. That day in Hiroshima the two worlds nearly converged' (1986: 715). *Hiroshima mon amour*'s powerful force in relation to traces of always just died and always going to die derives from its bodily manifestation of both these living and dead 'worlds' within our own. Finally, and most significantly for life's survival and future becoming, the film witnesses life again alongside the ever ominous threat of future war and the silences of the last: 'There was a fearful silence', attests Hiroshima writer and survivor Yoko Ota, 'which made one feel that all people and all trees and vegetation were dead'; the 'silence', Rhodes continues, 'was the only sound the dead could make' (1986: 715).

Yet, for the living and dying, there can also be a 'wish to die' that becomes 'another way to express the desire to live', as Braidotti explains, if 'life being desire ... essentially aims at extinguishing itself, that is, reaching its aim and then dissolving' (2006: 151). To experience death as a becoming demands, however, that most frightening risk. This, Braidotti continues, is 'the ultimate crack' that forces us (2006: 151), and *Hiroshima mon amour*'s protagonist, to the limit or crack's edge between personal destruction and impersonal life, death and love, to that 'mobile and precise' point at which death might lose itself in itself (LS: 153) as a 'city of the dead' (Rhodes 1986: 746) becomes at last a 'city made to the size of love' (Duras 1961: 77).

 à♥

It will begin again. 200,000 dead and 80,000 wounded in nine seconds. Those are the official figures. It will begin again. (HMA)

The character has become a kind of viewer. He shifts, runs and becomes animated in vain, the situation he is in outstrips his motor capacities on all sides, and makes him see and hear what is no longer subject to the rules of a response or an action . . . He is prey to a vision . . . possessed by an almost hallucinatory sensuality . . . a visionary, a sleepwalker. (C2: 3)

They held their arms [in front of them] . . . and their skin – not only on their hands, but on their faces and bodies too – hung down . . . wherever I walked I met these people . . . Many of them died along the road . . . like walking ghosts . . . They didn't look like people of this world . . . (Rhodes 1986: 718)

In distinguishing a 'basely sensual appetite from the most beautiful of loves', Deleuze considers a destructive encounter and its decomposition of relations vis-à-vis the symbiotic, proliferating relations of a 'true' love (1978a). This distinction between a degenerative and truly beautiful 'love', negative and affirmative encounter, speaks also to the ever 'blossoming industry of memorialization' that Adrian Parr and others observe (Parr 2008: 1). Against a 'reterritorializing Memory machine' through which past negates future as it recodes and reterritorialises the present by 'imposing upon the present too much remembrance and not enough forgetting' (Parr 2008: 107; 89), *Hiroshima mon amour* reveals the lovers' transformative, intensive encounter that exposes the affective possibilities of a woman and city's continuous survival and eternal becoming. And so, as through the opening sequence image of a beaming bus tour guide whose uniform bears an embroidered 'H', *Hiroshima mon amour* acerbically yet subtly rebukes a reductive commercialisation of remembrance that might overwhelm and constrain future life as the film poignantly evokes the loving encounters of woman-man, woman-city.

Hiroshima mon amour's sensual presentation of the woman and city's emergent awareness of their thresholds of intensity – the limits, degrees, lived passages and affects between the increases and decreases of their joys and sorrows – derives from the 'power of forgetting' (see ATP: 84) the human lovers release who come, again, to exceed them*selves* through their transitory encounter. If the lovers' fleshly skins come to embody that 'boundary between the outside and the inside', 'the internal world and . . . external world', a border, limit or 'skin . . . uniquely suited to receive new excitations', the process of the lovers-becoming-world remarkably corresponds to Deleuze's remarks through Nietzsche pertaining to the 'distinction between the conscious and unconscious' (NP: 112).

For if the 'reactive unconscious', as attests Deleuze, 'is defined by mnemonic traces, by lasting imprints', then the 'active super-conscious faculty' the woman of *Hiroshima mon amour* gradually assumes is 'the faculty of forgetting' without which 'there could be no happiness, no cheerfulness, no hope, no pride, no *present*' (NP: 112–13). Temporally, corporeally, *Hiroshima mon amour* reveals the death of death within itself as actual death gives way to virtual becoming and life's affective 'melodic line of continuous variation' (Deleuze 1978a)[5] via this essential, active, positive force of forgetting and untimeliness. As such, the film provocatively engages with the after-effects and affects of the lovers whose singular and creative encounters effect movements and means towards positive new becomings.

Against Hiroshima's exoticisation as a profitable tourist site, *Hiroshima mon amour* then explores potentials for life that arise and exist among the intangible remnants and ashes of the city's sufferings. This furtive quest, underscored by characteristic Resnais tracking movements interspersed with handheld shots that suggest a naïve tourist's curiosity, becomes *Hiroshima mon amour*'s immanent excavation. Through such means, the film not only relives but also reactivates and newly repeats the events of Hiroshima and the woman's pasts as it contemplates the *between*: the duration, affect and excess of an eternity between past-future, death-life, and our loves and events that forever eternally return. Which is to say, while 'history and memory reduce the intensive to the extensive', as Constantin Boundas writes, *Hiroshima mon amour*'s will to seek 'the eternal truth of the pure, virtual events' (1996: 332) that are actualised in the states of affairs it reveals opens to a multiple forgetting and virtual past.

Boundas' distinction between the 'eternalized past' and the virtual past, which is 'always already production' and 'made out of forgetting', 'all things being simultaneous in it' (1996: 333), corresponds to the 'considerable difference' Deleuze determines between an 'empirical forgetting' and 'essential forgetting'. Forgetting, writes Deleuze, 'exists within essential memory as though it were the "nth" power of memory' (DR: 140), as it forces each faculty to confront 'that which is its "own"': 'Discord of the faculties . . . each confronts its limit, receiving from (or communicating to) the other only a violence which brings it face to face with its own element, as though with its disappearance or its perfection' (DR: 141). This positive force and power of forgetting bespeaks an eternity or infinite 'within time' through the eternal 'life-force present in all things' (Braidotti 2006: 148) that comprises the actual continuum of life and time. This 'infinite which belongs to a single time, the eternity which belongs to an instant, the unconscious which belongs to consciousness, the "nth" power', propels the Deleuzian-Nietzschean principle: 'whatever you will, carry it to the "nth" power – in other words, separate out the superior form by virtue of the singularity of repetition in the eternal return itself' (DR: 8). Discover an immanent eternity and affirm the future through a becoming *with* the world and active forgetting; live intensely, eternally, sensorily, within this world. Push to the limit, the 'nth' power, while yet enduring.

'Such is the paradox', admits Braidotti, 'of nomadic subjectivity at the height of its process of becoming other-than-itself, suspended between the no longer and the not yet' as it aims towards a becoming-imperceptible, absolute deterritorialisation and repetition in the eternal return through an essential forgetting whose horizon is 'beyond the immediacy of life' (2006: 156). 'Becoming-imperceptible is the event for which there is no immediate representation' writes Braidotti; 'all a subject can do is mark his/her assent to the loss of identity' (2006: 156; 157).

And so, while an eternalised 'enslaving past' of reminiscence, History and nostalgia 'weigh . . . down memory', the 'lifeless present' and determine a future 'already continuous' with such a past through a 'forgetting of forgetting' and 'memorial repetition' (Boundas 1996: 333, 332), the constitutive power of the virtual past opens to life's singularity and power to differ through a 'repetition of the future which breaks up the hold [of past and present]' (1996: 332). Repetition through the eternal return corresponds again, to return to Boundas' words, to the 'virtual past [which] does not distinguish things in terms of before and after, all things being simultaneous in it. Not present and not lived, the past made out of forgetting is always already production' (1996: 333) that differs, eternally. Via Nietzsche Deleuze reiterates:

> It is not some one thing which returns, but rather returning itself is the one thing which is affirmed of diversity or multiplicity . . . The eternal return must be thought of as a synthesis; a synthesis of time and its dimensions . . . of diversity and its reproduction . . . of becoming and the being which is affirmed in becoming, a synthesis of double affirmation. (NP: 48)

If the eternal return, as Deleuze further contends, is 'an answer to the problem of *passage*' in relation to becoming and a 'passing moment [that] could never pass if it were not already past and yet to come – at the same time as being present' (NP: 48), then the returning corresponds as well to the passages, transitions, 'continual durations or variations of perfection' called affects between affections (SPP: 49). Which is to say that the eternal return's 'synthesis of time and its dimensions', which again affirms 'diversity and its reproduction', 'difference and its repetition' (NP: 48; 49), affirms also the irreducibility of experiences that potentially empower or overwhelm a self as it pushes towards its limits and a becoming-other. The eternal return, that is, expresses the singularity of life through a creative forgetting of self that is affirmed via becoming and a Will to Power. Of such a life of intensity and conscious forgetting through an event and erotics of love, François Zourabichvili movingly attests: 'existence has its intense passages and its ruptures: loving, and also forgetting, forgetting as what makes us capable of loving' (Zourabichvili 1996: 203).

With each cut, *Hiroshima mon amour* draws closer to such a virtual process of love. As it nears the skeletal remains of a domed ceiling whose bared wiry 'vertebrae' or rafters prefigure the vaulted edifices of Marker's *La Jetée*, the film's eye glimpses clouds that pass over the arms of the exposed arches. The French woman still ruminates: 'Why deny the obvious necessity of remembering?' (HMA), while the film's audio-visual layers resist causal coherence, recognition or memory flashback. As Deleuze observes, Resnais' 'work as a whole [is] based on the coexistence of sheets of past' (C2: 122) so that the woman's seeming flashbacks in *Hiroshima mon amour* rather suggest the film's own leaps among various regions of virtual past. As superimposed images surface of the River Ota, *Hiroshima mon amour*'s score seemingly sighs while the lovers' intertwined bodies re-emerge through the strata and sheets of past.

ॐ

Affect is constituted by the lived transition or lived passage from one degree of perfection to another. (Deleuze 1978a)

And again a return to the perfect embrace of the bodies. (Duras 1961: 7)

Between the series of successions, ideas and images that comprise our lives, the 'corporeal affections' (SPP: 73) or effects of other bodies upon our own, are our *affects*. Between representational modes of thought, in other words, are the non-representational, continual *durations* and *variations* that constitute our lived transitions and passages from one degree of perfection, reality or 'power of acting' to another. 'The feeling affect (joy or sadness)', Deleuze once more explains through Spinoza, 'follows from the image affection or idea that it presupposes (the idea of the body that agrees with ours or does not agree); and when the affect comes back upon the idea from which it follows, the joy becomes *love*' (SPP: 50).

What then of the lovers in relation to such a joy, such a *love*? What of their caresses, touches, connections, the ephemeral yet intense transfer of love between the two, simply 'she' and 'he', nameless virtual sensations and assemblages of lives lost and traumatised in Nevers-Hiroshima? As they emerge from the Hotel New Hiroshima into a forever new Hiroshima, the lovers pause while *Hiroshima mon amour* itself lingers between past-future worlds of recognisable-imperceptible, hate-love. Later, the lovers observe as production filming continues for the 'film about peace' in which the French woman has a part. It is yet another film, like the museum's filmed re-enactments, engendered by the atomic blast that *Hiroshima mon amour* enfolds within its audio-visual series. An actor, costumed and painted as a bomb victim, suddenly appears beside the lovers, watching the passing parade staged for this film-within-a-film; the lovers' seeming obliviousness to the man suggests the perpetual virtual coexistence of durations and experiences through which past, continuous world horrors exist threateningly alongside affirmative becomings of life. Duras writes: 'They [the lovers] suddenly find themselves involved again with their own story. This personal story always dominates the necessarily demonstrative Hiroshima story' (1961: 39).

Yet through their singular, ever-foreign love, enabled through a power of forgetting that confronts the imperceptible, unknown and untimely, the lovers' becomings ultimately exceed self and personal identity. '*Between the two*' is 'a natural play of haecceities, degrees, intensities, events, and accidents' (ATP: 253), and through the film's series of flutterings, vibrations and movements of *thisness* and affect, the lovers' well-formed subjects are forever shattered.

The film tracks along Hiroshima's streets, passageways, railways; it pans the French countryside and woman's past; it searches the lovers' faces across sections of time. They, the woman-man, Nevers-Hiroshima lovers, exist between times, past-future; theirs is a series of eternally returning virtual objects, 'shreds of pure past' (DR: 101) and singular experiences of future. The score murmurs its lovers' theme, its ever-new repetitions a series of 'whispering voices' itself among the lovers' becomings and encounters. Through Deleuze and Guattari we might suggest that to live is 'perhaps to bring this assemblage of the unconscious to the light of day, to select the whispering voices, to gather the tribes and secret idioms from which I extract something I call my Self' (ATP: 84). Movements actualised 'in the present of bodies', within 'the limits of worlds, individuals, and persons', argues Deleuze, imprison their singularities (LS: 167).

Yet there is movement through the excess of a well-formed, actual structured self, through the virtual events, sensual intermingling and becomings of bodies, their transitory happenings or dynamisms that underlie an actualisation. The 'event implies something excessive in relation to its actualization, something that overthrows worlds, individuals, and persons', writes Deleuze (LS: 167–8). Inasmuch as 'actually existing, structured things live in and through that which escapes them', as observes Massumi (1996: 229), this something which escapes, this affective *thisness*, evokes experience at its most intense and intimate, at that limit of a self and its becoming-other between personal-impersonal, actual-virtual, life and death.

Inside the lovers embrace. As their bodies fade from sight, superimposed images of the outside emerge. At dusk along the River Ota people rest, fish and gaze motionlessly at the water's passage while haunting woodwinds replay their nearly mystical, fleeting refrain. The lovers reappear in a tearoom at night as the Loire surfaces through layers of the woman's past. And as a camera tracks along the French countryside and river, 'a completely unnavigable river' the woman claims (HMA), the film's soundtrack yet remains in Hiroshima as once again *Hiroshima mon amour*'s series of time-images, images of pure time, virtual becoming and movement, transcend place, spatialised time and death. 'There is something which transcends time', Braidotti proposes through Deleuze, and 'once this insight is acquired', in *this world*, 'there is little to fear from actual death' (Braidotti 2006: 150).

From the untimely, unnameable *between*, between the film's audio-visual images and incessantly variable assemblages of Hiroshima-Nevers, he-she, their relations ever disjunctive, overlapping and exploratory, the film's affective power then surges. The lovers-becoming-other, becoming-woman, becoming-imperceptible and world open to the virtual potentials of all that may happen within this single existence. *Amor fati*, 'to want the event', declares Deleuze, 'has never been to resign oneself . . . but to extract from our actions and passions that surface refulgence, to *counter-effectuate* [or *counter-actualise*] the event, to accompany that effect without body, that part which goes beyond the accomplishment . . . A love of life which can say yes to death' (D: 65). Such is the eternal, continual return and production of love, love of one's fate and world wherein, 'once again', writes Duras, there will be 'an overlapping of Nevers and love, of Hiroshima and love. It will all be mixed, without any preconceived principle' (1961: 12).

In place, then, of a mere human love are the lovers' *unconscious erotics* and series of ever-new connections outside the self, its possessions and decisions. *Hiroshima mon amour, Hiroshima (my) unknown connections*. Between the two, between the singularities, qualities, memories of the human-city lovers, arise new sensations, intensities, creations or life. The 'relation between individuals', observes Williams,

> is neither one of a shared experience or a shared world, nor is it a shared understanding, nor an empathy. Instead, it is an interference between different dynamic processes that neither pole fully grasps. The encounter with the other makes my world more strange and, hence, more intense, not more comfortable or communal or better known (Stop trying to know me – you'll destroy everything.). (2003: 209)

She grips his hands, claws the cave cellar's walls. 'Memory is in these walls, one with the stone, the air, the earth', writes Duras (1961: 96), these walls that recall the scratched, gnawed, cursed, murdering walls of the concentration camps within Resnais' *Nuit et Brouillard*, while the woman's shorn head newly repeats images of bomb and Holocaust victims from both *Hiroshima mon amour* and *Nuit et Brouillard*. She sucks her bloodied hands, grasps and releases his. The images collide. Ages and layers of past surface and interchange. 'The only memory I have left is your name', she continues.

Yet now, as the French woman repeats her past love to her new love for a first time, she moves beyond memory and affixed identity via an impersonal process of subjectification that 'has no other memory than that of the material' (ECC: 66), the plurality of becomings and sensations that comprise her affective assemblage. Deleuze writes of a 'cartography-art built on "things of forgetting and places of passage"' (ECC: 66), and through the interpenetrations of woman-man, woman-city, *Hiroshima mon amour* plummets the depths and breadths of physical bodies while it traces their incorporeal surfaces and 'metaphysical events' (D: 64). 'Love', Deleuze maintains, 'is in the depth of bodies, but also on that incorporeal surface which engenders it' (D: 65). If the event, as he proposes, 'is always produced by bodies which collide, lacerate each other or interpenetrate, the flesh and the sword' (D: 64), it is an 'incorporeal, impenetrable battle', a 'fog of a million droplets', variations or becomings that constantly both await and precede us (D: 64–5).

'For my pathetic wish to be loved', proclaims Deleuze, 'I will substitute a power to love', to extract the pure event 'which unites me with those whom I love, who await me no more than I await them, since the event alone awaits us, *Eventum tantum*' (D: 66). Torn open, no longer 'persons, characters or subjects', via the film's tactile analysis of both actual depth and virtual surface, 'between the cries of physical pain and the songs of metaphysical suffering' (D: 66), the eternal return of life and threat of death, the *Hiroshima mon amour* lovers embrace creation and a love beyond identification.

As the film reveals, the woman has already begun to open to such an immanent awareness and self-knowledge. For as she leaps layers within her past, a cat enters the cellar of the woman's memory. 'Little by little' the woman 'enters the stare of the cat' as they encounter one another. Like the human lovers, the cat and woman do not know or identify with each other; from within even the confines of her childhood home, the woman embraces a woman-becoming-animal[6] as Nevers, and then Hiroshima, come to exist not as external places distinct from the woman but as parts and compounds of her becoming and movement from transgression and fixation. From the transfixion of her affective potential and power for survival upon traces of death and sadness, the woman's discovery of 'eternity within time' then opens to self-freedom and perception through a special love of forgetting and passage.

ॐ

I'll remember you as the symbol of love's forgetfulness. (HMA)

Against a blithe waltz that fills the Hiroshima tearoom, *Hiroshima mon amour* cuts to France and a replaying of the woman's humiliation. As the townspeople jubilantly, brutally shear the woman's hair, the music plays on; the position of the woman's figure itself recalls earlier museum footage of Hiroshima women as their hair is easily yet forcibly torn from their heads. What evidence is this of a nation's scarring, moreover of the women who bore their country's wounds deep within their bodies, skin and hair? 'I hear nothing but the sound of the scissors on my head', she tells her Japanese lover. 'It eases the pain of your death a bit, like . . . like for my nails . . . the walls . . . my anger. What pain.' Then, later, she admits, 'I tremble at forgetting such love.' She tells him more. 'I'll remember you as the symbol of love's forgetfulness', he vows.

And now the lovers truly live through their love, their 'a-parallel evolution', that something, as Deleuze infers, 'which is between the two' (D: 7), between 'two beings that have absolutely nothing to do with each other' (ATP: 10) and yet everything. For between the two arises a symbiosis of affect and effect as the lovers intuit the imperceptible affects that draw them to each other and beyond their selves. When in 'full, formal possession' of our power to act or 'perfection', Deleuze imparts, we experience an eternal 'active joy' no longer explained by duration but an 'eternal mode' (SPP: 51). Again, as Braidotti claims, this is not an eternity of forever or duration but the knowledge or realisation of 'eternity within time' (2006: 150). In consciousness of what our bodies are capable, 'in joy' in other words, as writes Deleuze, 'our power expands, compounds with the power of the other, and unites with the loved object' (SPP: 101).

They walk the streets as if to join the staggering ghosts of Hiroshima's past while the film's soundtrack discovers a new sombreness. 'Sometimes we have to avoid thinking about the problems life presents', claims the French woman as she speaks through scars of the ages, memory-ages of this world. Her lover stands behind. They speak 'ironically', as Duras' screenplay notes (1961: 70), of a war to come that might reunite them. The woman realises that this love, this singular, new love of their human forms and constructions, has at last enabled her to experience her past and self, for a first time. She hides in the dark, in the streets; the score's earlier refrain returns differently. They walk the streets, Hiroshima-Nevers, as the film's images reveal crystallisations of past-present-future time that the woman now fully apprehends. A funereal march overcomes the score. A 'time will come', she pronounces, 'when we can no longer

5 *They walk the streets,* Hiroshima mon amour *(Resnais 1959)*

name what it is that binds us. Its name will gradually be erased from our memory until it vanishes completely.'

'Somehow', a Hiroshima survivor has testified, 'I became a pitiless person, because if I had pity, I would not have been able to walk through the city, to walk over those dead bodies' (Rhodes 1986: 723). The streets, sounds and shadows of *Hiroshima mon amour* in its concluding sequences evoke the 'uncanny world of the dead', not only of Hiroshima's past, with its 'bloated corpses' that drifted along the river's waters (Rhodes 1986: 724; 725), but also Nevers', where once a German lover lay dying aside the banks of the Loire. *Hiroshima mon amour* revisits these layers as it presents, from the depths of the earth and from the ashes, a perpetually new love, a love of endless affective virtual power, pain, hope, loss and, finally, forever eternally, life. 'Hi-ro-shi-ma. Hiroshima'. Quietly she confronts her lover. 'That's your name.'

Notes

1. The film's score was largely composed by Giovanni Fusco. Georges Delerue's contribution was the film's jukebox waltz, as the accompanying booklet to the 2003 Criterion Collection DVD release indicates. See Russell Lack, 'About the composer: Giovanni Fusco' (*Hiroshima mon amour* DVD booklet 2003: 25).
2. With respect to his use of *sense* and *virtual*, Williams clarifies: 'I use "virtual", defined as the real but non-actual condition, because of its dominant role in Deleuze interpretation after *Difference and Repetition*. However, sense replaces this term in *Logic of Sense* and is in many ways a more subtle and precise term which, through its two-sidedness, counters the dualism or overvaluation of the virtual (and devaluation of the actual) that can be read, in error, into the virtual-actual distinction' (2008a: 89).
3. A certain 'datedness' imbues a number of both Resnais and Chris Marker's works with an anachronistic yet prescient edge, a quality that has occasionally been observed in Marker's works but seemingly not in Resnais'.
4. This breakdown of distinction between perceiver-perceived relations develops throughout Marker's oeuvre as well, as in characters in *La Jetée* and *Sans Soleil*, for instance, who, like the woman in Resnais' *Hiroshima mon amour*, come to perceive their own self-perception and dissolution. Marker reiterates his challenge to any dichotomy between seeing and seen through his own self-image which can be glimpsed for a moment in *Sans Soleil*; the rare sight captures reclusive Marker with camera in hand.
5. See also Smith 2006: 57.
6. Duras writes of 'the stare of the cat-Riva', so-named for actress Emmanuelle Riva (1961: 98).

4

Mad Love

The nature of emotion as pure element . . . in fact precedes all representation, itself generating new ideas. It does not have, strictly speaking, an object, but merely an *essence* that spreads itself over various objects, animals, plants and the whole of nature. (B: 110)

From its foreboding first strains[1] and the black and white still image of a deserted airport pier, *La Jetée*'s cumulative audio-visual-tactile image, a *free indirect discourse and vision* (see C2, ch. 7) overwhelms both screen and viewer as it evokes an experience akin to its music – that which is ever-new and of 'great variety . . . unexpected progressions, and expressive of every motion, and accent; almost savage in strength and spirit at times, but more often melancholy'.[2] Perhaps the most renowned and arguably most beautiful of Marker's several films and multi-media works, *La Jetée* (1962) derives its multi-sensory passionate force from its aura or *essence*, a particular *thisness* or sensual singularity that 'pierces' and wounds a body. As its contemplation of experience in an often intolerable world profoundly calls upon the senses, this short film imagines an emancipatory freedom or potential beyond our bodies' corporeal, fragile human suffering through the most productive and creative means possible. Via a vibrating screen that expresses itself synaesthetically through its details, traces and *essence* that are not bound to characters or subjectivities but affect and are affected by other bodies in this Spinozian sense, *La Jetée* newly discovers sensations of happiness, peace and sadness, intangibles at once so elusive and yet tactile.

If 'feeling is that which is in continual exchange' as Deleuze contends, feelings in fact 'become characters', and music, as he similarly notes, 'becomes specially important' (C2: 124–5). As do the preceding chapters pertaining to Resnais' cinema, the following chapters probe the notion of autonomous emotion and feeling as divorced from fixed subjective positions in Marker's cinema in relation to Deleuze's concepts of independent *affect*, by way of Spinoza, and *desire*. Affect in this sense suggests that which is always in continual exchange as an active or reactive force, as Deleuze and Nietzsche claim, with corporeal-incorporeal effects; desire then is an experimental, affirmative incessant process or force of affects that creates assemblages and empowers bodies by productive connections. Desire, in this sense Deleuze insists uniquely apart from Kant and in ways through Nietzsche and Spinoza but also Bataille, Marx, Freud and Lacan, is not a nostalgic or romantic longing but a process that continuously forms, deforms and reforms (see Holland 2005: 61).

With respect to a cinema and most especially a film as moving and seemingly melancholic as *La Jetée*, this chapter seeks to discern how the film ventures beyond fixations of tragedy and loss. Detailed discussions of the film's sequences will consider affect and sensation vis-à-vis the production of multi-dimensional experiences that speak to the potential of cinema and its embodiment of time and movement through its dance of sensory images, signs and encounters. In other words, this chapter ruminates upon the film's poignant whispers, its music, voices, noises, lights and shadows and their relations of speed and slowness, or *durée*, that not only comprise music and the living cinematic medium but also the human bodies they indelibly affect.

Deleuze's filmic analyses, it may be noted, face accusations of a partiality towards a canonical hierarchy of modernist 'art-house' cinema. Yet this seeming preference principally reflects Deleuze's fascination with the capacities of certain films to directly present not merely the flow of non-localised movement but also time itself through time-images or signs that liberate a human body from its self-imposed limits as it begins to perceive its world and self differently through select cinematic experiences. Interestingly however, despite evident admiration for the works of Marker's collaborators and friends, notably Resnais, Deleuze's writings do not acknowledge Marker's cinema although Marker's films, particularly *La Jetée*, remarkably exemplify Deleuze and Guattari's considerations, as does Marker's persona itself.

Self-effacing, moreover, always self-redefining, becoming-other or 'deterritorialising', the persona that is 'Chris Marker, the artist' is itself perhaps most synonymous with this beautiful short film. Inasmuch as Marker playfully recreates his persona through various assumed names and puns, in its musings upon memories and ordinary moments, *La Jetée* presents an equally myriad assemblage of things, a hundred tiny details, as Deleuze and Guattari might suggest, which collectively and impersonally effect and affect a body, be it, as Dorothea Olkowski observes, 'chemical, biological, social, or political' (1994: 120). The beautiful, writes Melissa McMahon, 'obliges us to think (its singularity poses a *problem*), without there being any concept for thought to settle on' (2002: 7). As it attempts to trace what is beautiful and intangible, what is not again a 'what' but rather *this*, a *thisness*, sign or 'trigger', as Steven Shaviro proposes (2002: 12), or haecceity as Deleuze and Guattari contend, Marker's cinema obsesses over lists of 'things that quicken the heart', as his *Sans Soleil* explains.[3]

This essential 'criterion', as *Sans Soleil*'s disembodied voice terms it, marks Marker's entire practice as one of futurity fully immersed within a creative past and memory. The beautiful, singular, fragile, affective and forever haunting populate Marker's oeuvre with details, faces and places, worlds of detail or the 'infinitesimal' which constitute, as explain Deleuze and Guattari, 'an entire realm of sub-representative matter' (ATP: 218–19). Upon scrutiny, these faces and places can dissolve; to reiterate Deleuze and Guattari's description, 'they are haecceities in the sense that they consist entirely of particles, capacities to affect and be affected' (261), the ever transient quality of which comprises a pure, incommunicable, aconceptual affect that may, by its 'event' in piercing and moving the soul, evoke Barthes' concept of *punctum*.

Foreign and yet familiar, obscure though simple, ephemeral albeit acute, Marker's cinema repeats itself ever newly through explorations that often assume for their points of interpenetrating directions indeterminate meanings of peace, happiness, dreams and memory. Perhaps in contrast to Resnais' cinema that also confronts the shocking horrors and traumas of twentieth- and twentieth-first century experience, Marker's films more fully interrogate the simple beauty of a present moment always already past and yet to come, and its lingering sensations of loss where peace, sensitivity and feeling, freed as these sensations may be from unified subjects, are to be found in an affective process that endlessly passes through and reconfigures the bodies of the films and those they encounter. This process of creation that speaks not only to what a body is but also to what it can *do*, to paraphrase Deleuze and Guattari via Spinoza (ATP: 257), inspires the following exploration of *La Jetée*'s affective beauty, an *essence* that inevitably evades this account of its incommunicable singularity.

ﻣ

The directors of the experiment tighten their control. They send him back. Time rolls back again. The moment happens once more; this time she is near him. He says something. She doesn't mind, she answers. They have no memories, no plans. Time builds itself painlessly around them. As landmarks they have the very taste of this moment they live . . . and the scribbling on the walls. (LJ)

The '*punctum*', Barthes writes, 'is a kind of subtle *beyond* – as if the image launched desire beyond what it permits us to see . . . toward the absolute excellence of a being, body and soul together' (1981: 59). An experience of *punctum*, a non-signifying intensive charge that takes us beyond our*selves*, may well be contemplated in relation to that *thisness* Deleuze and Guattari discern as *affect* that viscerally shocks a body, a body that may be defined as any whole aggregate of relational parts and speeds that affect and are affected by both internal and external actions-reactions or encounters with other bodies. All that remains beyond transcendent truths and illusions are 'bodies', Deleuze writes, 'which are forces, nothing but forces' (C2: 139).

To assess the means and effects of a violent singular beauty and love as released through Marker's film the 'relation between one force and others' must be considered, 'the shock of forces, in the image or of the images between themselves', as Deleuze explains (C2: 139). To conceive of an image or body without form, an assemblage of heterogeneous parts without binding organisation, a *body without organs* as Deleuze and Guattari propose through Artaud, is to dismantle the notion of a hierarchised organism, traditional psychoanalysis and its theory of subjectification and the dominance of linguistic signs through which language and meaning are most often structured. Although a body can never entirely free itself in that its becoming exists within the regime it endeavours to crack, inherent to a body's dynamism and movement is nevertheless a risk of madness through the incorporeal wounding and very real scarring of a corporeal body. Of such madness *La Jetée*'s voice speaks:

Nothing tells memories from ordinary moments. Only afterwards do they claim remembrance on account of their scars. That face, which was to be a unique image of peacetime to carry with him through the whole wartime, he often wondered if he had ever seen it or if he had dreamed a lovely moment to catch-up with the crazy moment that came next . . . Only later did he realise that he had seen a man die.

Upon these words the screen darkens to a blackness pierced only by a subtle subterranean reverberation over which the droning voice continues: 'And soon afterwards Paris was blown up.' The irrationality and sheer madness of Paris' destruction resounds through the

6 *Ruins and requiem,* La Jetée *(Marker 1962)*

sensory image as its emerging light reveals a startling sight of an uninhabitable new Paris beset by radioactivity. The visual image track, momentarily layered with the cavernous tones, fully materialises with light and a choral reprisal whose majestic a cappella refrain augments the disconcerting tone of the entire stratigraphic image. Black and white still images of an unrecognisable Paris dissolve into one another; their merging superimposed skies of deadly, deathly dust and clouds extend the limits of the screen. This ominous image surge that profoundly infringes upon the senses drives thought beyond dualisms of authenticity and representation as it infuses the screen with an emotive immediacy. A suppliant cry, the flow of ruins and requiem persists at a steady yet pausing pace as the visual images linger briefly while the elegy soars and the camera ascends along the remains of the Arc de Triomphe. Such sublime effect embodies Deleuze's apt description:

> It is a matter of giving 'emotional fullness' or 'passion' back to the intellectual process . . . 'intellectual cinema' has as correlate 'sensory thought' or 'emotional intelligence', and is worthless without it . . . we go from a thinking of the whole which is presupposed and obscure to the agitated,

mixed-up images which express it . . . the drunkenness, the pathos which bathes them. (C2: 159)

As the camera ventures beneath ground along the galleries of the Palais de Chaillot, tremors that echo through the sinister soundtrack and visibly trembling shots[4] give way to nearly imperceptible whispers, their sharp enunciation of frenzied German made more pronounced by the quickening rhythm of cuts between images.

> [*whispers*. Then:] The prisoners were submitted to some experiments of great concern apparently to those who conducted them. The outcome was disappointment for some, death for others and for others madness.

Through the experimenters' frantic whispers, a score of plaintive strings and a series of shadows that reveal mere skeletal silhouettes in a prophetic unmasking of faces, identity and personalisation,[5] the agitation of the audio-visual-tactile image, as actualised through such virtual intensifications of sight, sound and bodily sensation, escalates only to fade and accede to a moment's silence. An affective anxiety continues to pervade the image; its ghostly ethereality emanates alongside the man's bodily fear and these incorporeal and corporeal forces, at once unearthly, indistinct and visceral, jointly engulf the image in an 'internal monologue' that, as Deleuze infers, 'goes beyond dream, which is much too individual, and constitutes the segments or links of a truly collective thought' (C2: 159).

Which is to say, analogous to Deleuze and Guattari's project as well-defined by Daniel Smith, *La Jetée* is also an 'analysis of delirium . . . the delirium that lies at the heart of the self (schizophrenia) [which] is one and the same thing as the delirium that exists at the heart of our society' (2007: 75). This is a Paris in decay and decomposed, an urban embodiment of a self's unravelling and confrontation with mortality whose immanent survival indeed lies only through time and madness.

❧

> If the human race survives, future men will . . . look back on our enlightened epoch as a veritable age of Darkness . . . They will see that what we call 'schizophrenia' was one of the forms in which . . . the light began to break through the cracks in our all-too-closed minds. (R.D. Laing 1967: 154–5, cited in AO: 131)

The 'price to be paid, in cinema as elsewhere' Deleuze suggests, is 'always a confrontation with madness' (C2: 201). The inanity of the man's outer world, a ravaged Paris, finds its counterpart in the recesses of the underground galleries from wherein the man, held captive by the experimenters but moreover by the restraints of fixed identity, self and ego, seeks flight through the haunting memory of a woman's face. The man yet fails to perceive that a 'line of flight' or new becoming lies through an endlessly double process, coincidence or *between* of two terms or forces, beauty and fear, for instance, hope and despair, life through death, 'a process that produces the one within the other and couples the machines together' (AO: 2),[6] an encounter, becoming or 'nuptials' that fractures the limits of a well-defined 'self' and identity as it invents, zigzags or, again, 'passes or happens *between* two' (D: 6–7; emphasis mine). Deleuze explains:

> an encounter is perhaps the same thing as a becoming, or nuptials. It is from the depth of this solitude that you can make any encounter whatsoever. You encounter people (and sometimes without knowing them or ever having seen them) but also movements, ideas, events, entities. (D: 6)

If existence is an endlessly connective synthesis of 'machines', and each thing itself a machine connected to the flows of another body or machine, as Deleuze and Guattari propose, life might be viewed as a moving assemblage of bodies and machines propelled though desire, a *desiring-machine* that 'causes the current to flow ... flows in turn, and breaks the flows' (AO: 5). Only through self-experimentation and the making of his body as one without organs, a decoded, dynamic body that would extend the limits of his perception and mortality, can the man in *La Jetée* discover a freedom that would challenge the illusions of chronological time and a stable self.[7] In this sense madness is not a psychological disorder but a disordering of political and historical consequence and revolutionary potential (see Holland 1999: x), a breakthrough rather than breakdown,[8] a decoding and destroying of repressive codes and beliefs that constitute a self and society and that delimit the flows of life's movement.[9]

From amongst the prisoners the man is selected and as he awaits his fate at the hands of the experimenters, his audible heartbeats punctuate the image.

> He was frightened. He had heard about the Head Experimenter. He was prepared to face the Mad Scientist, a Dr Frankenstein. Instead, he met a reasonable man who told him in a relaxed way that the human race was doomed. Space was off-limits. The only link with survival passed through Time.

This line between madness and reason is as illusory, *La Jetée* suggests, as the notion of truth through representation, a repressive construction that fragments life's dynamism and contingency. 'There are mad faces', Deleuze and Guattari write, 'that do not conform to what one assumes madness should be' (ATP: 177). When sensory experience and creative possibilities are diminished through immutable morals, codes and theories of madness, truth and subjectivity, the profound connections and sensations between all things cannot be sensed. Definitions of the real and perceptible constrict life and movement and yet, to reiterate a contention of this book as explored in Chapter 2, if thought might perceive that that which takes place 'takes place in one world', or 'univocally' as Deleuze stresses, the seemingly separate worlds of reality and representation would coalesce (C2: 130).

The cinematic image, again, would not seem to exist distinctly from 'real life' and a 'body' might, once more, be recognised as Bergson proposes, as an 'aggregate of the material world, an image which acts like other images, receiving and giving back movement' (1991: 19). To glean this revolutionary concept of life is to perceive that all memories, imaginings, perceptions and fictions are as 'real', as this book has attempted to illustrate, as the Histories, Truths and Universals society holds dear. The degrees to which 'we' are affected and affect ever newly comprise the very real sensations and intensities of life, each moment of a synthesised past-present-future forever open to a future freed from any totality of ego-centric time.

As it assesses these affective, asubjective, impersonal forces, sensations and 'machines' that constitute our bodies and give rise to intensely intimate, touching encounters, *La Jetée* plummets beneath ground to plumb an obscure underworld of such coexistent temporalities, unidentifiable processes and endless imperceptible momentary events that underlie the world of entrenched thought and reason. The film performs, that is, a geological quest to discern the indiscernible, the material remnants and minutiae of quotidian life, as it sifts through debris and layers of subterranean strata. Deleuze and Guattari might define such an experiential, sensory exploration of certain *thisnesses* and forces as anti-historical:

> Nietzsche opposes history not to the eternal but to the subhistorical or superhistorical: the Untimely, which is another name for haecceity, becoming, the innocence of becoming (in other words, forgetting as opposed to memory, geography as opposed to history) . . . Creations are like mutant abstract lines that have detached themselves from the task of representing a world, precisely because they assemble a new type of

reality that history can only recontain or relocate in punctual systems. (ATP: 296)

In pursuit of the ephemeral and ever-new, *La Jetée* explores the power then of a 'pure ontological' memory whose creative force emerges from stratigraphic planes of such subhistorical layers of past in the face of which conventional time and faces and bodies themselves lose organisation and resist the reterritorialising of social production and overcoding. In a world where all known truths have vanished, the man locates in this madness a truer truth that eluded simple expression in the world he knew. He confronts not his own personal memory but this vaster world-memory, an architecture of memory (C2: 117), through a tactile sensuality, *beauty*, *thisness* or *haecceity* emanating from his encounters with a foreign world and otherness of self, life and language, a becoming that surfaces most intensely through a face.

This woman's face, a corporeal landscape and intensive surface evocative of Deleuze and Guattari's concept of faciality and the layers that engender a face, is itself a politics that breaks through and dismantles the 'black hole' of subjectivity, human consciousness and memory, reason and language (ATP: 186–9). There is risk, of course, in becoming trapped in an alluring idealisation of a face without seeing through to the traits, zones, becomings and details of its composition. 'A language', write Deleuze and Guattari, 'is always embedded in the faces that announce its statements' (ATP: 179); how tempting it is, that is, 'to latch ... onto a *face*' and be guided by the seduction of aesthetic interpretation and its qualifications of beauty and authenticity (ATP: 187).

How can we then see beyond a face, can the man gaze past such a 'unique image of peacetime' (LJ) and loveliness to look 'no longer ... at or into the eyes but ... swim through them' as Deleuze and Guattari urge? (ATP: 187). Inasmuch as *La Jetée* asks how we might think beyond psychological definition and aesthetic idealisation to exceed ourselves through strange encounters of love, faces and bodies, the very means of this questioning via the film's release of certain singularities from their formal properties into a pure realm of affect demand that the film itself be seen as a living form, body or aggregate of singularities and affects that might generate empowering joy or disempowering sadness, a true cinema of ethics and ethics of cinema.

ﻉ

In the underworld he first assumes to be overrun by madness, the man's captors shield his face with a mask, an act that manifests the process of the man's becoming towards 'asignifying, asubjective, and faceless' sensory experience wherein faces become nothing but haecceities (ATP: 187), 'set[s] of nonsubjectified affects' (ATP: 262), series of movements, speeds and slownesses, images and interactions. Even a mask, Deleuze and Guattari write, can become 'the face itself', an 'inhumanity of the face', once more a politics whose unravelling entails a definite risk of madness (ATP: 181; emphasis mine). What then is love's relation to such madness? 'Schizophrenia is like love', Deleuze and Guattari claim, both flows a productive and reproductive desiring-machine (AO: 5). Indeed, love too seems an affective decoding, a series of flows coupled by desire that, by their associations and conjunctions, enhance certain bodies whose encounters multiply their own bodies – not through union or juxtaposition, as Deleuze explains (D: 18), but in the surfacing and proliferation of *thisnesses* that pass *between* two, 'that something [that] happens between them' (D: 15).

'If you cannot grasp the small trace of madness in someone, you cannot be their friend', Deleuze maintains. 'But if you grasp that small point of insanity . . . that point of madness is the very source of their charm.'[10] Can it be *this* that moves the soul and extends the crack between the self and its beyond, incorporeal life and corporeal death, or immanent dying and personal death, bringing us nearer the potential to fully, selflessly embrace the singular, beautiful and different while not compromising mortal life, language and survival?

There are ways, Deleuze suggests, 'in which the association of the two [faces of personal and impersonal death] may be brought about', among these madness, suicide, drugs or alcohol (LS: 156). Although art is not, Deleuze and Guattari admit, 'an end in itself' (ATP: 187), the cinema, as an art of automatic movement unlike other arts, does possess the potential to expose this cracking of experience via its images of time de-chronologised and 'out of joint'. These direct time-images reveal becoming itself, the past and future on either sides of the crack, as they expose coalescing lines of the personal and impersonal. Yet again, to break through walls of a face, identity and unified organisation is to confront the limits of 'what a body can do' as it crosses through its-self towards a singular beyond. The violence is undeniably real as its incorporeal virtuality becomes actualised in a corporeal body.

By its evocation of a love that is 'itself inseparable from an experience of mortality' (Fynsk 1991: xv), *La Jetée* enacts this risk of a becoming-imperceptible through an impersonal yet most personal death as it negotiates these faces of death and time: that of the 'most fully present' with respect to which the future and past are determined and, on the other hand, a contracted present of the 'mobile instant' (LS: 151), simultaneously always past-future. Such shatters existence ever preoccupied with mortal death as it 'calls the subject out and beyond itself' (Fynsk 1991: xv; see also Houle and Steenhuisen 2006: 22).

There is, Deleuze explains, a dualism that 'corresponds to the two aspects of the time-image: a cinema of the body, which puts all the weight of the past into the body, all the tiredness of the world and modern neurosis; but also a cinema of the brain, which reveals the creativity of the world, its colours aroused by a new space-time, its powers multiplied' (C2: 205). There is, in other words, potential for a 'line of flight' or new becoming via the cinema whose time-images might reveal the double process or encountering of both the despair and exhaustion of a past and the hope of a present 'with all its future potentialities . . . the two making up one and the same world, ours, its hopes and its despair' (C2: 205). If what is important is 'no longer the association of images . . . but the interstice between two images', once more it may be said that this coincidence or *between* of two terms or forces, hope and despair, speaks to the potential of life through death, an impersonal immanent death through a becoming-imperceptible or becoming-other, a folding and taking into the self of every element of nature (C2: 200).

Ian Buchanan asks how an externalisation 'of an impulse which, when released in the world, takes on an exuberant life and existence of its own', can be 'conceived as an inward fold, when surely that must imply internalisation?' (2000: 52). This folding, this coupling process of producing one within another, in fact, as Buchanan clarifies, is both an externalisation of a self's becoming-other beyond it-self, and an internalisation of the subject as the self is enfolded into a larger fold. As Chapter 2 vitally stresses in relation to the figure of the *Muselmann*, through a truer death than the one the self internalises and personalises, a body might find freedom through a depersonalised death, which necessitates, as Buchanan further states, 'a disavowal of an individual past (one's memories) in favour of a common future' and a 'coming to terms with a common past so as to have an individual (but not personal) future, one's own death' (2000: 137).

If we might become 'worthy of what happens to us', as Deleuze urges, 'and thus to will and release the event, to become the offspring of one's own events', we might indeed perceive that one's personal death is at once a rebirth (LS: 149–50). This is the point, to again repeat Deleuze's words, at which not only 'I disappear outside of myself' but also 'the moment when death loses itself in itself, and [. . . in] the figure which the most singular life takes on in order to substitute itself for me' (LS: 153).

ﻉ

One is exhausted before birth, before realizing oneself, or realizing anything whatsoever. (ECC: 152)

A means of encounter, making a line . . . shoot between two people, producing all the phenomena of a double capture, showing what the conjunction AND is, neither a union, nor a juxtaposition, but the birth of a stammering . . . AND . . . AND . . . AND . . . (D: 9–10)

Launched once more into the middle of a brightly coloured, sensual and tactile 'dateless world which first stuns him by its splendour' (LJ), the man finds that face, that 'loved or dreamed-of' landscape whose beauty overwhelms and affronts him and between the two, this man and this woman, a love arises more true than the self he was (ATP: 172–3). This is where madness also resides, in the smallest of connections and details, between things. In relation to the two processes or aspects of the crack that divide a self, Deleuze considers the notion of a human couple. 'Here is a man and a woman', he writes, 'and why couples, if not because it is already a question of movement, and of a process defined on the basis of the dyad?' (LS: 154).

With poignancy and a tactile ethereality, *La Jetée* reveals the otherworldly love of lovers whose interactions, forever without memories and plans, enact the process of a self's encounter with its limits. 'A truly perfect relationship', Deleuze and Guattari propose through D.H. Lawrence, 'is one in which each party leaves great tracts unknown in the other party' (ATP: 189). And the images flow now as if in a dream. The man in fact no longer knows 'whether he is driven, whether he has made it up, or whether he is only dreaming' (LJ). Cinema 'spreads', Deleuze suggests, 'an "experimental night" or a white space over us; it works with "dancing seeds" and a "luminous dust"; it affects the visible with a fundamental disturbance, and the world with a suspension, which contradicts all natural perception' (C2: 201).

'As in a dream', the film continues, 'he shows her a point beyond the tree, hears himself say, "This is where I come from", and falls back, exhausted' (LJ). 'Being exhausted is much more than being tired' writes Deleuze in relation to Samuel Beckett's characters (ECC: 152) who, having disconnected from or renounced 'any order of preference, any organization in relation to a goal, any significa-tion', cannot, as Brian Evenson suggests, 'move beyond thinking over possibilities and beginning to act' (Evenson 1994) and so instead affirm disjunctions and 'disjointed terms' (ECC: 153).

Whereas the 'realization of the possible always proceeds through exclusion', either this or that, as in 'to go out or stay in' (ECC: 153), the 'exhausted person exhausts the whole of the possible', and so 'exhausts himself in exhausting the possible, and vice-versa' (ECC: 152). The 'disjunction has become *inclusive*; everything divides, but into itself' (ECC: 153), '"this *and* then that"' (C2: 180; emphasis mine). This once more becomes a form of stammering beyond memory, names and the self. 'In the process', writes Smith, the exhausted 'exhaust themselves physiologically, losing their names, their memory, and their purpose in a "fantastic decomposition of the self"' as the self, 'even without attaining this limit', becomes defined 'by a process of "becoming"' (Smith 1997: xxix).

This again, as Deleuze explains with regard to cinema of the time-image, is 'the method of BETWEEN, "between two images"', that 'make[s] the indiscernible, that is the frontier, visible' and 'which does away with all the cinema of Being = is' (C2: 180). The exhaus-tion of the self, image and 'possible', in other words, pertains once more to a *between* in which the man of *La Jetée* lingers, a between that is 'entirely in the domain of the virtual or the possible', as Smith once more observes via Deleuze's thoughts upon exhaustion in Beckett's oeuvre (Smith 1997: xxix). As the man of *La Jetée* exhausts him*self* and the possible and so 'passes entirely into the virtual cha-osmos of included disjunctions' (Smith 1997: xxix), he again then opens to a between of terms and the 'between' of exhaustion itself through which one 'arriv[es]', as Deleuze claims, 'at the self, not as a term in the series, but as its limit':

> between two terms, between two voices or the variations of a single voice – a point that is already reached well before one knows that the series is exhausted, and well before one learns that there is no longer any possibility or any story, and that there has not been one for a long time. (ECC: 157–8)

In other words, exhausted, indeed already 'dead', and launched by the experimenters through various zones of time towards a confrontation with his own self and self as child, a 'vital degenera-tion' and 'most extreme dissolution' (ECC: 154), the man exists in a space released from 'sensory-motor schemata', a 'space before action, always haunted by a child', as Deleuze writes in relation to the cinema of the body, and with uncanny resonance for *La Jetée* (C2: 203). This 'space', once more, is the 'between' the time-image can expose, 'between', Deleuze continues, 'one death and the other, the absolute inside and the absolute outside' (C2: 208), where 'memory is no longer the faculty of having recollections' but the 'membrane which . . . makes sheets of past and layers of reality cor-respond, the first emanating from an inside which is always already there, the second arriving from an outside always to come, the two gnawing at the present which is now only their encounter' (C2: 207).

By way of this in-between 'between one death and the other', where 'the absolute inside and the absolute outside enter into contact, an inside deeper than all the sheets of past, an outside more distant than all the layers of external reality' (C2: 208), by way of this inter-stice and void exposed through exhaustion and a method of 'between two images' (C2: 180) that fractures the self and 'abolish[es] the real' (ECC: 154), the possible itself and the man's notion of any unified world or 'whole undergoes a mutation' (C2: 180). Ultimately the man begins to perceive a multiplicity of relations within this single world of interconnections which 'thus merges with that Blanchot calls the force of "dispersal of the Outside"', 'that void which is no longer a motor-part of the image' (C2: 180). The 'whole becomes', that is, as continues Deleuze, 'the power of the outside which passes into the interstice' to become 'the direct presentation of time' (C2: 181), as the man's body embodies an '*immense* tiredness of the body' (C2: 189; emphasis mine), a time-image itself that at once manifests the exhaustion of the man's self, his thought of a once pos-sible world, and the image's sensory-motor action.[11]

It is extremely difficult to make a pure and unsullied image . . . by reach-ing the point where it emerges in all its singularity, retaining nothing of the personal or the rational, and by ascending to the indefinite as if into a celestial state. *A* woman, *a* hand, *a* mouth, *some* eyes . . . (ECC: 158)

I no longer look into the eyes of the woman I hold in my arms but I swim through, head and arms and legs, and I see that behind the sockets of the eyes there is a region unexplored, the world of futurity. (ATP: 171)

Through the experimenters' whole series of tests, the man meets the woman at different times. 'She welcomes him in a simple way. She calls him her ghost' (LJ). The lovers walk as children run along their path. 'Is it another day? He doesn't know. They shall go on like this, on countless walks in which an unspoken trust, an unadulterated trust, will grow between them, no memories, no plans. Up to the moment, where he feels ahead of them, a wall' (LJ). For the man yet clings to an actual corporeal present within the limits of his self and body, a present in which he is doomed to die, and so he exists between the personal illusions he retains and the moment of his violent encounter with his actual self's fatal destruction and decomposition at the film's end, a death that at last releases him from the constraints of identity and pedantic time.

'There was no way to escape Time' (LJ), the ominous voiceover claims with seeming reference to human mortality, except through, *La Jetée* paradoxically evinces, a death of the self and its immanent becoming in time. Through Beckett once more, Deleuze writes of 'many authors [who] are too polite and . . . content to announce the total work and the death of the self. But this remains an abstraction as long as one does not show "how it is": how one makes an "inventory", errors included, and how the self decomposes, stench and agony included' (ECC: 154–5).

Yet the man's opening towards immanence and *a* life, beyond the agony of the actual and 'before birth, and before the other begins' (ECC: 156), lies through a beautiful, 'sensual catastrophe'[12] and love that exhausts memories, plans, words, space and the image itself. For as the lyrical visual images of the lovers' moments, glances and gazes coalesce with the haunting melody of the soundtrack, from between the fluidity of the audio and visual tracks, and the woman and her 'ghostly' lover, there arises a 'ghostly dimension of an indefinite impersonal': 'a woman, a man, and a child, without any personal coordinates' (ECC: 166).

The man 'never knows whether he moves towards her, whether he is driven, whether he has made it up, or whether he is only dreaming' (LJ). He lies exhausted, seemingly asleep, his mask removed. The shot fades, and another at once resurfaces with the sounds of several birds and an image of the sleeping woman who lies upon a pillow and beneath sheets, her hand at her head. Another image then emerges against the first as a series of slowly superimposed images and affects, of delicacy, softness and serenity, overcome the screen. 'The image', Deleuze suggests, 'is precisely this: not a representation of an object but a movement in the world of the mind. The image is the spiritual life' (ECC: 169). In a manner akin to the cascading series of images that revealed the film's earlier glimpses of the woman as she lay asleep outside in the sun, through this new series of sensual superimpositions that flow ever more rapidly as each image of the sleeping woman gives way to the next with briefer and briefer pause, *La Jetée* once more embodies the limit, 'polarized membrane' or 'memory' between one aspect of the direct time-image, again, a cinema of the body, and another, that of the mind (see C2: 207).

'The identity of world and brain', Deleuze explains,

> does not form a whole, but rather a limit, a membrane which puts an outside and an inside in contact, makes them present to each other, confronts them or makes them clash. The inside is psychology, the past, involution, a whole psychology of depths which excavate the brain. The outside is the cosmology of galaxies, the future, evolution, a whole supernatural which makes the world explode. The two forces are forces of death which embrace, are ultimately exchanged and become ultimately indiscernible. (C2: 206)

As *La Jetée* embodies this limit through which the self confronts its other as past collides with future, the image 'attain[s] the indefinite' (ECC: 160) as it opens not to any end but an infinite flow. For the life *La Jetée* exposes through its evocation of a personal, permanent death is a flow, an image as process, a spiritual life freed from the personal that persists through and beyond the body of the film itself. While a seeming immobility is evident within each still frame of the film – a photograph of life made mobile through the medium's movement – the cuts between the film's images themselves also refer to the limit between personal death and immanent life. And at last in this second sequence of the sleeping woman, the images express not only a 'world-brain' (C2: 206), or movements in the world of the mind whereby the process of the man's becoming-other becomes also an exploration of the world as brain itself, but they also relate to that which Deleuze describes, again through Beckett, as a *language III*. 'The image', writes Deleuze,

> is not defined by the sublimity of its content but by its form, that is, by its 'internal tension', or by the force it mobilizes to create a void or to bore holes, to loosen the grip of words, to dry up the oozing of voices, so as to free itself from memory and reason: a small, alogical, amnesiac, and almost aphasic image, sometimes standing in the void, sometimes shivering in the open. The image in not an object but a 'process'. We do not know the power of such images, so simple do they appear from the point

of view of the object. This is *language III*, which is no longer a language of names or voices but a language of images, resounding and coloring images. (ECC: 159)

Images of the sleeping woman flow against the sounds of the bird-song as the interaction of the audio and visual tracks in this sequence grant a new affective immediacy, directness and presence to the film made more pronounced by the extreme high pitch of the birdsong, its intensifying 'extremely brisk tempi' (Bogue 2003b: 29),[13] and, moreover, the quickening pace of the images. These are not memories but flashes of pure intensities.

The camera draws closer to the woman's face which appears now in close-up tilted towards screen left; her left hand rests against her right shoulder; her eyes remain shut; the birdsong persists. As *La Jetée*'s images flow, the woman seemingly turns, shifts and sighs in her sleep.[14] The birdsong further intensifies. She lifts her eyelids slowly, and then blinks repeatedly, her gaze affixed upon 'ours'. This image, this singular 'microfraction of time' (ECC: 161) that intimates and exceeds the most tender and intimate of human experiences, witnesses the film's most profound, intense collision of its personal and impersonal forces. For the momentary transition from still to moving image underscores the image's processual becoming as it at last also fully embodies *La Jetée*'s virtual embrace of intensive, spiritual life by means of an exhaustion or freeing of the image from possession or signification.

The 'image is more profound', observes Deleuze, 'because it frees itself from its object in order to become process itself; that is, an event as a "possible" that no longer even needs to be realized in a body or an object, somewhat like the smile without a cat in Lewis Carroll' (ECC: 168).[15] Later, again à propos Beckett, Deleuze adds:

It is not enough simply to think of something or someone ... What is required is an obscure spiritual tension ... since it raises the thing or the person to the state of an indefinite: *a* woman ... Nine hundred and ninety-eight times out of a thousand, one fails and nothing appears. And when one succeeds, the sublime image invades the screen, a female face with no outline. (ECC: 169–70)

By way of this 'pure intensity that pierces the surface' (ECC: 173), this 'flash of a pure image', this woman's face, 'unbound and destratified' (Evenson 1994), becomes *a* woman's face that effects a man's self-shattering and liberation via *a* death made singular.

৵

And deep in this limbo, he got the message from the men of a world to come. They too travelled through Time, and more easily. Now they were there, ready to accept him as one of their own. But he had a different request: rather than this pacified future, he wanted the world of his childhood, and this woman who perhaps was waiting for him. (LJ)

Far off, far off, as if he had landed on another planet, as a man might after death. (ATP: 189)

Suspended in this 'limbo', in between past-present-future time and forever affected by 'the memory of a twice-lived fragment of time' (LJ), lost and yet free and driven by a love for a woman that takes him beyond himself as their love manifests a 'process of *their passing into each other*' (Massumi 2002a: xviii), the man rushes inevitably towards *a* death. By such a death the man enacts a substitution of his self for a liberation of the singularities that affect the collective dimensions and multiplicities of his body, and we, the film's viewers, are potentially also moved (N: 6–7). For at the heart of this lovely film, from between its mesmerising, lyrical images and most affective sequences, a beauty arises and strikes us by its flowing series of emotively evocative moments, each 'unexpected flash', as Barthes might suggest, another *punctum* (1981: 94–6).

And so, through confrontation with the body of this film, 'I' feel my own body moved; 'something inside me' is touched by my relationship with this intensive screen of affects comprised of 'liberated singularities ... things, animals, [and] little events' (N: 7). In reference to the gap between content and expression, Brian Massumi writes of 'the immanence of their mutual "deterritorialization"' (2002a: xviii), and through the smallest of details, *La Jetée* embodies as much by way of two lovers whose process of passing into each other through the unravelling of a self reveals a potential opening to new experience and perception via such a startling singular love. The encounters between the man and woman, the man and his self, myself and the film itself enact a 'depersonalization through love' through the lovers and the ways they 'understand and complement, depersonalize and singularize – in short, love – one another' (N: 7).

ॐ

He wanted to be returned to the world of his childhood, and to this woman who was perhaps waiting for him ... he thought in a confused way that the child he had been was due to be there too, watching the planes. (LJ)

As it liberally etches time's past-future fissure within itself, that 'silent trace of the incorporeal crack', *La Jetée* deepens this scaring within the body of the man. Through a production of an affirmative *desire*, the 'fugitive beings' (ATP: 271) and bodies of *La Jetée* preclude distinct definition, understanding or categorisation. Inasmuch as the lovers resist such definitive description and analysis, the man's 'memory' then is more accurately an assemblage of singular sensations, bodily encounters of connections, actions and reactions. He is a prisoner within an unimaginable, unrecognisable world of crumbled ruins that once were known as Paris, his virtual images seeming remnants of this past existence.

Yet, as Deleuze and Guattari write, '*becoming is an antimemory*', and through his process of depersonalisation, the man discovers a contemporaneousness of his adult and child as he becomes *a* body, a multiplicity, a man becoming-woman, other, imperceptible (ATP: 294).[16] The child whose story the film tells is *a* child, '"a" molecular child', whose assemblage or block of singular sensations and perceptions are not of the man's childhood but of a new world becoming, a new memory-world formed by the lovers' encounter whose virtual images permeate a vast virtual and impersonal world-memory and past (ATP: 294). 'Is it possible to maintain the inherence of the incorporeal crack while taking care not to bring it into existence, and not to incarnate it in the depth of the body?' Deleuze demands (LS: 157). Perhaps *La Jetée*'s beauty is the potential it extends to its viewer to 'extend the crack' a little further, 'not enough to deepen it irremediably' within ourselves, but to at least 'go farther than we would have believed possible' towards new life through a haunting love (LS: 157–8; 161).

La Jetée's heartbeat, its tracing of love, indeed evinces Bergson's classification of an 'image' as that which exists 'halfway between the "thing" and the "representation"', once more a *thisness* (Bergson 1991: 9). The film's experiment, the perception of a self within time by a self, deepens the crack within the 'thickness' of the film, the man's 'noisy body' and my own (see LS: 156–7). I am deeply moved by this film whose love and tender vulnerability touches me by its sensual 'telling of memories from ordinary moments' (LJ), its most sensitively embodied movements across personal-impersonal lines and its tenuous balance along the crack's edge between two deaths that calls me from myself.

The film maps a love through death, and we are called to consider such experience anew. The man's quest, and that of the film, may

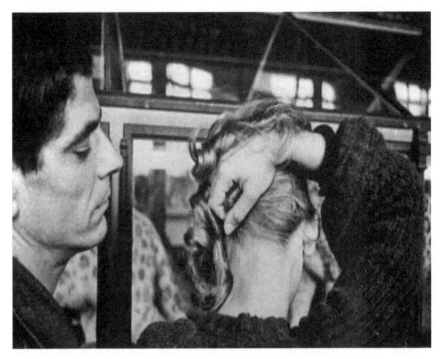

7 Thisnesses *that pass* between *two*, La Jetée *(Marker 1962)*

seem to be a tracing of a deeply wounding scar and yet the film's joyful revelation of a love encounter exceeds personal space-time dimensions, discounting any melancholy affect. Our 'capacity to be affected' is diminished, Deleuze explains through Spinoza, if '*our power of action is reduced to attaching itself to ... traces*' (EPS: 246); such is a 'diminution of the power of acting ... called *sadness*' (SPP: 50). The film does not then recover, re-present or redeem a memory, truth or authenticity but reverberates effortlessly via its flowing *punctum*, its series of images that request a death of ourselves, and via its vulnerability and fragility 'we' are infected by its mad love.

Notes

1. The film's credits identify the 'Russian Liturgy of the Good Saturday'.
2. N. Lindsay Norden writes that 'those who have heard [the Russian Liturgy] never forget it, so forceful and so wonderful is the impression it creates'. She quotes another who states that the music 'contains melodies of great variety, full of unexpected progressions, and expressive of

every motion, and accent; almost savage in strength and spirit at times, but more often melancholy in character. The Russian people have not found their existence an altogether happy one.' Indeed, as Norden claims, 'the imagination and emotion of the Russian people have found their freest expression in music' (1919: 426).

3. 'By learning to draw a sort of melancholy comfort from the contemplation of the tiniest things, this small group of idlers left a mark on Japanese sensibility much deeper than the mediocre thundering of the politicians. Shonagon had a passion for lists: the list of "elegant things", "distressing things" or even of "things not worth doing". One day she got the idea of drawing up a list of "things that quicken the heart". Not a bad criterion I realise when I'm filming; I bow to the economic miracle, but what I want to show you are the neighbourhood celebrations' (SS).

4. This unsteadiness of the camera indeed recalls the instability or shakiness of both still and moving images within Resnais' *Nuit et Brouillard*.

5. Marker's fascination with masks and a certain 'unmasking' or analysis of societal and fascist forms of oppression and self-repression can be traced from Marker and Resnais' 1953 *Les Statues meurent aussi* through Marker's 2001 *Le Souvenir d'un avenir*, the latter which will be examined briefly, also in relation to masks, in Chapter 6.

6. Here Deleuze and Guattari also explain that 'Everything is a machine. Celestial machines, the stars or rainbows in the sky, alpine machines – all of them connected to those of his body. The continual whirr of machines' (AO: 2).

7. See *Dialogues II*: 'experimentation on oneself, is our only identity, our single chance for all the combinations which inhabit us' (D: 11).

8. See *Anti-Oedipus* for a passage in which Deleuze and Guattari acknowledge Foucault and quote Laing: 'Madness need not be all breakdown. It may also be breakthrough' (AO: 131).

9. See Deleuze 1971: 'At this stage, psychoanalysis proves less and less capable of understanding madness, for the madman is really the being of decoded flows.'

10. See Charles J. Stivale's summary of the Deleuze and Parnet filmed interviews, *L'Abécédaire de Gilles Deleuze, avec Claire Parnet* (1996), Web Resources, Wayne State University, available at <http://www.langlab.wayne.edu/CStivale/D-G/ABC1.html> (accessed 1 November 2005).

11. Despite their disparate means and affective qualities, both *La Jetée* and Resnais' *Nuit et Brouillard* expose such an 'immense tiredness', a tiredness examined in Chapter 2. Both films, through the man of *La Jetée* and the *Muselmann* of *Nuit et Brouillard*, reveal a process of becoming, a crystallisation of past-future time, through bodies that linger in the in-between of personal death and immanent life.

12. I borrow this term from James Williams' 'Deleuze on J.M.W. Turner' (1997: 239).

13. See Ronald Bogue's discussion of 'The Music of the Birds' in relation to Deleuze and Guattari's thoughts on the composer Oliver Messiaen, 'whose approach to rhythm and birdsong in his musical compositions and theoretical writings opens the way toward a conception of music as an engagement of cosmic forces' (Bogue 2003b: 14). 'The same thing that leads a musician to discover the birds', Deleuze and Guattari remark, 'also leads him to discover the elementary and cosmic' (ATP: 309).

14. For additional discussion pertaining to an indiscernibility between mobility and immobility, life and death, an indiscernibility that enables the direct presentation of time and affect in the films of Marker and Resnais, see again Chapter 2. However, whereas Resnais' moving images of the *Muselmänner* in *Nuit et Brouillard* appear as stills, and so affront by their sudden movements, these still images of the sleeping woman in *La Jetée* indeed appear as moving. *La Jetée* then further startles its viewer by the actual sudden movements of its images as the film inserts moving images amongst the still during the climactic moments of the woman's blinks.

15. For further discussion of Cats, their virtual potentials and actual embodiments, see Chapter 6.

16. Elsewhere Deleuze and Guattari write: 'The BwO [body without organs] is a childhood block, a becoming, the opposite of a childhood memory. It is not the child "before" the adult ... it is the strict contemporaneousness of the adult, of the adult and the child, their map of comparative densities and intensities, and all of the variations on that map' (ATP: 164).

5

Signs Without Name

Poetry is born of insecurity: wandering Jews, quaking Japanese; ...
moving about in a world of appearances: fragile, fleeting, revocable, of
trains that fly from planet to planet ... That's called 'the impermanence
of things'. (SS)

The artist tells him- or herself that this world has had different aspects,
will have still others, and that there are already others on other planets;
finally, the artist opens up to the Cosmos in order to harness forces in a
'work.' (ATP: 337)

Lawrence ... writes: 'To be alone, mindless and memoryless beside the
sea ... Far off, far off, as if he had landed on another planet, as a man
might after death.' (ATP: 189)

I'm writing you all this from another world. (SS)

A seemingly otherworldly, fleeting yet haunting series of visual, voice
and sound assemblages amassed with the 'relentlessness of a bounty
hunter' constitute the opening moments of Marker's 1983 *Sans Soleil*
during which the narration announces: 'He wrote: I've been round
the world several times and now only banality still interests me' (SS).
At once specific, explicit and cryptic, the film's narration and images
of time deftly manifest doublings and paradoxes of life, creation
and experience: death and survival, memory and forgetting, horror
and beauty, fragility and indestructibility, joy and loss, layers of life
that simultaneously, collectively comprise, as *Sans Soleil* suggests,
familiar *and* indecipherable aspects of existence that the films of this
book seek to momentarily glimpse and distinguish. Via its embrace
of spiritual cosmic 'worlds' within our own whose language of 'electronic graffiti' delineates 'the contours of what is not, or is no longer,
or is not yet' (SS), *Sans Soleil* sensorily evokes a melancholy whose
disembodied wounds bespeak the loss of actual limits and survival of
virtual remains. By such affecting embodiment, *Sans Soleil* effectively
unearths the untranslatable and impermanent, that invisible *between*
or 'poignancy of things', the 'Japanese secret' that implies 'the faculty
of communion with things, of entering into them, of being them for

113

8 'Fragments of war enshrined in everyday life', Sans Soleil (Marker 1983)

a moment' so that, 'in their turn[,] they should be like us: perishable and immortal' (SS).

Persistently, Sans Soleil attempts to convey paradoxically enduring yet evanescent sensations and melancholies, those poignant 'immobile shadows' (SS) begot by disembodied wounds. At the margins of our world between all things past and future, visible and invisible, the film then encounters that ceaselessly double process, coincidence or between of forces as it glares at the 'partition that separates life from death' and that 'last state – before their [actual] disappearance – of the poignancy of things' (SS). This pursuit, that is, of Sans Soleil and all films of this study through their respectively innovative and new means is, as insists Sans Soleil's narration, 'not a search for contrasts' but a 'journey to the two extreme poles of survival' (SS). Yet while Sans Soleil purportedly examines the two 'extremes' of Japan and Africa, it more profoundly contemplates the dynamic movements of actual-virtual relations with their doublings and faces of horror and beauty that reveal the two sides of all things, that twofold synthesis of actual and virtual split continually into two like time's past-future divide itself.

Microscopically and intensely, the film pursues the 'virtual counterpart' (SS) and poignancy of all things corporeal and incorporeal,
seen and unseen; through the unexpected and ever-transitive, *Sans
Soleil* discerns virtual extensions, *thisnesses* that defy name, and
signs that forever impinge upon the soul that line the actual mundane
quotidian. 'He wrote me: coming back through the Chiba coast I
thought of Shonagon's list, of all those signs one has only to name
to quicken the heart, just name' (SS). A sign, as Deleuze following
Spinoza proposes, 'can have several meanings' but is always 'an
effect', 'the trace of one body upon another' (ECC: 138). With regard
to the impossibility of naming or affixing affective experience, *Sans
Soleil* respectively remarks: 'To us, a sun is not quite a sun unless it's
radiant.' In quest, then, of the ineffable, of signs without name or
dynamic unfoldings and revelations of the routinely imperceptible, of
thisnesses, haecceities and piercing moments 'held . . . at arms' length
. . . zoom's length, until [. . . their] last twenty-fourth of a second'
(SS), *Sans Soleil* perseveres. 'If they don't see happiness in the picture,
at least they'll see the black' (SS).

'The *white or black screen*, finally', writes Ronald Bogue à propos
modern cinema, 'is the interstice made visible' (Bogue 2003a: 179).
'The first image he told me about', begins *Sans Soleil*, 'was of three
children on a road in Iceland, in 1965. He said that for him it was the
image of happiness and also that he had tried several times to link it
to other images, but it never worked' (SS). *Sans Soleil*'s first series of
unlinked images, that of three Icelandic children, a US war plane and
finally 'a long piece of black leader' (SS), indeed overtly exposes, in
direct relation to Marker's *La Jetée*, the screen and the filmic cut, that
between of images that potentially becomes, as Deleuze explains, the
screen itself.

In relation to the means through which *Sans Soleil* foregrounds
the cuts between its images, as through its long piece of black leader
in these opening moments, it is vital to return to Deleuze's writing
on modern cinema and the postwar time-image. For, once more,
Deleuze identifies a 'reversal where the image is unlinked and the cut
begins to have an importance in itself . . . there is no longer linkage
of associated images, but only relinkages of independent images
. . . one image *plus* another . . . The cut may now be extended and
appear in its own right, as the black screen, the white screen and their
derivatives and combinations' (C2: 213–14). Through this method of
between or AND that this book has hitherto discussed, what Deleuze
terms a 'whole new system of rhythm', or 'serial or atonal cinema',

9 *'Cat, wherever you are, peace be with you'*, Sans Soleil *(Marker 1983)*

modern cinema, moreover *Sans Soleil* itself, gives rise to not only the emergence of a direct presentation of time but also the time-image's direct encounter with the limits of thought itself (C2: 214).

For this encounter between thought and image, as staged through-out all films explored by these pages, also discovers particular signifi-cance via *Sans Soleil*. Unlike the films of this book's earlier chapters that each emerge from a certain definitive horror – the Holocaust, Hiroshima, an atomic apocalypse – *Sans Soleil* marks a shift towards a more comprehensive, layered interrogation of both strangely familiar *and* indecipherable aspects of life that exist in relation to sufferings past and yet to come. *Sans Soleil*'s acute scrutinisation of the banal does indeed reveal unexpected horrors and excesses that bespeak not a single monumental historic event but countless unique injustices and sorrows and their everlasting reverberations.

To reiterate a primary contention of this book and Deleuze's cine-philosophy, the time-image in effect 'puts thought into contact with an unthought, the unsummonable, the inexplicable, the unde-cidable, the incommensurable' (C2: 214), that breakdown or crack we confront as our corporeal *and* incorporeal reality, which death's virtual/impersonal, actual/personal aspects most profoundly embody. Engendered in response to the actual horrors of our world, their lingering affective effects and our complicity, complacency and banality, the modern cinema's expression of an 'impotence' or powerlessness precipitated the breakdown of the cinema's sensory-motor organisation, the method of linear, rational or 'sutured' continuity championed in classic cinema. What the modern cinema of the time-image 'advances', claims Deleuze, 'is not the power of thought but its "impower"' (C2: 166).

Modern cinema in effect encounters what Deleuze by way of Artaud recognises as the 'powerlessness at the heart of thought', that which Deleuze through Artaud believes cinema 'essentially suited to reveal' (C2: 166). For the cracks or cuts of the image in modern cinema expose time's fissure of an actual present into both future and virtual past, that domain of all past events that doubles or mirrors the present, as well as the self's own confrontation with the very limits of rational thought that fracture the limits of the self and effect its personal-impersonal split. 'What the modern cinema forces thought to think', writes Bogue, 'is the outside, that dispersive, spacing force that passes into the interstice' (2003a: 176).

At the 'two sides of the limit' of the self and of thought demarcated by the irrational cut, 'thought outside itself and this un-thought within thought' (C2: 278), *Sans Soleil*'s long piece of black leader and the disjointed images of its sequences correspond then to the fundamental importance of the 'interstice between two images' and the irrational, autonomous cuts that mark neither beginning nor end (C2: 200). The 'object of cinema', declares Deleuze, 'is not to reconstitute a presence of bodies, in perception and action, but to carry out a primordial genesis of bodies in terms of a white, or a black or a grey (or even in terms of colours), in terms of a "beginning of visible which is not yet a figure, which is not yet an action"' (C2: 201).

This making perceptible of the imperceptible is again a reversible process of becoming or movement through which novel actualisations and virtual differenciations surface. As this book interrogates the multiple forces and interpenetrating bodies, *thisnesses* and things that comprise our world through its engagements with Marker and Resnais' films, its analyses resonate with what Deleuze acknowledges as the cinema's 'essence' (see Chapter 4), or at least 'one of its essences: a proceeding, a process of constitution of bodies from the neutral image, white or black, snowy or flashed' (C2: 201) that ultimately, vitally, restores 'our belief in the world', *this* world.

For despite Deleuze and Marker's seeming invocations of worlds beyond our own, their poetic cine-philosophy crucially examines creative means of becoming and living in *this* world through revelations of the virtual, untimely affects, forces and singularities of our incorporeal sensations and events and their corporeal effects. 'The problem', Deleuze asserts, 'is *not* that of a presence of bodies, but that of a belief which is capable of restoring the world and the body to us on the basis of what signifies their absence' (C2: 202). The problem, that is, is not one of appearances but of 'inconspicuous perceptions' (FLB: 89) that make visible the invisible, the interstice, the *between* two images. To repeat Deleuze's words through Godard: 'make the indiscernible, that is the frontier, visible' (C2: 180), and so stare directly, once more, into the 'partition that separates life from death' while surveying that 'last state', before their disappearance, 'of the poignancy of things' (SS).

What we alternatively recognise as whole – continuous 'images in a chain . . . an uninterrupted chain of images each one the slave of the next', and whose slave we are' – merges again with that which, to repeat, Blanchot calls 'the force of "dispersal of the Outside"' (C2: 180). This fissure, crack or '"dissociative force"', a '"hole in appearances"' (C2: 167), forever fractures that which *Sans Soleil* terms our own 'world of appearances' (SS), which parallels imperceptible worlds of disappearances. As it perceives this doubling of 'worlds' through its 'constant comings and goings' about the globe (SS), and through which we encounter the self's impossibility or impotence at the limits of habitual thought, chronological time and assured subjectivity, the film's epistolary narration remarks: 'In a way the two worlds [of appearances and disappearances] communicate with each other. Memory is to one what history is to the other: an impossibility.'

ॐ

The first image he told me about was of three children on a road in Iceland, in 1965. He said that for him it was the image of happiness. (SS)

Sans Soleil's title screens, in vivid red, purple and yellow, Russian, English and French respectively, silently follow the film's opening sequence with its fleeting glimpses of a T.S. Eliot quotation – 'Because I know that time is always time / And place is always and only place'[1] – three Icelandic children, US warplane base and black leader that concludes the sequence. The pervasive blackness of both the

leader and lengthy interstices between the disparate images underscores, as aforementioned, the film's explicit confrontation with
the ineffable limits of cinema and thought that pushes, as Bogue
contends with regard to the limits of cinema, 'the visible "to a limit
which is at once invisible and yet can only be seen"' as it discloses
a speech that '"is at once, as it were, the unspeakable and yet what
can only be spoken"' (Bogue 2004: 23; see also C2: 260). If, that
is, 'thought, in cinema', may be 'brought face to face with its own
impossibility', as Deleuze states by way of Jean-Louis Schefer, then
thought draws from this powerlessness 'a higher power of birth'
through a *'suspension of the world'* and a *'disturbance*, which, far
from making thought visible . . . are on the contrary directed to what
does not let itself be thought in thought, and equally to what does not
let itself be seen in vision' (C2: 168).

How then can cinema make visible the invisible through images of
time and movement? How does *Sans Soleil* pierce, rupture, reverber-
ate and sensuously affect *beyond* any categorisation, recognition or
'image of happiness' through its haunting pursuit of life's doublings
and paradoxes? And what does this portend for film, life and its
intercessions with 'the web of time' and death (SS)? 'What becomes
essential in modern art', Daniel Smith maintains, 'is no longer
the matter-form relation, but the *material-force* relation' (Smith
1996: 43), that which makes us sense unsensible forces, those forces
of the Outside beyond apprehension and reproduction that compro-
mise reason and effect the pre-individual.

Such a violent encounter with the intolerable and unthought that
precipitates the cinema's sensory-motor break gives rise to that 'confrontation of an outside and an inside' through thought itself, that
which, once more, is 'born from an outside more distant than any
external world' and which 'confronts an inside, an unthinkable or
unthought, deeper than any internal world' (C2: 278). At the frontier of the self's crack or disintegration and the cinema's own break
with indirect representation, empirical and chronological succession
(C2: 155) via its irrational cut that foregrounds the 'two sides of
the limit' (278), new kinds of subjectivity emerge which open to a
freedom and 'joy' of life.

Through collision with the outside or limit from which they
derive, these subjectivities or 'folds' of outside and inside, world and
self, engender nonhuman becomings. Despite conventional readings
of the film, *Sans Soleil*'s myriad disjunctive connections, or 'relinkages of independent images', do not then convey a contrast between

119

certain homogenised peoples and lands by way of a multi-level narrative or protagonist frequently regarded as a 'fictional stand-in for Marker' (Alter 2006: 103).[2] Rather, the film's deterritorialisations of once-historicised images expose the singularities, forces and relations that unfold through actualisations at various levels, before and beyond human consciousness and experience, and that comprise individualities. This break with a phenomenology grounded in subjectified, clichéd perception (see WIP: 150) seeks to expose the effects of the virtual relations underlying our states of affairs and bodies that we commonly fail to perceive.

In other words, Marker and Deleuze, with Resnais and Guattari, advance thinking beyond the subject and consciousness as they realise a force of becoming through pure optical and sonic descriptions in cinema and concepts in philosophy. These cinematic affects and percepts, and philosophical concepts, evoke both the before and after via the enduring prominence of the interstice or frontier itself, through which a direct presentation of time surfaces, a continuum that senses pure duration and directly captures invisible force, *thisness* and sensation – *red*ness, not blood (see Smith 1996: 46). How then does the artist's material, as Smith questions, 'become capable of "bearing" the sensation?' (1996: 42).

With regard to the cinema, we must again also consider what Deleuze claims as 'the essence of cinema – which is not the majority of films'. For the essence of cinema, he contends, 'has thought as its higher purpose, nothing but thought and its functioning' (C2: 168), which operates by way of affect and sensation. 'As soon as it takes on its aberration of movement', Deleuze continues, the cinematic time-image

> carries out a *suspension of the world* or affects the visible with a *disturbance*, which, far from making thought visible ... are on the contrary directed to what does not let itself be thought in thought, and equally to what does not let itself be seen in vision ... thought, in cinema, is brought face to face with its own impossibility, and yet draws from this a higher power of birth. (C2: 168)

Once more, this 'experience of thought', which 'essentially (but not exclusively) concerns modern cinema' and which is 'a result of the change [or break from sensory-motor organisation] which affects the image' (C2: 169), requires 'not imaginary participation' (C2: 168). Rather, as Chapter 4's exploration of *La Jetée* also reveals through *thisnesses* and 'things that quicken the heart' (SS), this experience of thought corresponds to 'the rain when you leave the auditorium'; it is 'not dream, but the blackness' (C2: 168). This 'encounter with the unthinkable' (C2: 171) through sensation then pertains to the capture of *thought outside itself*, a self-less seeing and becoming from which *pure* visual situations and a *free indirect discourse* emerge to disclose a new relation between film and thought. The artist's task is always sensation itself, not the sensational, not 'Happiness' but 'the black' that may bear the sensation, should it 'not let itself be seen' (SS).

The cinema's interaction of two *unlinked* images that trace 'a frontier which belongs to neither one nor the other', as Deleuze writes with regard to a modern cinema such as Godard's (C2: 181), again distinguishes dimensions of *thisnesses* that can only be sensed, that something in the world 'not of recognition but of a fundamental *encounter*' that forces thought (DR: 139) and 'reach[es] the body before discourses, before words, before things are named: the "first name", and even before the first name' (C2: 172–3). Might we name the unnameable, 'those signs one has only to name to quicken the heart, just name' (SS)?

'What then', persists *Sans Soleil*, 'shall we call this diffuse belief, according to which every fragment of creation has its invisible counterpart?' (SS). In pursuit of these 'things' or *thisnesses* that quicken the heart, *Sans Soleil*'s experimental foray across intersecting virtual-actual lines of dynamic movements and relations encounters not forms and subjects but what Deleuze and Guattari may term 'a mode of individuation' that is 'very different from that of a person, subject, thing, or substance', and for which they reserve the name *haecceity* (see ATP: 261–3).

And so, from the rhythms, masks, chants and crowds of an African festival to outer space, an ocean's depths and the performativity of a Japanese parade, *Sans Soleil* traces the frontiers of our globe with an eye seemingly attuned to the exuberant, yet more evocative of the minute. For, with 'a sort of melancholy comfort [derived] from the contemplation of the tiniest things', the film locates its heartbeat in these 'neighbourhood celebrations' (SS), between the liberated elements – speeds and affects – of forms, subjects and things that flash across the interstices of the film and its audio-visual forces, and through which the oft indiscernible yet persistent pulsation of a heart, resonant even through the sounds of a ferry, train or festive parade, may be heard and even felt. 'It might suffice', *Sans Soleil*'s world-traveller adds, 'to pick up any one of the telephones that are lying around to hear a familiar voice, or the beating of a heart.' Yet how to name this ubiquitous throbbing of a 'chaotic universe',[3] the uprooted materials and affects of events and becomings, the assemblages, 'climates, winds, seasons, hours' that 'we' and all things and animals populate (ATP: 263), the 'unthinkable which cannot even be spoken' (C2: 171)?

If the limit or ineffable itself as a force of becoming, again what Deleuze terms the 'power of the outside', passes into the interstice to directly realise time in the image (181), each interstice is then, as Bogue concludes, 'an expression or unfolding of the outside' (2003a: 176). Once more at the limit of personal and impersonal, this force of thought and becoming effects a becoming-imperceptible, a becoming-molecular, becoming-animal, becoming-child, before self-apprehension, memory, language – a *becoming everybody*': 'For everybody/everything is the molar aggregate, but *becoming everybody/everything* is another affair', maintain Deleuze and Guattari,

> one that brings into play the cosmos with its molecular components. Becoming everybody/everything (*tout le monde*) is to world (*faire monde*), to make a world (*faire un monde*) . . . To be present at the dawn of the world . . . To reduce oneself to an abstract line, a trait, in order to find one's zone of indiscernibility with other traits, and in this way enter the haecceity and impersonality of the creator. (ATP: 279–80)

In relations of speed and slowness, *Sans Soleil*'s traveller-becoming-world skirts from one end of the globe to another across planes and spaces of territorialisation, deterritorialisation and reterritorialisation, those destructive yet also productive movements of social change that the film assesses and towards which it imparts positive force. 'Here', *Sans Soleil* interjects, 'to place adjectives would be so rude as leaving price tags on purchases.' 'Japanese poetry never modifies', the narration continues. 'There is a way of saying boat, rock, mist, frog, crow, hail, heron, chrysanthemum that includes them all.' Hence, the story of a man from Nagoya who lost his love and killed himself; inasmuch as 'Happiness' exceeds and resists articulation, 'They say he could not stand hearing the word "Spring".'

As *Sans Soleil* continues to trace and 'map out' the limits of actual-virtual frontiers, the doublings or foldings of life through which one lives 'in two times, at two moments at once' (LS: 158), the film gives rise to liberative dissolutions as truths of memory and history falter and life-affirming 'powers of the false' (see C2: ch. 6) and foreignness emerge within the familiar.

He wrote me that the pictures of Guinea-Bissau ought to be accompanied by music from the Cape Verde islands. That would be our contribution to the unity dreamed of by Amílcar Cabral. Why should so small a country – and one so poor – interest the world? . . . They traumatized the Portuguese army to such an extent that it gave rise to a movement that overthrew the dictatorship, and led one for a moment to believe in a new revolution in Europe. Who remembers all that? History throws its empty bottles out the window. (SS)

If the truthful man wants 'nothing other than to judge life', as Deleuze argues through Nietzsche (C2: 137), to impose morality as a truth and right to self-appointed justice and repressive sovereignty, *Sans Soleil*'s making strange or 'world' via images that disclose a coalescence between virtual and real (see C2: 68) shatters any ideal of truth, and with it our world of appearances whose essential message is 'the code'. 'It's a coded hypocrisy', claims *Sans Soleil*. 'The code is the message. It points to the absolute by hiding it. That's what religions have always done.' The following pages rather find that the 'essential point', as Deleuze sees it, is 'how the new regime of the image (the direct time-image)' shatters such censoring 'truths' in our actual world and states of affairs as it forges a metamorphosing power of the false (C2: 134–5).

To return to Chapter 4's discussion of an inclusive method of between through exhaustion, what remains are bodies, forces, 'nothing but forces' and their relations, 'the power to affect and be affected', 'the shock of forces, in the image or of the images between themselves' (C2: 139). As these forces of relations, visions of the unseen, or pure affects and percepts, once again encounter an outside, '*the outside* of language, but . . . not outside it' (ECC: 112), they forge a foreign language in the interstices, cracks and breaks of the film that gives rise to a vital space of creative becoming and productive reinvention within the actual pre-existent world.

For *Sans Soleil*'s travels about the globe effectively happen *between* or *outside*; they encounter effects and affects, *thisnesses*, that pass or happen 'between two as though under a potential difference', not one term or thing becoming the other but each encountering the other, 'a single becoming which is not common to the two' but *between* the two, something between or 'outside the two, and which flows in another direction' (D: 6–7). This 'double capture' of the conjunction AND is once more 'neither a union, nor a juxtaposition, but the birth of a stammering, the outline of a broken line' (D: 9–10) and the creative emergence of an *anomalous*, minor people of geography, of 'orientations, directions, entries and exits' (D: 2) and 'very varied lines' (D: 10), an unpeopled people of desert islands,[4] of waves that fold into each other, of people 'populated by tribes' yet deserted and alone in a continual process of self-perceiving perception that forever repeats defining identity while defining movements of difference. 'The desert, experimentation on oneself', to repeat Deleuze's declaration, 'is our only identity, our single chance for all the combinations which inhabit us' (D: 11).

As the following sections will discover, *Sans Soleil* effects its own becoming through a dynamic image of itself that engenders a perpetual movement and 'pure consciousness' (DI: 10) through an immanent, connective process of bringing together differentiating and identifying relations. This process of transforming identity through difference lies through an *auto*-perceptibility, of perceiving and being perceived, and affectivity, of affecting and being affected, across, through and over lines of remembering and forgetting, separation and creation.

The nomads of *Sans Soleil*, and the film's nomadic correspondent 'himself', occasion a 'movement [that] does not go from one point to another' but that rather 'happens between two levels as in a difference of potential' (D: 31), in a space of 'involution' or of being 'between' (D: 29), a space of becoming, a deserted space of neither evolution nor regression, past nor future, nor even present, a space in the middle created and reached 'by losing, by abandoning, by reducing, by simplifying', by purifying oneself of one's self through a consciousness that precedes one's self and through which one becomes, a personal-impersonal process of actual contact and potential separation, a vital line, *a* life. Written in the interval before his own death, Deleuze's final essay, 'Immanence . . . a life', a piece that resurfaces throughout these pages, gives life to Deleuze's life's doctrine as it renews *Sans Soleil*'s own open-ended becoming.

> *A* life is everywhere, in all the moments that a given living subject goes through and that are measured by given lived objects: an immanent life carrying with it the events or singularities that are merely actualized in subjects and objects. This indefinite life does not itself have moments, close as they may be to another, but only between-times, between-moments; it doesn't just come about or come after but offers the immensity of an empty time where one sees the event yet to come and already happened, in the absolute of an immediate consciousness. (PI: 29)

Across and through the islands of deserted peoples it discovers, through nomads who have only geography and so have 'neither past nor future' as they exist 'always in the middle' without history (D: 31), *Sans Soleil* probes the *inverse* or *underside* of the actual as it inevitably identifies and yet sees anew while stuttering and pushing the terms of its cinematic means and 'language' 'to its limit, to its outside, to its silence' (ECC: 113). As *Sans Soleil*'s journey 'to world' becomes a quest to chart and attain *pure sensation* in terms of remembering and forgetting, repetition and re-creation, Tom Conley's remarks regarding Deleuze's own 'multi-faceted or multi-layered ground plan of the relation of sensation and imagination to location' (Conley 2005: 209) resonate remarkably. For the film's rhizomatic, experimental mapping expresses virtual potential – those qualities of possible sensations that defy name: Happiness, unhappiness, emptiness, thirst, Spring, war, the 'great orchestral masses and accumulation of details', 'overcrowded, megalomaniac, inhuman', 'rhythms, clusters of faces', horror and beauty, both of which have 'a name and a face' (SS).

If *Sans Soleil* may be conceived as a series of performative encounters, an intensive map via its living screen of intensities and affects, its mapping is 'entirely oriented toward an experimentation in contact with the real' as opposed to any 'tracing'; for a map, as Deleuze and Guattari propose, is that which remains 'open and connectible in all of its dimensions' (see ATP: 12–15). While the cinema can re-present and re-fortify identity through redundancy, a practice that transforms a map into image, or 'rhizome into roots', *Sans Soleil* alternatively looks to the microscopic events, 'hallucinatory perceptions' and synaesthetic sensations that 'extricate themselves from the "tracing"' and 'balance of power' (ATP: 15) as it endlessly finds itself in an interval between geography and history, the seeing and non-seen.

Of those unseen, *San Soleil* demands: 'How can one claim to show a category of Japanese who do not exist? ... their real name – eta – is a taboo word, not to be pronounced. They are non-persons. How can they be shown, except as non-images?' (SS). In ways parallel to Deleuze's creative lines of thought, *Sans Soleil* pushes repeatedly towards limits, towards the *'sentiendum'*, *'memorandum'*, *'cogitandum'* (DR: 141) or, as Bogue writes, 'the insensible that the senses alone can experience', 'the immemorial that memory alone can remember', 'the inconceivable that understanding alone can conceptualize' (Bogue 2004: 23). To render these paradoxes, to again push cinema 'to a limit which is at once invisible and yet can only be seen' (C2: 260), should one speak then, as Deleuze suggests, of 'a nonstyle' or the '"elements of a style to come which do not yet exist"' (ECC: 113), of new foreign means of reaching limits of language and cinema through a people and microscopic events yet to come, of rhizomatic maps, networks and fissure-veins in worlds beyond our sight and sun? 'He wrote: Tokyo is a city crisscrossed by trains, tied together with electric wire she shows her veins' (SS).

෨

> It is because this world is intolerable that [. . . thought] can no longer think a world or think itself. The intolerable is no longer a serious injustice, but the permanent state of a daily banality. (C2: 170)

> I've been round the world several times and now only banality still interests me. On this trip I've tracked it with the relentlessness of a bounty hunter. (SS)

> And if the writer is in the margins or completely outside his or her fragile community, this situation allows the writer all the more possibility to express another possible community and to forge the means for another consciousness and another sensibility. (K: 17)

'Art, and especially cinematic art', declares Deleuze, 'must take part in this task: not that of addressing a people, which is presupposed already there, but of contributing to the invention of a people' (C2: 217). On the margins of the communities he observes, *Sans Soleil*'s nomadic correspondent witnesses 'a people of wanderers, of navigators, of world travellers' whose fragile indestructibility ceaselessly fascinates him (SS). 'He didn't like to dwell on poverty', admits the film's narration, 'but in everything he wanted to show there were also the 4-Fs of the Japanese model. A world full of bums, of lumpens, of outcasts, of Koreans.' More specifically, he speculates: 'how to film the ladies of Bissau?'

Whilst he negotiates the two poles of survival, again, no more Japan and Africa than the intolerable in the everyday and unthinkable in thought, *Sans Soleil*'s global journeyman gives life to a 'being of thought which is always to come' (C2: 167) as he envisions the world and our becomings through it in ever-new ways. 'We are not in the world, we become with the world', suggest Deleuze and Guattari; 'we become by contemplating it. Everything is vision, becoming. We become universes. Becoming animal, plant, molecular, becoming zero' (WIP: 169; see also Zourabichvili 1996). As an 'alien thinker within the thinker' (Bogue 2003a: 177) in the process of becoming-other, a *spiritual automaton*[5] with dismantled, paralysed speech and sight torn from any individualised perspective, *Sans Soleil*'s unseen protagonist perceives, reports and facilitates new kinds of selfless subjectivity, life and worlds that fold into themselves inasmuch as 'memory lines forgetting' (SS).

For as the protagonist encounters the film's worlds, they fold into this wandering traveller so that 'he' and 'we' are enveloped in an affective, nonhuman becoming-other, a zone of 'indetermination, of indiscernibility' (WIP: 173) from which emerge pure affects, intensities and sensory becomings – 'otherness caught in a matter of expression' (WIP: 177). Which is to say, while the film's actualisations of virtual events participate in, incorporate and embody the virtual, giving it a body, a life, a universe, the actualisation yet emanates a virtual excess and force of the new which gives rise to new ever-differing worlds; such is, as *Sans Soleil* reveals, 'the impermanence of things' (SS). 'It is the edge of virtual, where it leaks into actual, that counts. For that seeping edge', claims Massumi, 'is where potential, actually, is found' (1996: 236). In this respect, *Sans Soleil*'s voyaging seer peers into the realm of the imperceptible and incommunicable as he interrogates the 'partitions', 'thresholds', 'poles', 'rifts', limits, frontiers and borders, the *folds* and 'coexistences' of our world with its 'subterranean tunnels that . . . run parallel to the city' and youth, the 'baby Martians', who 'live in a parallel time sphere' (SS).

These doubles and other dimensions of time forever repeat or refold to produce new becomings, interactions and transformations within our world, foldings, unfoldings and refoldings that *Sans Soleil* strives to assess and express. And so, as the virtual escapes the permanent, its immanent potential is in fact its impermanence and endless vitality, escape and excess in that *between*, zone or passing – again, that 'something passing from one to the other' – through which 'living beings whirl around and [that] only art can reach and penetrate . . . in its enterprise of co-creation' (WIP: 173).

The 'walls between the realms are so thin that one can in the same breadth contemplate a statue, buy an inflatable doll, and give the goddess of fertility the small offering that always accompanies her displays' (SS), perhaps while also beginning to perceive the virtual-actual realms and dimensions of the imperceptible, that zone of doublings and indiscernibility that *Sans Soleil* constructs with 'blocs' of affects and percepts. To perceive the imperceptible while becoming-imperceptible, to perceive one's own self perception while becoming-other and self-less, is to enter into relation with the 'undeterminable, the unreferable . . . "the reverse side of thoughts", which itself is what dreams come up against and rebound, break' (C2: 167). Such is to confront the 'two poles of survival' (SS) and, by so doing, free and bear witness to *a* life 'in this world as it is' (C2: 173).

This encounter with the limits of self and thought at once invokes a painful actualisation and virtual potential whereby the *'intolerable'*, as Smith indicates, is 'a lived actuality that at the same time testifies to the impossibility of living in such conditions' (1997: xliii). In *Sans Soleil*, such lived actuality or 'everyday banality' (SS) attests to the importance of the banal in its continuous form. As with the ultimate event of death, so too may *affect* be experienced punctually as 'localized in an event', as writes Massumi; yet 'it is also continuous, like a background perception that accompanies every event, however quotidian' (Massumi 1996: 229). The virtual-actual two-sidedness to which Massumi refers, the 'simultaneous participation of the virtual in the actual and the actual in the virtual, as one arises from and returns to the other' (Massumi 1996: 228), is nothing other than *Sans Soleil*'s affective, self-perceptive and continuous contemplation of these two poles of survival, the two sides of all things that manifest a synaesthetic participation of the senses in each other.

And so, as the film cuts abruptly from its title screens to an image of a loudspeaker affixed to a boat, we suddenly experience the camera's roaming eye, whose nonhuman perception, split from any subjective positioning, releases a *percept*, an impersonal seeing also observed via Resnais' cinema in Chapters 2 and 3. Water visible below comprises much of the shot, an image punctuated by the noise of the soundtrack with its intense rhythm redolent of *La Jetée*'s own quickening heartbeat and audible pulsations. 'He wrote: I'm just back from Hokkaido, the Northern Island. Rich and hurried Japanese take the plane, others take the ferry. Waiting, immobility, snatches of sleep. Curiously all of that makes me think of a past or future war' (SS).

The world traveller, whose letters the film's narrator reads, writes of the 'small fragments of war enshrined in everyday life' that he perceives. The 'fragility of those moments suspended in time' embody thresholds of reality, sleep, dream and fantasy that bespeak reality's two-fold oscillation and exchange between actual-virtual dynamic relations, the two poles or sides of all things that fundamentally speak to potentials and dangers of existence, and *Sans Soleil*'s own revelatory becoming and movement between a 'world of appearances' and its incorporeal transformations.

As the film's unearthing eye discharges affect from a world of appearances, the earthly and commonplace, it interrogates such reversible relations between actual-real and virtual-real – the ephemeral excesses of experience, the extraordinary beyond ordinary, beauty through horror, life through death – as the film takes on an ethereal, otherworldly sensory quality that exceeds any individualised perspective or place. For through the film, affect becomes an imperceptible yet deeply penetrating force[6] that manifests itself in *Sans Soleil*'s moments of greatest resonance and poignancy that are at once both profoundly banal and surreal, intimate and unearthly. Despite all disjunctions, violences between and within the image, the film exudes a grace as it stares, and stares often, in an 'invisible' style evocative of Mr Yamada's 'action cooking', whose way of 'mixing the ingredients' in a restaurant in Nishi-nippori could usefully apply, *Sans Soleil*'s voyager conjectures, to 'certain fundamental concepts common to painting, philosophy, and karate' (SS).

If 'Mr Yamada possessed in his humble way the essence of style' through use of his 'invisible brush' (SS), *Sans Soleil*'s own style, or *nonstyle*, again exposes the foreign within the familiar as it endlessly pushes towards the invisible, that invisible counterpart of all things on the other side of actual. At the margins of the fragile communities he observes, the frontiers between a world of appearances and 'swarm of appearances', *Sans Soleil*'s disembodied visionary indeed expresses new potential worlds 'before the fall' through worlds 'inaccessible to the complications of a Puritanism whose phoney shadow has been imposed on it by American occupation'; through worlds beyond our 'castrating censorship' and televised, 'portable and compact ... already inaccessible reality' (SS); through worlds wherein participants within and without the film – viewer, Marker and those yet to come – enact and construct new truths and consciousnesses via transformative *becoming-others* in that passage between translatable and untranslatable, truth and 'Happiness'.

I paid for a round in a bar in Namidabashi. It's the kind of place that allows people to stare at each other with equality; the threshold below which every man is as good as any other – and knows it. (SS)

All consciousness is a matter of threshold ... If life has a soul, it is because it perceives, distinguishes, or discriminates, and because a whole world of animal psychology is first of all a psychology of perception. (FLB: 88; 92)

It was in the marketplaces of Bissau and Cape Verde that I could stare at them again with equality. (SS)

In fact, the self is only a threshold, a door, a becoming between two multiplicities. (ATP: 249)

Like the drunken man the film observes directing traffic at a crossroads, *Sans Soleil* materialises at a crossroads between 'roads' or ways of common perception. For through its encounters with the thresholds of actual-virtual processes and borders between thought and non-thought, the film's expression of the people, animals and worlds it experiences exposes the minute, particular and imperceptible perceptions we fail to commonly perceive through our molar or macro apprehensions. We hear, for instance, as Deleuze writes, a sea's sound, those 'conscious, clear, and distinct apperceptions' and 'macroperceptions' to which we are 'overly accustomed', yet not the 'murmurs of each wave' (FLB: 86–7).

As *Sans Soleil* strives to discern the 'pricklings', 'murmurings' and 'little foldings' of molecular perceptions to effect its own *becoming-animal* and so extract affects and percepts from conventional limited perception, the film cuts from a close-up of an emu to a graphic close-up match of a young African woman, a 'match' or becoming that at once evokes a new transformation via a 'becoming-emu' or animal of woman that suggests a 'phenomenon of bordering' and 'affectability ... no longer that of subjects' (ATP: 245; 258). For the graphic match moves beyond a representation of resemblance or analogy, beyond what may be seen, interpreted and faithfully reproduced, towards the liberation and extraction of the virtual sense or pure affects and sensations of an *anomalous* animal, an 'animal' at the edge, fringes, borderline or *between*.

This is not to say that the woman becomes animal. 'Becomings-animal are basically of another power', explain Deleuze and Guattari, 'since their reality resides not in an animal one imitates or to which one corresponds but in themselves, in that which suddenly sweeps us up and makes us become – a *proximity, an indiscernibility* that extracts a shared element from the animal' (ATP: 279). The relations between animal and human throughout the film, as foreshadowed by this early graphic match, express *Sans Soleil*'s becoming, its intensive production of ever-new virtual potentials and multiplicities of affects that exceed the thresholds and borders of our rigidly defined perceptible existence with its visible-invisible controls that perpetuate our illusory truths and freedoms.

'Let us at least say that there is counterinformation', to repeat Deleuze's intervention, if people may move '"freely" without being at all confined yet while still being perfectly controlled' by communication and information 'we are told . . . we are supposed to be ready or able to . . . believe' (Deleuze 1998b: 18). Alternatively, the *anomaly*, non-individuality, singularity or becoming of the animal and woman that manifests neither an individual nor a species is 'affect in itself' (ATP: 259), a becoming-animal 'which arrives and passes at the edge' (ATP: 244) to forge means for new ways of thinking and seeing, for 'another consciousness and another sensibility' (K: 17).

To see and think anew through such revolutionary means, as presented by *Sans Soleil*, Deleuze and Guattari, is not to look, gaze or stare and concede to power-relations and terms of equality as hierarchically, historically constructed and articulated, but rather to free life's flow of images and perceptions from our reductive apprehensions of their actualised forms. Perception, in this impersonal, living, non-representational and non-interpretational sense, is always a new mode of becoming – a *becoming-animal* – that senses virtual elements before and beyond recognisable distinction, designation and actualisation. The release of such virtual potential through perception creates new worlds and releases inconspicuous perceptions at the road, threshold or crack between perceptible and imperceptible, communicable and incommunicable.

How then to communicate 'the simplicity' and 'lack of affectation' of the couple who came to perform the rite that would 'repair the web of time' so that their runaway cat Tora would be protected (SS); how to film a 'people of nothing' and 'emptiness' (SS); how to convey the 'built-in grain of indestructibility' of the women who choose their fiancées and deny 'the magical function of the eye' at the centre of all things (SS); how to conceive of survival, unity and equality alongside happiness, beauty and an ever-proliferating population of cats and animals?

'He wrote me that in the Bijagós Islands it's the young girls who choose their fiancées. He wrote me that in the suburbs of Tokyo there is a temple consecrated to cats' (SS). The film cuts from the close-up side profile of an emu in France gazing off screen right to a woman in Guinea-Bissau gazing off screen left to a cats' temple in Japan with its 'Maneki Neko' cats aligned in rows beckoning off screen right. The assemblage of audio-visual images at once takes 'the temporal form of an instantaneous counteractualization' (N: 170) as the images counteract and deterritorialise a notion of difference entrenched in nationalistic and colonialist discourses.

By *Sans Soleil*'s global 'mapping', as 'open and connectible in all of its dimensions', the film does not so much contrast 'African time to European time and also to Asian time' (SS) as it newly reconfigures these 'extreme poles of survival' through evocations of their singularities, affects and virtual possibilities. Africa, Europe and Asia become undefined landscapes of a 'deterritorialised world', a world wherein 'all faces envelop an unknown, unexplored landscape' (ATP: 172) and exist within a time of the Aion, a 'floating', 'nonpulsed' time 'against pulsed time or tempo, experimentation against any kind of interpretation', a 'state where forms dissolve, and all that subsists are tiny variations of speed between movements in composition' (ATP: 267).

Upon this virtual imperceptible plane or surface of consistency or immanence, a field or space of possibilities, becomings and productive interactions on the other side of the plane of organisation, development or transcendence, liberated 'particles of an anonymous matter' communicate 'through the "envelope" of forms and subjects, retaining between them only relations of movement and rest, speed and slowness, floating affects, so that the plane itself is perceived at the same time as it allows us to perceive the imperceptible (the micro-plane, the molecular plane)' (ATP: 267).

Here too the face is an open surface and series of layers, a white or blank 'map' that may become a deterritorialised space and intensive map of progressive new becomings and potentials through which may emerge a people of nomadic thinkers and survivors. 'The face is a map', exclaim Deleuze and Guattari (ATP: 170), and while the film's traveller acknowledges 'the unbearable vanity of the West, that has never ceased to privilege being over non-being, what is spoken to what is left unsaid' (SS), *Sans Soleil* never ceases to ascertain revolutionary becomings through the faces of the lands, peoples and animals it encounters, the 'face-landscapes' that perceive and are perceived.

The entire city is a comic strip; it's Planet Manga. How can one fail to recognize the statuary that goes from plasticized baroque to Stalin central? And the giant faces with eyes that weigh down on the comic book readers, pictures bigger than people, voyeurizing the voyeurs. (SS)

I see that behind the sockets of the eyes there is a region unexplored, the world of futurity. (ATP: 171)

The more you watch Japanese television . . . the more you feel it's watching you. (SS)

Now the face has a correlate of great importance: the landscape, which is not just a milieu but a deterritorialized world. (ATP: 172)

The film cuts to a shot of a volcano whose conical mountain seems an island itself above the clouds. On the islands of Cape Verde, *Sans Soleil*'s faceless explorer confronts the faces of other wanderers, navigators, world travellers, a 'people of nothing' and 'of emptiness' (SS), and as we stare openly with the film's vagabond, the faces compellingly return our glares. Immediately preceding this early sequence in the film, a series of 'frozen' still shots exemplifying such perceiver-perceived relations are presented, each image 'stilled' upon a staring face: that of a young African woman in a boat who glances ever so briefly towards the camera before lowering her gaze ('How can one remember thirst?'); an elderly man who stares for a moment at the camera in the bar in Namidabashi ('the kind of place that allows people to stare at each other with equality; the threshold below which every man is as good as any other – and knows it'); and the two women at the jetty on Fogo in the Cape Verde Islands who glare forthrightly at the lens. Each 'frozen' still shot punctuates its sequence's end as it ironically reiterates the 'great concrete freeing of nonpulsed time' that Deleuze and Guattari suggest (ATP: 269) through a seeming pause or halting of time in the image.[7]

Prior to the third of these frozen still shots, *Sans Soleil*'s narrator remarks: 'Frankly, have you ever heard of anything stupider than to say to people as they teach in film schools, not to look at the camera?' This act of looking and being looked at repeatedly surfaces throughout the film and Marker's entire oeuvre yet these relations between perceiver-perceived emerge perhaps with greatest force and intensity in *Sans Soleil*. For through the auto-perceptive doubling or folding of gazes whereby the perception of an other becomes also a perception of one's self and self-dissolution, we once again experience a perceptual perpetual process of identity and separation.

There is potential for reinvention of one's self *or* the reclamation of a self's identity that occurs whenever 'Marker's camera', the nomadic traveller's gaze, chances to rest upon a gaze that explicitly returns 'his' own, be it human, animal or otherwise. While a mirroring gaze may repeat organising determinations and great redundancies of human segregation and classification, those a face most outwardly announces at its most blank, male/female, black/white, it potentially

10 *Auto-perceptive doubling,* Sans Soleil *(Marker 1983)*

also realises and facilitates a self's separation and becoming-other, becoming-animal, becoming-imperceptible.

'I see her; she saw me; she knows that I see her; she drops me her glance, but just at an angle where it is still possible to act as though it was not addressed to me and, at the end, the real glance, straightforward, that lasted a twenty-fourth of a second, the length of a film frame' (SS). If this is the stare of equality to which *Sans Soleil* ultimately refers, the glance and look of a face exacted from a woman of Bissau, the market lady of Praia, such 'equality' may then be the reflexive, transitive equivalence relation between perceiver-perceived – film, screen, camera, viewer, filmmaker – as all bodies become-other through each other in an a-parallel or non-parallel evolution not of imitation or assimilation but of a differing doubling, a 'double capture' through which '"what" each becomes changes no less than "that which" becomes' (D: 2–3). 'One might say', as does Deleuze, 'that something happens between them, at different speeds and with different intensities, which is not in one or other, but truly in an ideal place', such as the 'zone' of *Sans Soleil*, 'which is no longer a part of history, still less a dialogue among the dead, but an interstellar conversation, between very irregular stars, whose different becomings form a mobile bloc which it would be a case of capturing, an inter-flight, light-years' (D: 15–16).

On the 'landscape of another planet', *Sans Soleil*'s seeing nonhuman, unseen eye sees in fact the face of 'our future', a world wherein 'to call forth a vision, to be moved by a portrait, to tremble at the sound of music, can only be signs of a long and painful pre-history' (SS). Such a world, the film's narration suggests, could be told through 'one who has lost forgetting', such as the protagonist of 'the film to come' *Sans Soleil* describes who, at each moment through his impossible memory, might seem able to 'comprehend' (SS), as Deleuze proposes, 'all violence in a single act of violence, and every mortal event *in a single Event*' (LS: 152). Yet, as such is the ultimate task, to will, embrace and become worthy of all that happens to us, to remember yet always also to forget, 'naturally', as *Sans Soleil* concedes, this protagonist of 'the film to come' will fail. 'The unhappiness he discovers is as inaccessible to him as the poverty of a poor country is unimaginable to the children of a rich one' (SS).

To survive, to live, one must always, to repeat Deleuze's own repetitions, achieve a productive balance *between*, between the 'incorporeal crack at the surface' and the 'thickness' of a body, or risk self-destruction (LS: 156). 'If there is a crack at the surface, how can we prevent deep life from becoming a demolition job and prevent it from becoming it as a matter "of course"? . . . is it possible to limit ourselves to the counter-actualization of an event . . . while taking care to prevent the full actualization which characterizes the victim or the true patient?' (LS: 157). Is this then the 'secret' to which *Sans Soleil* repeatedly refers, 'the poignancy of things [that] implied the faculty of communion with things, of entering into them, of being them for a moment' (SS), the poignancy, the *between*, the balance, the survival and proliferation of life which demands always a remembering and a forgetting, and an always becoming-other through a double becoming of the virtual-actual aspects of our bodies that are forever 'perishable and immortal' (SS)?

Sans Soleil relates the only recourse remaining for this would-be protagonist of the film to come, 'that which threw him into this absurd quest: a song cycle by Mussorgsky . . . it was then that for the first time he perceived the presence of that thing he didn't understand which had something to do with unhappiness and memory, and towards which slowly, heavily, he began to walk'. While the imperceptible presence of *Sans Soleil* admits, 'of course I'll never make that film', he has nonetheless given it a title, 'indeed the title of those Mussorgsky songs: *Sunless*.[8] How far must we go between life and death to shed light on the 'sunless' while preserving the 'secret' of the *between*, of survival and 'happiness'? 'How long will it take to forget the secret?' (SS).

৵

Like the pyramid, the desert island exists before and after the advent of humans or their incursions in the world. The island is a '[c]onscience of the earth and the ocean . . . ready to commence the world' (DI: 11). (Conley 2005: 214)

Is it a property of islands to make their women into the guardians of their memory? (SS)

There remains the possibility of the author providing himself with 'intercessors' . . . of taking real and not fictional characters . . . putting these very characters in the condition of 'making up fiction', of 'making legends', of 'story-telling'. The author takes a step towards his characters, but the characters take a step towards the author: double becoming. (C2: 222)

I think of a world where each memory could create its own legend. (SS)

On the desert island of Sal, 'a salt rock in the middle of the Atlantic' bestowed with seemingly countless days of unrelenting sun (SS), *Sans Soleil*'s voyager writes again to the film's female, faceless, nameless voice. Like the travelling 'he' of the film, 'she' is often also referred to as a 'me', a self, never individualised, always other, who exists between viewer and the nomad wanderer. As a 'character' himself, seeing but unseen, the travelling, letter-writing nomadic 'man' and our correspondent through the film's excursions is 'continually becoming other, and is no longer separable from this becoming which merges with a people' (C2: 152), a becoming or folding that imbricates the filmmaker Marker himself. For inasmuch as 'each film-maker is a movement in himself', in this sense Marker 'too becomes another' (C2: 221) 'as he takes real characters as intercessors and replaces his fictions by their own story-telling, but, conversely, gives these story-tellings the shape of legends, carrying out their "making into legend"' (C2: 152).

Through their becomings, fabulations or makings into legend, the people of *Sans Soleil* strive to intercede in the intermission or interstice between life and death as they acknowledge that 'moment that is only that of *a* life playing with death' (PI: 28), when quotidian life takes on an impersonal, singular life. 'Tokyo is full of these tiny legends, and of mediating animals' (SS), and as the people's rituals and legends take flight to reveal something more to do with happiness and forgetting than unhappiness and memory, their spiritual becomings temporarily free the film from its melancholy contemplations. If 'legends are born out of the need to decipher the indecipherable' and 'memories must make do with their delirium, with their drift' (SS), *Sans Soleil* derives a certain joy and anarchic madness through the signs of memory and sacred signs it senses and encounters that break through the 'wall' of a hierarchically signified stratified face.

And so, while we become implicated and other through these foldings, layerings and reinventions of filmmaker, narrator, wanderer and character, a *free indirect discourse* arises, akin to that of *La Jetée*. In this pure act of speech torn from visual association and self, we hear *Sans Soleil*'s narrator obtain an 'original irreducible dimension' that resists the first person, even as she speaks in first person (C2: 242). This female voice of a becoming-other, becoming-woman, becoming-animal beyond the dominant authoritative male voice of ethnographic documentary film and majoritarian univocality[9] is *Sans Soleil*'s voice of the 'fourth person singular' (DI: 143; see also *The Logic of Sense* and *Dialogues II*). It assumes Deleuze's general description of such a voice in modern cinema, a voice that 'speaks as if [she] were listening to [her] own words reported by someone else, hence achieving a *literalness* of the voice, cutting it off from any direct resonance, and making it produce a free indirect speech' (C2: 242).

The visual and sound images of *Sans Soleil* then become pure, 'autonomous components of a single, truly audio-visual image' that 'depends on a more complex link between the visual image *and* the sound image' (C2: 252). Once again, becoming is always a matter of *AND*, the making of a line between two bodies, an encounter between two, not of the two, in the two or common to the two, for in fact the two relations have nothing to do with each other (D: 7); rather, a joyful, wondrous encounter and becoming is an encounter with the animals, affects, intensities, movements, sensations and vibrations that move, touch, pierce and wound us; we are never the same. We are islands, Japan-becoming Africa, Africa-becoming Japan . . . 'We are deserts', writes Deleuze, 'but populated by tribes, flora and fauna' (DI: 11). Back on the desert island of Sal, 'He wrote me: I've understood the visions. Suddenly you're in the desert the way you are in the night; whatever is not desert no longer exists' (SS).

In Bissau, 'where the magical function of the eye was working against [him]' (SS), *Sans Soleil*'s wanderer again contemplates the African women whose faces escape that magical eye, the 'faciality machine', as Deleuze and Guattari conceive it, whose 'social production of the face', based upon 'our semiotic of modern White Men, the semiotic of capitalism', would assimilate the women's faces to dominant signification and subjectification (ATP: 181; 182). 'All women have a built-in grain of indestructibility. And men's task', *Sans Soleil* observes, 'has always been to make them realise it as late as possible. African men are just as good at this task as others.' As the women throughout the film glare at the camera, their collective corporeal polyvocality, vitality and force shatters any pretence of face, exotic mystery, ethnic othering or fetishisation as the intensities and affects of their faces and bodies resist capture. 'After a close look at African women', the unseen or faceless female voice continues, 'I wouldn't necessarily bet on the men' (SS).

If the women, children, animals and islands of *Sans Soleil* that see and are seen then embody virtual worlds or potentials, 'desert islands' as populated with actual bodies and virtual anomalous survivors, these bodies form asubjective, 'collective assemblages of enunciation' that still evince the fragilities and insecurities of actual bodies. 'Such a creature on a deserted island would be the deserted island itself, in so far as it imagines and reflects itself in its first movement', Deleuze writes (DI: 11). As the peoples and lands of *Sans Soleil* constitute such double becomings of self-consciousness and renewal, reinvention and *fabulation* as *a people yet to come*, a singular people of more than 'twelve million anonymous inhabitants' (SS), their vital becoming-imperceptible and immanence perhaps lies through the spiritual, sacred worlds of the islands the film discovers. We might proclaim with Deleuze that this is the 'constitution or reconstitution of a people, where the film-maker and his characters become others together and the one through the other, a collectivity which gradually wins from place to place, from person to person, from intercessor to intercessor' (C2: 153).

Islands, their cities and people in *Sans Soleil* become then sites of the double, retrospective, auto-perceptive becomings of filmmaker, narrator, wanderer and character whose folds envelope us. 'The *élan* that draws humans toward islands extends the double movement that produces islands in themselves', Deleuze notes (DI: 10). This double movement of separating and creating extends again and as well to a remembering and forgetting, repetition and difference, a 'dreaming of islands' that is a 'dreaming of pulling away, of being already separate . . . of being lost and alone' while 'dreaming of starting from scratch, recreating, beginning anew' (DI: 10). As James Williams writes, 'to connect and to discard are joint actions – we cannot do well at one without doing well in the other' (Williams 2003: 5).

Once more then, the doubling process is always one of a repeating difference that produces the effect of a counter-actualisation, a doubling of actual self and virtual impersonal other as doubled by a memory-image's doubling of each perception-image, a virtual doubling of present launched simultaneously towards future and past, that whole virtual past of our memories, experiences and 'images already affected by the moss of time' (SS) that *Sans Soleil* strives to perceive. 'I've spent the day in front of my TV set, that memory box', 'he' writes, whose commercials seem 'a kind of haiku to the eye' with their gazes that forever return his own.

Like the whole of time itself, memory, as Bogue writes following Bergson and Deleuze, 'is not inside the individual mind, but each mind is inside memory, like a fish in the ocean. The ocean of memory is the virtual past, which gushes forth at each present moment in a perpetual foundation of time' (Bogue 2003a: 119). As *Sans Soleil*'s traveller journeys across ocean from island to island listening to 'all the prayers to time' issued throughout his trip while 'collecting' materials for the film to come that he will 'never make', he increasingly perceives his self's existence within time, within the 'zone' or 'web' (SS) of perpetual time, within which all life moves, lives and changes.

Through these travels across lands and lines of time, the film encounters layers and strata of landscapes and faces that expose the paradoxes and strange doublings of this stratigraphic, archaeological time as well, the junkyards with inoperative vehicles in a city of incessant transport; the imposed names and other faces of 'horror' that flicker and flash in incessant waves upon Japanese television; the anachronistic faces of a megalopolis that, at nightfall, 'breaks down into villages, with its country cemeteries in the shadow of banks, with its stations and temples', each district 'once again a tidy ingenuous little town, nestling amongst the skyscrapers' (SS).

Against his increasing perception of his self within time, and as the face-landscapes he discerns forever stare back, the film's correspondent visits a small bar in Shinjuku that reminds him 'of that Indian flute whose sound can only be heard by whomever is playing it. He might have cried out if it was in a Godard film or a Shakespeare play, "Where should this music be?"' (SS). This again is 'the impermanence of things', a release and perception of affect through a singular body's encounter with the world. What remains imperceptible to representation and recognition becomes sensate through a self's othering and openness to worlds and sensations beyond its own, the worlds of an other. Although always between two, the process of becoming, creation or life itself is always also a solitary affair, 'because, when it comes down to it, you are always alone, and yet you are like a conspiracy of animals . . . you have never been more populated'; such solitude is once more 'a means of encounter' with the self and its always becoming-other that arises *between*, between one AND an-other (D: 9).

We then are oceans around islands, deserted bodies and waves of encounters encountering other deserted bodies, either deserted islands of 'collective imagination, [which is] what is most profound in it, i.e. rites and mythology' (DI: 11), or islands of deserts whose deserts offer no means for possible life. We encounter other bodies whose affects either affirm our power and make us become, or reduce us to a powerlessness and incapacity for new life. Once again,

> we know nothing about a body until we know what it can do, what its affects are, how they can or cannot enter into composition with other affects, with the affects of another body, either to destroy that body or to be destroyed by it, either to exchange actions and passions with it or join with it in composing a more powerful body. (ATP: 257)

The uncommon in *Sans Soleil*, the mystical, cosmic, spiritual and sacred worlds and rites of the people-islands it discovers, reveal the solitary collectivity of becoming Deleuze identifies. The 'people' and consciousnesses of the film's various reflective screens and surfaces, the faces of the television sets, billboards, the eyes of all the worlds the traveller confronts, engender a movement, not of human transport but the 'very moment of things' (DI: 10), a consciousness of pure duration itself, an *élan* that produces the desert and our 'beings' as deserted for, as Deleuze discerns, 'humans do not put an end to desertedness, they make it sacred' (DI: 10). 'Those people who come to the island indeed occupy and populate it', he continues,

> but in reality, were they sufficiently separate, sufficiently creative, they would give the island only a dynamic image of itself, a consciousness of the movement which produced the island, such that through them the

island would in the end become conscious of itself as deserted and unpeo-pled. The island would be only the dream of humans, and humans, the pure consciousness of the island. (DI: 10)

The 'uncommon humans' of *Sans Soleil* that the Noro, or Japanese priestess, communicates with – the spectres, monsters, spirits, 'gods of the sea, of rain, of the earth, of fire' (SS) – are resonances and rever-berations of the virtual, again that invisible counterpart of every frag-ment of creation that may only be accessed through the uncommon 'beings' that outwardly bare their singularities: the women, children and animals of *Sans Soleil* who effect our own becoming-woman, becoming-animal, *becoming everybody, becoming world*. 'I learned that, as in the Bijagós, it is through the women that magic knowledge is transmitted . . . Everyone bows down before the sister deity who is the reflection, in the absolute, of a privileged relationship between brother and sister. Even after her death, the sister retains her spiritual predominance' (SS).

To that question so dear to the old explorers – 'which creatures live on deserted islands?' – one could only answer: human beings live there already, but uncommon humans, they are absolutely separate, absolute creators, in short, an Idea of humanity, a prototype, a man who would almost be a god, a woman who would be a goddess, a great Amnesiac, a pure Artist, a consciousness of Earth and Ocean, an enormous hurricane, a beautiful witch, a statue from the Easter Islands. There you have a human being who precedes itself. (DI: 11)

And then in its turn the journey entered the 'zone', and Hayao showed me my images already affected by the moss of time, freed of the lie that had prolonged the existence of those moments swallowed by the spiral. (SS)

In Iceland, a volcanic island in the northeastern Atlantic bestowed with few days of unrelenting sun, and where 'he' had 'laid the first stone of an imaginary film', *Sans Soleil*'s voyager writes again: 'And that's where my three children of Iceland came and grafted them-selves in.' The traveller becoming-filmmaker retrieves the shot adding the footage he had cut, 'the somewhat hazy end, the frame trembling under the force of the wind beating us down on the cliff, everything I had cut in order to tidy up', only to discover that the remnants, the discarded shots and debris of the 'tidied' version 'said better than all the rest what I saw in that moment, why I held it at arms' length, at zoom's length, until its last twenty-fourth of a second' (SS).

11 'At arm's length, at zoom's length, until its last twenty-fourth of a second', Sans Soleil *(Marker 1983)*

The children observe the camera curiously as it ventures towards their blissful lack of self-apprehension and recognition; sensing the risk, the impermanence and fleetingness of the irrevocable, ephemeral moment with its affective aura of peacefulness that might at any moment vanish in time, the camera remains at a distance, an arm and zoom's length away from grasping the forgotten, the immanent unseen on the other side of seen. 'Small children', writes Deleuze, 'through all their sufferings and weaknesses, are infused with an immanent life that is pure power and even bliss' (PI: 30). Earlier on, again, as the age-weary traveller watches the youth dance in the park at Yogogi, he shares in their secret: 'The youth who get together every weekend at Shinjuku obviously know that they are not on a launching pad toward real life ... they are life, to be eaten on the spot like fresh doughnuts' (SS).

Left to this world, a world also of sufferings and weaknesses whose profound difference from that of a child's lies through a self-consciousness cultivated as a means for narcissistic self-interest rather than reinvention, *Sans Soleil* then 'performs its own Dondo-yaki', its own fiery 'farewell to all that one has lost, broken, used' (SS) in pure

Markeresque style. As the films' images enter Hayao's zone of 'electronic graffiti', the first transformed image a Maneki Neko cat from the shrine in Japan, the voyager remembers: 'Cat, wherever you are, peace be with you.' The electronic ashes fill the film's final frames as the images assume new life. While the contours of their actual forms dance in flames or flashes of light, *Sans Soleil* at last honours the deserted islands of its journey, its virtual spirits and collective souls whose magic secret may simply be the name for happiness.

Notes

1. This newly repeats Deleuze's account of the time-image as that which 'always gives us access to that Proustian dimension where people and things occupy a place in time which is incommensurable with the one they have in space' (C2: 39). The quotation from Eliot's *Ash Wednesday* appears in the English version of the film; a Jean Racine quotation appears in the original French version. For both film versions and text of the complete quotations, see the 2007 Criterion Collection DVD collective release of *La Jetée* and *Sans Soleil*, under exclusive license from Argos Films, and 'Racine/Eliot' in its accompanying booklet (DVD booklet 2007: 31).
2. Several assessments of *Sans Soleil*, by Nora Alter and Catherine Lupton, for instance, present such an argument. While their extensive analyses of Marker's works are very thorough and useful, Lupton's position pertaining to what Jon Kear (1999: 15) terms a 'structure of reflective consciousness', and what Lupton regards as a 'process of sorting things out and linking them together' via 'a kind of global, disembodied consciousness', seems to propose a cohesive structure for the film through an *embodied subject* or *subjects* located in the film's albeit 'multivocal properties' (Lupton 2005: 149–57). Elsewhere in a nuanced analysis extending to animals and places, Sarah Cooper ventures beyond notions of the film's cohesion to problematise continuity *and* change within *Sans Soleil* (see Cooper 2008: 116–18). Conceptualisations of selfless consciousness, point of view and the author/creator/filmmaker 'Marker' himself will continue to be assessed throughout this chapter.
3. Smith writes: 'Divergences, bifurcations, and incompossibles now belong to *one and the same universe*, a chaotic universe in which divergent series trace endlessly bifurcating paths: a 'chaosmos' and no longer a world' (1997: xxvi). (See also Chapter 2 and WIP: 204).
4. See Deleuze's 'Desert Islands' (DI: 9–14), and Tom Conley's 'The Desert Island' (2005).
5. See C2: ch. 7 and Bogue 2003a, with regard to Deleuze's concept of the 'spiritual automaton'.

6. With regard to the 'autonomy of affect', or, once more, 'that which is imperceptible but whose escape from perception cannot but be perceived, as long as one is alive', Massumi's analyses again are valuable (1996: 229).
7. Such stillness again recalls the stills of *Nuit et Brouillard* and *La Jetée*, and anticipates those to be examined in Chapter 6 through Marker and Bellon's *Le Souvenir d'un Avenir*.
8. Of Mussorgsky's *Sunless* Cycle, James Walker notes that 'Mussorgsky's remarkable talent for observing and truthfully conveying in music the innermost movements and moods of the soul' may be found in all the songs of *Sunless*, although Mussorgsky's 'inspiration understood best the moods of pain and unhappiness' (Walker 1981: 387).
9. For further discussion pertaining to minoritarian 'voices' and faces, see MacCormack 2000.

6

Of Scars, Smiles and Past-Future Signs

'Memory is not in us; it is we who move in a Being-memory, a world-memory.' (C2: 98)

By way of brief returns to *Hiroshima mon amour* and *Sans Soleil*, through Marker's *Le Souvenir d'un Avenir* (2001) and an extended analysis of his *Chats Perchés* (2004), this final chapter replays and newly explores thoughts pertaining to counter-actualisation and dramatisation, signs, faciality, repetition, temporal synthesis, depth and surface, as well as the encounter of film and philosophy itself. While discussions of these concepts, themes and singular expressions have resurfaced throughout these pages, this chapter emerges and develops most notably from the last upon *Sans Soleil*. Which is to say, as it examines Marker's more recent works against Resnais' canonical *Hiroshima mon amour*, a film that indeed, as Chapter 3 evinces, defies rigid terms of classification or interpretation, this chapter moves towards a broader examination of virtual potentials and means of resistance through considerations of past-present-future uprisings, hypocrisies, wars and their lasting resonances. The process of thinking Marker and Resnais' works together, particularly in this chapter, discovers ever-unique forms of resistance to orders and forms of repression that distinguish modern existence. As attuned then to this book's concern with the paradoxically irrevocable and fleeting, haunting yet transient, this chapter turns once more through repeating concepts to repeating connections between and through Marker and Resnais' bodies of works.

The mystical experience, as Tom Conley observes, 'is characterized . . . by an individual's account of his or her voyage to and from an ineffably universal event, which set the body in a trance, and which has left marks, scars, or other physical evidence that confirm the individual's tale of passage' (1993: xii). Memories wound and scar.

Such experience, Conley continues, defies language, representation and meaning as a 'virtual sensation of a somatic moment of totalization and dispersion', what Deleuze and others identify as an *event*. 'Why', writes Deleuze, 'is every event a kind of plague, war, wound, or death?' (LS: 151). If certain experiences and sensations exceed our understanding and our selves, if terror, violence, shame and suffering pervade our lives and memories, how might we live? How might we escape the intolerable, that which is 'no longer . . . a serious injustice, but the permanent state of a daily banality' (C2: 170), to believe in this world, to discover becomings, 'even within ourselves', in the face of human misery and its memories? (see N: 172–3).

The enduring sensations of our wounds for all time must be borne and embodied, Deleuze fundamentally asserts. We may return to Deleuze's ethical doctrine of counter-actualisation whereby to 'will and release the event', to redouble or counter-actualise what happens to us, is to read and exist in the time of the Aion, that which is 'always still in the future and already in the past', so as to act out, like an actor or 'anti-god', 'something perpetually anticipated and delayed, hoped for and recalled' (LS: 150).

It may be argued that *sensations* themselves directly pertain to memories and sensory cultural evocations, be they cinematic, musical, painterly or literary, yet the sensation *itself* of an artwork alone persists. 'Even if the material [of the painter, musician, sculptor, writer, filmmaker] lasts for only a few seconds', Deleuze and Guattari suggest, 'it will give sensation the power to exist and be preserved in itself *in the eternity that coexists with this short duration*' (WIP: 166). 'Not the resemblance but the pure sensation', pure percept wrested from a subject's perceptions, pure affect extracted from the affections among transitory affective states (WIP: 167).

Through multiple interconnections with all preceding chapters, this chapter then newly explores art, primarily filmic, and its singular enactments of events or wounds, wars and deaths that demand anamnesis or a recounting that dramatises and reencounters as it counter-actualises and delimits the original event so as to keep 'only its contour and its splendour', the event's virtual impersonal immateriality, incorporeality, futural potentiality and sensual singularity (LS: 150).

This is not a recounting of memory as nostalgic reminiscence. In lieu of a focus upon memory conceived as a reproduction of the same and similar, this chapter contemplates what this book has advanced throughout as an ethical futural synthesis of time, what

Deleuze terms a third synthesis or 'theatre of repetition' (DR: 10). Through such we might access a pure non-psychological memory and inhabit the 'present without thickness, the present of the actor, dancer, or mime', and so experience, counter-actualise and liberate the pure forces of events along Aion's past-future line. Actual present events forever transform the virtual past, the 'pure past' Deleuze distinguishes by way of Bergson, inasmuch as this virtual past affects the actual 'present' (LS: 168). To encounter, dramatise or actualise virtual memory, to '*redoubler la doublure*' (LS: 168) and 'witness the birth of memory' as a 'function of the future' (C2: 52), this chapter will reveal and confront, again by way of Marker and Resnais' creative practices, the violent sensations, very real forces and affects that comprise the planes of memory and directly impinge upon body and soul.

ॐ

The present is the actual image, and *its* contemporaneous past is the virtual image ... According to Bergson, 'paramnesia' (the illusion of *déjà-vu* or already having been there) simply makes this obvious point perceptible: there is a recollection of the present, contemporaneous with the present itself, as closely coupled as a role to an actor. (C2: 79)

If the 'present is incomplete unless ... considered in relation to all the things it passes away into (the pure past)' (Williams 2005: 69), then the present and our actual existence doubles or 'duplicates itself along with a virtual existence, a mirror-image' (C2: 79). In this way, as these pages have repeatedly reiterated, time is always actual and virtual, a beyond of psychological memory (C2: 109) that continually 'corresponds to the most fundamental split in time ... the differentiation of its passage into two great jets: the passing of the present, and the preservation of the past' (Deleuze 2002: 151). 'Whoever', Deleuze explains, 'becomes conscious of the continual duplicating of his present into perception and recollection ... will compare himself to an actor playing his part automatically, listening to himself and beholding himself playing' (C2: 79). The subject's perception of perception, a perception of perception facilitated through the cinematic time-image, finds expression particularly through the time-image's *crystal-image*, a 'mobile mirror' through which cinema exposes time's ceaseless division, this virtual-actual doubling or folding of all events, time, memory and the self.

'It is not memory that is needed but a complex material that is

147

found not in memory but in words and sounds', Deleuze and Guattari state (WIP: 168). 'Amnesia, hypnosis, hallucination, madness, the vision of the dying, and especially nightmare and dream' – European cinema, Deleuze writes, has confronted such phenomena since its early formations (C2: 55). If a spectator's sensory-motor schema and reflexes organise the cinematic *movement-image* that Deleuze identifies, an image whose moments are perceived to be constitutive parts of a whole duration, it is the cinematic *time-image* that, again, profoundly disturbs and suspends this sensory-motor flux as any centre or fixed point disappears.

'When we cannot remember', Deleuze explains once more via Bergson, 'sensory-motor extension remains suspended, and the actual image . . . does not link up with either a motor image or a recollection-image which would re-establish contact'; the actual 'enters into relation with genuinely virtual elements, feelings of *déjà vu* or past "in general" . . . dream-images . . . fantasies or theatre scenes' (C2: 54). From these memory disturbances and recognition failures there emerges a 'new type of character for a new cinema' (C2: 19), a visionary mutant overcome by forces too powerful, unjust or beautiful, in any case 'too great for us, like too strong a pain', 'a limit-situation . . . but also the most banal, a plain factory, a waste-land' (C2: 18).

As this encountering of the intolerable and unbearable in 'its excess of horror or beauty' (C2: 20) fragments the self and its psychology, beliefs and memory, this new cinema of the postwar time-image confronts the difficulty of 'get[ting] out of the black hole of subjectivity, of consciousness and memory' (ATP: 187). Time itself unfolds and takes on its own excessiveness. The 'time is out of joint', insists Deleuze by way of *Hamlet* through Kant; 'like a serpent' it unfurls and dispels all subordination to movement or nature (see Deleuze 1978b). This liberalisation of time is both an 'empty form of time', or 'third synthesis', as well as a temporal totality *and* a series (DR: 88–9); as with all things, time is divided and 'at the intersection of a twofold synthesis' of actual qualities and virtual extensions, or species and parts, specification and organisation beneath which are spatio-temporal dynamisms, 'agitations of space, holes of time, pure syntheses of space, direction, and rhythms' (DI: 96).

Yet what to make of this chaotic, unknown world wherein a self loses its self, this *cruelty* that Artaud surmises, this *strange theatre* that Deleuze discerns 'comprised of pure determinations, agitating time and space, directly affecting the soul, whose actors are larva'?

(DI: 98). 'What to make of this world of threats and ambush' muses *Le Souvenir d'un Avenir*, Yannick Bellon and Marker's 2001 film. Masks, foreign faces and an intensifying sense of fright pervade Bellon and Marker's film that traces relations of visibility and invisibility, actuality and virtuality, exteriority and interiority, history and memory, testimony and fiction, associations that forever fragment binary divisions. A sinuous series of black and white photographs, the film recalls Marker's 1962 *La Jetée* and what Deleuze is wont to term an *architecture of the memory*.

The film presents not a 'remembrance of things past' but indeed a *Remembrance of Things to Come* – a time of futurity and *difference* in itself, an *untimeliness* that brings only the new, eternal repetition of the different. Resistant to archetypal representation, the film's multiple faces, including those of France, Africa, colonialism, exploitation, disease, sadness and ruin as well as childhood and innocence, become virtual affects of lives lost or wounded in a pre- and postwar world ever at war, the traumas of each locale and body presented succeeding iconic reference to become pure forces of, as the voiceover suggests, 'cold, hunger, [and] deprivations of every kind' (LSA).

ॐ

In the case of writer Joë Bousquet the wound is invisible . . . Simone Weil writes to him: 'You have war lodged in your body. To dwell upon misfortune it must be borne in the flesh.' (LSA)

Joë Bousquet must be called Stoic. He apprehends the wound that he bears deep within his body in its eternal truth as a pure event. To the extent that events are actualized in us, they wait for us and invite us in. They signal us: 'My wound existed before me, I was born to embody it.' (LS: 148)

If there is a double structure to every event, the present actualisation and past-future counter-actualisation, then the world of 'impending war' (LSA) that Bellon and Marker's film evokes indeed imparts the poignancy and vital duality of this ambiguity, that of the definitive, concrete subjective present embodied in a state of affairs or person and the conceptual, ideational still-future and already-past 'mobile instant' that embraces the *singular* and 'splendor of the event itself', that which is 'both collective and private . . . neither individual nor universal' (LS: 152). 'No one has shown better than Maurice Blanchot that this ambiguity is essentially that of the wound and of death', Deleuze writes; 'Every event is like death, double and impersonal in its double' (LS: 151–2). While actual wounds manifest themselves with a personal and oft-times brutal materiality that memory sensorily retains, reality contains both this violent physicality of such events and intensities experienced in the present as well as their virtual re-enactments and re-workings that subsist in an empty pure form of radical time, that 'straight-line labyrinth' which corresponds to death and divides perpetually into past-future via impersonal memory and dramatisation (DR: 111).

Death then persists not in mournful commemorative memory but, as these pages insist, as that 'neither present nor past but always coming' dying that forever encounters the future (DR: 112). As Deleuze repeats through Blanchot, death's two aspects enact a radical reversal whereby one's most intimate, intense and violent confrontation with one's own power through personal death in a present gives way to a more profound violence that unroots oneself from one's self in an 'abyss of the present' (DR: 112). In relation to this impersonal face of death and dying, a liberative, self-destructive dying that negates corporeal death, how might a wound of war be multifariously 'lodged in a body' (LSA)? How can one escape one's self for a self to become, as writes Ronald Bogue, 'the locus of an internalization of chance, becoming, and force' (1994: 3), a 'locus of resistance' through which time as subject itself is produced and affected? What, again, is a body and what are its relations to the very real wounds of experience and memory?

As preceding pages and chapters have diversely endeavoured to demonstrate, through an ethics of affirmative production, and alongside and beyond various other philosophic voices, Deleuze maintains that the virtual is always as real as the actual, that a self is an internalisation of metamorphic, variable, mobile forces whose movement and body must be conceived in terms of what it can do, as any aggregate of singularities, forces, affects and encounters. A film, then, is as much a transient body as is its audience, and memory a creative power that actualises and makes conscious virtual images through recollection, a process that reconstitutes and transforms past and future.

If a body is forever in motion as it undergoes incessant metamorphosis, memory, subjectivity, desire and death may be immanently and creatively reconceived inasmuch as an *event* may also be newly regarded as a transformative change that expresses time's constant folding and unfolding, rhythms and speeds of incorporeal virtualities and bodily intersections, dynamisms which comprise an event's corporeal actualisation. A thinking of time that can only be sensed surfaces when certain actual events, those of war, depression, illness and various crises, become inscribed in the 'depth' of a body. The cracked line of time, Aion's past-future course eternally split, deepens in the flesh of a sensate body whose own power and capacity for joy and life has been diminished. 'In fact', solemnises Deleuze, 'a lot has happened, outside as well as inside: the war, the financial crash, a certain growing older, the depression, illness, the flight of talent' (LS: 154–5). In all, 'what this means is that the entire play of the crack has become incarnated in the depth of the body' (LS: 155).

What then to make of life's wounds, memories and faces? How might remembrance recall a future? As Marker's films directly imagine and effect a future, each of his works builds upon and through the last so that his entire oeuvre itself may be regarded as a virtual past, a Bergsonian 'cone' of layerings of various pasts that forever open to a future, while the faces and surfaces of the films bear traces of multiple past pains that echo through time. 'They are called the shattered faces' (LSA). An image from *Le Souvenir d'un Avenir* reveals the disfigured faces of war veterans; through their faces one might recall the distorted faces of Francis Bacon's art. Distortions in Bacon's art were unintended; disfigurements arose through attempts to capture the imperceptible movements, flows and vitalities of bodies.[1] Deleuze quotes Bacon: 'paint the scream more than the horror . . .' (FB: 51; see also Sylvester 1993: 48). Could it be that these faces of viciously wounded men within the film suggest not only the tragic effects of war but moreover the affects, forces and signs of war itself, the scream incarnated at the level of the body and brought into conflict with other bodies, 'our' bodies, through this living cinematic screen and its flowing intensities of shame, suffering, fear, déjà vu yet also hope, possibility and freedom?

War and memory are indeed 'lodged in the body' and borne in the flesh of the film and the counter-attacks made upon our perceiving bodies. 'Feelings become uprooted from the interiority of a "subject"', Deleuze and Guattari insist, 'to be projected violently outward into a milieu of pure exteriority that lends them an incredible velocity, a catapulting force: . . . they are no longer feelings but affects [. . . that] transpierce the body like arrows, they are weapons of war' (ATP: 356). The film eludes all sentimentality in violent, rapid moves towards a 'smooth' haptic space of contact (ATP: 371) that the cinema reveals through time-images that oppose the rationality and causality of movement-images.

12 '*In the case of writer Joë Bousquet the wound is invisible*', Le Souvenir d'un Avenir *(Marker and Yannick Bellon 2001)*

As it releases a 'nonpulsed time', *Le Souvenir d'un Avenir* and its rhythms, sounds and visuals produce affects of shame and loss that viscerally, sensually affront the bodies engaging with the screen. Our bodies encounter the film's superhistorical worlds and an interminable, decentred, nonlinear time whose incorporeal past-future crack finds corporeal actualisation in the cracks or cuts between cinematic images as well as in the film's multiple faces and bodies that resist narrative and categorical assimilation as 'nonsubjectified affects' (ATP: 262; see also C2: 179).

As the film's own voiceover suggests, through its embodiment of various pasts specific to lands across the globe, *Le Souvenir d'un Avenir* exposes this interstice of pure time and difference that bespeaks the future: 'Denise Bellon has grasped this unique moment in time when postwar was becoming pre-war. Each of her photographs shows a past yet deciphers a future' (LSA). The film's pursuit of this futural time, abstracted from chronology and the hierarchical grounds of identity, sexuality, nation, race, religion and class, endangers these Truths and edicts of systematic teleological 'real' life as it at once distinguishes Marker's art as a multilinear system whose '*anti-memory*' encompasses regions of a world-memory (ATP: 294; see also Chapter 4). This virtual pure recollection indeed exists in a 'sheet' or continuum preserved in time beyond any single individual or group.

With regard to the cinema's capacity to reveal 'a little time in the pure state' via a continuum comprised of 'fragments of different ages' through which images become embodied within each other, Deleuze writes of transformations that take place between two sheets of virtual past. These constitute, he maintains, a sheet of transformation that 'invents a kind of transverse continuity or communication between several sheets, and weaves a network of non-localizable relations between them' to extract non-chronological time, that which is, again, at once past and always to come (C2: 123).

À propos *Le Souvenir d'un Avenir*'s expression of such an unlimited past-future through filmic moments revelatory of time's non-chronological divide, the voiceover of the film concludes: 'And in spite of everything, once again prophetic, the history of the century's end will be that of its masks' (LSA). The masks of the film's near final frame may seem to allude to the ever-persistent threat of an anaesthetised world of insensate beings we might too easily recognise. Yet might the masks' presence more profoundly imagine an ever-differing world without masked Truths, one of pure difference, repetition, 'disguise and displacement' that can only be sensed? (see DR: 105). If 'something in the world forces us to think', to again repeat Deleuze's proposition, 'this something is an object not of recognition but of a fundamental *encounter* [. . . that] may be grasped in a range of affective tones: wonder, love, hatred, suffering', and yet, in 'whichever tone, its primary characteristic is that it can only be sensed' (DR: 139).

Once more, this 'something', *thisness* or 'object of encounter' denies recognition, recollection, perception, preconception or imagination; as such, it is not a quality but a *sign*, contends Deleuze, and it is cinema, he furthermore stresses, that is 'itself a new practice of images and signs, whose theory philosophy must produce as conceptual practice' (C2: 280). Signs, stresses Deleuze, 'are the true elements of theatre. They testify to the spiritual and natural powers which act beneath the words, gestures, characters and objects represented. They signify repetition as real movement, in opposition to representation which is a false movement of the abstract' (DR: 23). 'Signs', in other words, as Deleuze and Guattari further explain, 'are not signs of a thing; they are signs of deterritorialization and reterritorialization, they mark a certain threshold crossed in the course of these movements' (ATP: 67). Elsewhere, with regard to such movement, the illusions of 'truthful' representation, and the creative, *differing* freedom of modern art, Deleuze clarifies:

Movement, for its part, implies a plurality of centres, a superimposition of perspectives, a tangle of points of view, a coexistence of moments which essentially distort representation . . . Difference must become the element, the ultimate unity; it must therefore refer to other differences which never identify it but rather differentiate it . . . Every object, every thing, must see its own identity swallowed up in difference, each being no more than a difference between differences. Difference must be shown *differing*. We know that modern art tends to realise these conditions: in this sense it becomes a veritable *theatre* of metamorphoses and permutations. A theatre where nothing is fixed, a labyrinth without a thread . . . The work of art leaves the domain of representation in order to become 'experience', transcendental empiricism or science of the sensible. (DR: 56)

Philosophy then becomes through the experiences of modern art and most profoundly those of cinema. These speak, as Chapter 3 explores, directly to what Deleuze terms the 'forgetting within memory', an 'essentially imperceptible' which can only be sensed, that virtual *being* of the past, a past of every time rarely perceived, *forgetting* as memory's own limit, the 'nth' power of memory (DR: 140–1).[2] Through uniquely cinematic moving images in time, the cinema's systems of signs, encounters and images – its *living forms* – command new 'practices' of philosophical theory: philosophy alone must isolate, identify and practice philosophical 'concepts adequate to the living [cinematic and non-philosophical] images they classify', as Bogue suggests (2003a: 202).

A 'theory of cinema', that is, 'is not "about" cinema', as Deleuze's *Cinema 2: The Time-Image* concludes (C2: 280). Rather, Deleuze proposes that a theory of cinema need address the very ontology of philosophy as it engages with the concepts cinema engenders. 'There is always a time, midday-midnight, when we must no longer ask ourselves, "What is cinema?"', Deleuze declares, 'but "What is philosophy?"' (C2: 280). The concepts of cinema then, 'are not produced in films themselves', as Bogue further elucidates, 'but those who make movies generate the concepts that belong to film' (2003a: 202). This is a productive, creative process and encounter between the images of film and concepts of philosophy, between philosophy and film, a film-philosophy that examines cinematically articulated images that incite philosophical concepts through specifically filmic, non-philosophical *signs*. Of these signs that extend beyond cinema towards life itself, as the affects of cinema and the concepts of philosophy shock us into perceiving the routinely imperceptible, Bogue continues:

directors enunciate a core of basic cinematic concepts, and philosophers work with those concepts to develop related concepts and construct from this collection of concepts a coherent cinematic theory ... The essential and positive relation between philosophy and the non-philosophy of the arts is evident throughout the noon-midnight hour of *Cinema 1* and *Cinema 2*, an extended hour in which 'What is cinema?' and 'What is philosophy?' are posed as a single question. (2003a: 202)

Via its signs, images, percepts and affects, cinema forces us to sensorily encounter *thisnesses* that can only be sensed, that '*sentiendum* or the being of the sensible' (DR: 140), the signs and objects of a fundamental encounter of which Deleuze writes and Marker and Resnais confront. Through the *faces* of people, places and all things in his works, Marker again brings us face to face with our selves and the imperceptible, the minute, banal made wondrous. For the face 'serves', as Bogue writes, 'as a sign, not as signifier to signified, but as the moon's visible surface to its dark side'. 'The face points toward possible worlds yet unspecified, and if I am to encounter that sign, rather than simply classify it (ignore it, reject it, imitate it), I must enter with it into the composition of a world enfolded in its possibilities' (Bogue 2007: 13).

If the face is then but an imperceptible sign, an intimation of untimely virtual real relations, the masks of *Le Souvenir d'un Avenir*'s final moments indeed conceal no transcendent truth or identity. The film's voiceover concludes: 'And in spite of everything, once again prophetic, the history of the century's end will be that of its masks' (LSA). The masks of the film's near final frame evoke worlds of simulacra, bodies and images, convergences between history and fable, fact and fiction that give rise to sensations and faces unknown and subjectless. We might concur with Deleuze that there 'are no ultimate or original responses or solutions' to inconceivable and unimaginable horrors that Marker and Resnais' cinemas newly envisage, but 'only problem-questions, in the guise of a mask behind every mask and a displacement behind every place' (DR: 107). 'Problems concern the eternal disguise', writes Deleuze; 'questions, the eternal displacement ... in conditions under which the false becomes the mode of exploration of the true, the very space of its essential disguises' (DR: 107). Ever-absorbed with the minutiae of life, the tendencies and movements that comprise our bodies and experiences in time, *Le Souvenir d'un Avenir* contests fixed truths of history it ironically surveys in relation and juxtaposition to cinema and photography. 'These photographs', the film reflects, 'may be the only traces which remain for history' (LSA).

Le Souvenir d'un Avenir effectively implies, then, that such 'traces' are not signifiers of authenticity or sufficient relics of evidence as the film's images themselves seemingly embody what Deleuze might term microscopic architectures of time whose encounters with asignifying intensities of forces and affects constitute and exceed each image. The 'too prophetic' surrealist world of which Denise Bellon was part, a world thoroughly enraptured by the 'opposition between dream and reality' and 'the cunning cruelty and darkness of the days to come', as the film's voiceover states, was enamoured with all aspects of 'darkness, weirdness' and 'suffocation' (LSA), sensations the surrealists strove to capture at their most shockingly real. For the surrealists and *Le Souvenir d'un Avenir*, one mask or representation assumed veritable would merely beget another. Against transcendent layers of history and veracity that shroud and limit perception, Deleuze and Guattari likewise claim: 'The mask does not hide the face, it *is* the face' (ATP: 115).

What can one do with essence, which is ultimate difference, except to repeat it, because it is irreplaceable and because nothing can be substituted for it? . . . Difference and repetition are only apparently in opposition. There is no great artist who does not make us say: 'The same and yet different.' (PS: 49)

SHE: I remember.
I see the ink.
I see the daylight.
I see my life. Your death.
My life that goes on. Your death that goes on. (Duras 1961: 63)

The lovers' bodies interpenetrate. 'Formless', 'anonymous' (Duras 1961: 8), smooth, bare limbs, ashes and dust. Amidst the ashes and dust of a foreign new world, the lovers lose themselves. The scarred, post-annihilated city of Hiroshima affronts thought itself – how can life wilfully desecrate life – as she struggles to recall what she thought she knew in an unrecognisable, post-apocalyptic world whose strangeness Resnais' *Hiroshima mon amour* suggests via the disconnects and incongruities of its musical score and achronological cuts. Even so, life persists: 'History tells, I'm not making it up, on the second day certain species of animals rose again from the depths of the earth and from the ashes' (HMA). In impossible attempts to negotiate the incomprehensible deaths and suffering, the woman demands perfect remembrance: 'Why deny the obvious necessity for memory?' And yet, as an actress and person without name (as is he, her new love), she embodies the very madness of emergent life and an ever-new creative 'love' amidst unfathomable decay.

Alongside the surfacing and proliferation of animal and plant life are the affective encounters between the woman and her loves and the *thisnesses* or becomings that pass *between* two, 'that something' that 'happens between them' (D: 15) that recalls the lovers' love of Marker's *La Jetée*. As does *La Jetée*'s mad love, *Hiroshima mon amour* refutes authoritative anamnesis as it reveals and witnesses the singular return or creative becoming of something new within a charred world through which the woman, an actress without proper name, encounters time's final third synthesis.

A fiber stretches from a human to an animal, from a human or an animal to molecules, from molecules to particles, and so on to the imperceptible. (ATP: 249)

If, as Deleuze explains, the first synthesis is that of habit and chronology on which conventional conceptions of past and future depend, the second synthesis pertains to memory and constitutes time as a pure past which causes the present to pass. In the third synthesis, 'the present is no more than an actor, an author, an agent destined to be effaced' (DR: 89–90; 94) whose loss of self always corresponds to a future. The cuts between *Hiroshima mon amour*'s filmic images also actualise this futural projection as they embody a cut that projects past into future, as Williams observes with regard to time's crack: a 'decision or an unconscious selection does not only cut away from the past, it brings something new into the past and brings the past into the future. So though there is a break, there is also an assembly. A discontinuous and continuous time are implied by selection' (2005: 70).

At first bewildered by the process of her becoming-imperceptible as she encounters Time and the events that have happened, the actress counter-actualises or opens herself up, as Deleuze describes, 'to the impersonal and preindividual' (LS: 150), to the virtual, persistent incorporeal intensities and forces underlying actual horrors. 'The actor thus actualizes the event, but in a way which is entirely different from the actualization of the event in the depth of things' (LS: 150). As Deleuze elsewhere reflects with regard to the third time in which the future appears, it is

> as though the bearer of the new world were carried away and dispersed by the shock of the multiplicity to which it gives birth: what the self has become equal to is the unequal in itself. In this manner, the I which is fractured according to the order of time and the Self which is divided according to the temporal series correspond and find a common descendent in the man without name, without family, without qualities, without self or I . . . Historians sometimes look for empirical correspondences between the present and the past, but [. . . such] involves repetition only by analogy or similitude . . . Repetition is never a historical fact, but rather the historical condition under which something new is effectively produced. (DR: 89–90)

In this new world wherein his body becomes hers and she the 'living denial of reason' (Duras 1961: 106), the woman's remembrance recalls a past, as does Bellon's photography, that deciphers a future 'always still in the future and already . . . past' (LS: 150), a 'demented' time (DR: 88) in which her dead lover's death forever 'goes on'. Which is to say, both *Le Souvenir d'un avenir* and *Hiroshima mon amour* open to a direct perception of an eternal return, a simultaneity of past-future time that discerns the abyss of which Deleuze through Blanchot writes: 'In this abyss they (*on*) die – they never cease to die, and they never succeed in dying' (LS: 152; Blanchot 1982: 155).

And 'this is how the story of time ends', claims Deleuze, 'by undoing its too well centred natural or physical circle and forming a straight line which then, fed by its own length, reconstitutes an eternally decentred circle' (DR: 115). Freed of name and measured time, the lovers of *Hiroshima mon amour* are 'reduced', as Duras describes, 'to a terrifying, mutual impotence . . . They simply call each other once again. What? Nevers, Hiroshima . . . They are names of places, names that are not names. It is as though, through them, *all of Hiroshima was in love with all of Nevers*' (Duras 1961: 13).

❧

> He wrote me: I will have spent my life trying to understand the function of remembering, which is not the opposite of forgetting, but rather its lining. We do not remember; we rewrite memory much as history is rewritten. How can one remember thirst? (SS)

> To connect and to discard are joint actions – we cannot do well at one without doing well in the other. (Williams 2003: 5)

> Virtual objects exist only as fragments of themselves: they are found only as lost; they exist only as recovered. Loss or forgetting here are not determinations which must be overcome; rather, they refer to the objec-

tive nature of that which we recover, as lost, at the heart of forgetting. (DR: 102)

Memoryless and yet prophetic, Marker and Resnais' cinemas newly conceptualise memory, death and time, a time of the before and after in which we exist and life persists. *Hiroshima mon amour*'s positive force of forgetting and selfless becomings resonate through Marker's works, and most remarkably in Marker's *Chats Perchés*, a work that in turn newly repeats *Sans Soleil*. Marker and Resnais' works indeed always at once confront a past and future as they affront norms of habitual perception and recognition through surfacings of little perceptions and minute imperceptibles that resist signification and identification. As *Sans Soleil*'s voiceover wonders, how can one remember thirst? Or really *know* what it was like to discover the sea, when you'd only seen it at the movies, as *Le Souvenir d'un Avenir* muses? Or know *everything*, as *Hiroshima mon amour* contests, or even have one's death to oneself, as *Nuit et Brouillard* most profoundly contemplates?

As this chapter has already intimated, Resnais' *Nuit et Brouillard* and *Hiroshima mon amour* express a more extreme encounter between the mundane and surreal than Marker's more mischievous and sardonic transformations of the commonplace and banal in *Chats Perchés*, a work which is always also nonetheless connected to considerations of tragedy, conflict and loss. However, inasmuch as Marker and Resnais' works jolt us from our everyday through their uniquely similar and dissimilar examinations of the horrific, oppressive and threatening, both artists' practices consistently evoke variations of a tenderness, gentility and sensitivity that enable the signs of life and becomings the films reveal.

As people, animals, places and all things open to new combinations and potentials – as a woman exceeds her self to become-other through her encounters with a foreign city; as an ephemeral yet ubiquitous world of cats embodies possibilities of creative resistance and metamorphosis – this chapter focuses upon 'superhistorical' voyages about the globe. Indeed, such voyages through which historical truths become uprooted distinguish all the films of this study inasmuch as the means of Marker and Resnais' works evince Deleuze and Guattari's definition of the *Untimely*, 'which is another name for haecceity, becoming, . . . forgetting as opposed to memory, geography as opposed to history' (ATP: 296). As this chapter then turns more towards Marker's multi-media practice that conceives and embraces possible other worlds beyond our own, wherein, for instance, the grin of a Cat may beckon a new Paris-world as a surpassing of fixed distinctions, as between human and animal, demand new perceptual processing, it yet recalls the immanent becomings of *Hiroshima mon amour*'s lovers.

While Marker's works continue to emerge from an alternative or subversive side of convention to probe the recesses of life's surface that fold and double transparencies of our world, *Chats Perchés*' frequently handheld, ubiquitous camera skirts the streets of Paris and its underground. 'As my lens slips inside the crowd like an inquisitive snake', Marker writes, 'what it frames is, despite the apparent cohesiveness of the groups, the everlasting face of solitude' (Marker 2007: 27). Ever captivated by faces, eyes and images that grasp at limits of perceptibility, Marker's images incessantly examine structures, movements, under- and over-ground trains, gazes and places that populate the disparate lands and ages the films' eye visits. The resulting images reveal highly physical, material worlds whose configurations and dimensions produce an overwhelming impression and affect of *solitude*, while the captured or filmed faces resist subjectification to become haecceities.[3]

With a searching, 'snaking' eye that explores, like *Sans Soleil*, the 'fragility of moments suspended in time' (SS), *Chats Perchés* assesses the banality, solitude and simplicity of the everyday against the powerful hierarchies we obstinately, strangely construct, and of which the film speaks:

> A Grinning Cat appeared on the wall of the church at St. Germain des Prés. Within a month he was erased. Does that iconoclastic rage ring a bell? Sure, the Taliban blowing out the Buddhas in Afghanistan . . . Given their respective environments, both obscurantisms show the two faces of the same coin. (Marker 2007: 44)

Resistance is never simple, but 'a cat', Marker elsewhere declares, 'is never on the side of power' (Marker 1977). 'Can one', as Deleuze asks, 'already glimpse the outlines of . . . future forms of resistance'? (N: 182). With regard to 'control societies that no longer operate by confining people but through continuous control and instant communication' (N: 174), Deleuze concludes that a 'snake's coils', or cat's grin, as Marker might suggest, 'are even more intricate than a mole's burrow' (N: 182).

৯

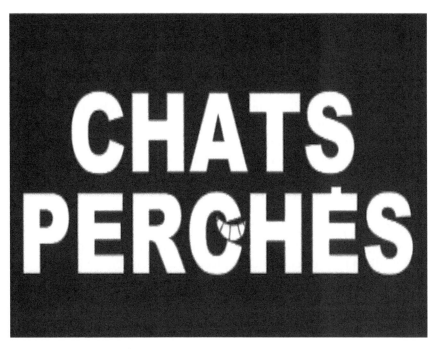

13 Chats Perchés *(Marker 2004)*

> The haecceity is the fact that it occurs as an event, but when it emerges, it has always-already been there, it is always everywhere. It's like the smile of the Cheshire cat in Lewis Carroll's *Alice*, it's everywhere, in the entire universe. (Stivale 1998: 215)

> Pure events . . . let an incorporeal rise to the surface like a mist over the earth, a pure 'expressed' from the depths: not the sword, but the flash of the sword, a flash without a sword like the smile without a cat. (ECC: 22)

> . . . and I'm looking for the Cats. (CP)

'And by the way', *Chats Perchés* asks, 'where did that grin come from?' During the film's first moments its title, C H A T S P E R C H É S, appears letter by letter, with a Cheshire Cat's grin, of course, in the cradle of the second 'C'. In a transmutation of technological means, within seconds the screen becomes a computer's as an owl and its message flashes: 'VOUS AVEZ UN MESSAGE EN ATTENTE'. Signs of cats and their ethereal smiles, owls as well as a Markeresque enigmatic voice comprise these opening shots of *Chats Perchés*, a film that trails several 'metamorphoses of the Cat' (CP).

While *Chats Perchés* proceeds to cunningly offer a certain

mock-historical genealogy of 'the Cat through the ages, from cave painting until constructivism' (CP), through its pursuit of the Cats' appearances and disappearances, the film moreover constructs an acute assessment of the perverse hierarchical structures and ideals that oppress the post-9/11 world in relation to the becomings, smiles and *signs* of 'the Cats'. Their sightings and erasures effectively inspire and underscore this undertaking that becomes no less than the film's expression of a contemporary cultural symptomatology. Through its materialisations of dynamic relations between actual and virtual, material and immaterial, *Chats Perchés* examines certain forces and tendencies that underlie societal institutions, their technologies of control, and various forms of resistance.

Fleetingly perceptible, the Cats and their grins embody a certain becoming-imperceptible as their appearances and disappearances refute all that is discernible, subjective and entrenched, their very tangible intangibility exceeding conventional and established classifications of 'cat'. For the Cats of *Chats Perchés* are more than mere cats, such as those Deleuze and Guattari might term 'individuated animals, family pets, sentimental, Oedipal animals each with its own petty history, "my" cat' (ATP: 240). Rather, as the voiceover states, 'to someone who landed in that gloomy city where smiling had become a kind of secret cipher between affiliates, the grin of the Cat was the gate to a different Paris' (CP). The film's Cats and their dynamic materialisations and vanishings express in effect an event's two sides, or life's depth and its slippery surface upon which the felines ephemerally balance as their peculiar smiles imagine new worlds. 'A cat on a roof. Then another. Then another' (CP).

A playful score accompanies this first sequence of the film that traces the synchronised, seemingly sudden emergence of a Paris 'flash mobbing'. The event, as an email text upon the screen and the film's voiceover informs, is to involve the opening and closing of umbrellas and a 'poetic' chant around a large pot. This 'second ParisMob', Marker's camera confirms, quickly materialises as a large, relatively impromptu assemblage of people gathers to enact the strange activity in front of the Centre Pompidou before rapidly dispersing, much like the Cats themselves. 'Et tout ça sous le regard d'un chat', the screen reads. As it cuts to a still close shot of the pot, with synthesised sounds recalling Marker's earlier works and a rapid zoom in upon a grinning, yellow cat painted or perched unexpectedly high upon the side of a chimney in the far background, *Chats Perchés* reveals its first powerful sign, a Cat, indeed a *sign*, a 'carrier of intensity that transmits a change in sense through a change in an actual moment' (Williams 2008a: 32).

The Cats are there, effecting and transmitting changes in between the film's myriad historical facts and actual moments. They become and embody transitory *thisnesses*, affects and sensations that exceed fixed states; they are virtual excess, after-images and minute 'flash-mobs' or flashes on the surfaces and thresholds of actual and virtual appearances and disappearances with smiles that linger. The Cats, *Chats Perchés* insinuates, dramatise and re-encounter our events, wars, protests, solitudes and sufferings. They redouble and expose aspects of virtual memory via novel counter-actualisations of our original corporeal wounds that incorporeally, singularly endure as persistently as a Cat's grin.

'Counter-actualisation', Hélène Frichot observes, 'which doubles the work of the event, is always in excess of that what which has been actualised . . . and effectively allows an opening for future actualisations' (2005: 67). With sensory resonances that penetrate 'rather like after-images, or effects of light that appear and disappear in a flash' (2005: 71), the Cats counter-actualise the actual events and states of our lives and memories as they convey the 'immaterial side of the surface of sense' (2005: 67), that mobile instant of an event and death itself that Deleuze discerns.

'UN **CHAT**?' With this title screen that the film's voice echoes, another Cat flashes. Then another. Then another. 'FLASHBACK' announces another title screen. And in between still images of graffiti cats proliferating throughout the city emerges a faintly superimposed moving image against the Paris skyline, a frightful image of past haunted by our diverse memories, a funereal bagpipe rendition of *Amazing Grace* and the film's ever-ironic narration. While the image flashes as briefly as the Cats themselves, it distinctly reveals the burning World Trade Towers with their cloud of devastation uniquely evocative of Hiroshima's. There was talk in November 2001, the film's voiceover continues, of a 'new age' of Us against Them, 'the Killers'. *Chats Perchés*' formally announced flashback underscores the film's ironic, pertinent and poignant relation to the future and more recent past. While the familiar delusion of a (westernised) global harmony rapidly faded post-9/11, the dualist position withstands.

We are forever grounded by our selves' limitations and their demarcations with respect to alien others. Deleuze's 'critique of truth', which thrives upon an ethics of *Amor fati* or a love of one's fate and the world *as is*, seemingly corresponds with *Chats Perchés'* interrogations of past, present and future, so that the question arises: how can we free our selves and break from the binds of subjectivity if our safe, practical, deluded and defensive strongholds of subjectivity are perpetually embedded in a self-destructive and aggrandising notion of difference: our righteousness, their demonolatry? While we revere our own tripartite gods – transcendent God, harmonious World, rational Self – how might we truly live? How might we enter into relation with genuinely virtual elements to 'witness that birth of memory' as a function of the future? (C2: 52).

If the flashback, as Deleuze defines it, 'is a conventional, extrinsic device' that 'indicate[s], by convention, a causality which is psychological, but still analogous to a sensory-motor determinism', and that 'only confirms the progression of a linear narration' (C2: 48), perhaps, as Deleuze and *Chats Perchés* insist, and *Hiroshima mon amour* corroborates, we 'live' when we *cannot* remember. For only when our sensory-motor extension remains suspended and the actual image 'enters into relation with genuinely virtual elements' can time, the virtual past and the 'birth of memory, as function of the future', emerge (C2: 52).

With ever-new multi-sensory sight we might then enter into a definition of 'the new dimension of [nomadic] subjectivity' of which Deleuze writes (C2: 54). In catlike step with the virtual, *Chats Perchés'* 'flashbacks' flash on the surface of the actual with sensations and perceptions that are 'as cut off from memory-based recognition as they are from motor recognition' (C2: 55). With 'floating memories, images of a past *in general* which move past at dizzying speed, as if time were achieving a profound freedom' (C2: 55), the film's resurfacings of past are as elusive and free from conventional assimilations of time and self as a Cat's grin.

෴

> The primordial element is the sonorous beauty and it is from there that the mind must leap to the image. (Bazin 1983: 180; see also Alter 2006: 27)

> To enlarge perception means to render sensible, sonorous (or visible), those forces that are ordinarily imperceptible. (Deleuze 1998a: 72; see also Ansell Pearson 2002: 171)

In constant pursuit of the Cats, Marker's camera descends below ground into the Métro's depths and characteristically lingers to survey the faces. As a string ensemble performs, the camera peruses the observing crowd and captures a woman's gaze; she returns the camera's look with a smile in a moment that strikingly recalls both *La Jetée* and *Sans Soleil*. Marker elsewhere admits: 'My dream was to be able to catch them [the reactions of people] as I did animals, in pure *naturalezza*' (Marker 2008: 30). In an extension of this singular moment with its two-way passage and mixture of curious glances, *Chats Perchés* temporally 'freezes' both gazes, the woman's and hence the camera's as well, in a close-shot freeze-frame of the woman's face and her surfacing smile, a dynamic moment and image that at once evokes not only the Cats' broad grins but also, again, the glances and extraordinary emergent expressions and smiles of women and animals throughout Marker's oeuvre.[4]

Effected through this interplay of bodies and gazes, this unexpected momentary flash of the woman's smile surfaces, as do the Cats and their grins, as an event whose 'essence is that of the pure surface effect, or the impassible incorporeal entity' that results 'from bodies, their mixtures, their actions, and their passions' but that 'differs in nature from that of which it is the result' (LS: 182). How, again, can one describe a singular momentary transition, remember thirst, seize upon a gust of air, arrest the 'effects of light that appear and disappear in a flash' (Frichot 2005: 71), or capture a vanishing cat?

With respect to Deleuze's conceptualisations of a fold and the continual virtual-actual doublings of all things, life, self, body, time, death and the event, Frichot considers French architect and theorist Bernard Cache's concept of inflection as that which '"changes qualities as soon as one tries to grasp it"' (2005: 70). Such a concept in fact corresponds to a haecceity, that 'curious mixture' of speeds and slownesses, 'unformed particles' and nonsubjectified affects (ATP: 262) that occurs, as Stivale remarks, as an event that has 'always-already been there' and is everywhere, once more like 'the smile of the Cheshire cat' (1998: 215). Deleuze, Frichot adds, responds to Cache's formulation by proposing that inflection 'configures an "elastic point"' and 'is the pure Event of the line or of the point, the Virtual' (FLB: 15; Frichot 2005: 70). 'The qualitative force that continues obstinately to escape us', Frichot continues, 'the breeze that animates these inflected folds . . . is the virtual' (2005: 70).

As virtual potential actualised and materialised in bodies and states of affairs, an event arises as an instantaneous surfacing or momentary intensity between forces and things. The event, writes Deleuze, is 'a very special *attribute* . . . noematic and incorporeal'

(LS: 182), and may also be regarded as a 'change in waves resonating through series' (Williams 2008a: 1) with the virtual 'cresting', 'in a liminal realm of emergence, [. . . as] half-actualized actions and expressions arise like waves on a sea to which most no sooner return' (Massumi 2002b: 31).

Once more, life is surface and depth, virtual potential and actual effect, and our bodies waves of resonances and vibrations, dilations and contractions of matter, rhythms of speeds and flows that comprise life's virtual-actual series and the 'noisy accidents' that have 'dug their way down' to that 'silent, imperceptible crack, at the surface' (LS: 155), the frontier at which we attempt to stay, perhaps somewhere between the two worlds *Chats Perchés* discerns, 'the real [actual] world' and that 'more familiar world, the world of cats' (CP). Through sly, stealthy embodiments, *Chats Perchés* then enacts Deleuze's ethical imperative as it nimbly explores events, dangers and *cat*astrophes – 'On April 21, catastrophe. The cat Bolero pinched his paw in the escalator' (CP) – catastrophes inherent to both 'worlds', the Cats' and our more apparent own.

And so, from within the more secretive world of the Métro's depths, *Chats Perchés* continues its search for the Cats amid the 'gremlins, zombies, and griffins' of the underground billboards and passageways (CP). Even a pigeon's seemingly trapped flight along a Métro corridor reveals a metamorphosis: 'The next surprise is to watch a pigeon transforming itself into a man' (CP), a transformation that animates *Chats Perchés*' line of flight or tracing of creative transformations and metamorphoses, feline and human alike. As Keith Ansell Pearson considers, 'how can time be something invisible or imperceptible? Although invisible forces – molecular affections and perceptions – are not time they are intertwined with its passages, intervals, echoes, and tunnels' (Ansell Pearson 2002: 171).

As Cats randomly appear and slip away from the interstices, tunnels, roofs, reverberations and surfaces of the worlds *Chats Perchés* scours while continually liberating perception from any conventional representative function, we witness the title screen, 'THE MORPHEYE', with what appears as an owl's eye lurking in the 'O'. The film's revelation of molecular affections and perceptions indeed 'enlarges perception' through an encountering of time *itself* 'as force' (Ansell Pearson 2002: 171), a sensory envisioning that Francis Bacon correspondingly, yet differently, realises via his art, as suggested earlier in this chapter.

This 'rendering sensible, sonorous or visible of forces that are ordinarily imperceptible' effectively becomes a process of counter-actualisation as the film enacts that excessive, 'slippery aspect of the event' (Frichot 2005: 67) that exceeds actualisation and that Deleuze most profoundly details. For amid the demonstrators, activists and mere observers, the Cats' surfacings resonate with Deleuze's distinctions between depth and surface, material and immaterial, fixed and processual, sounds and the sonorous qualities of things: 'To render language possible thus signifies assuring that sounds are not confused with the sonorous qualities of things, with the sound effects of bodies, or with their actions and passions' (LS: 181), those incorporeal qualities and sensations that flash, shock, puncture, wound and leave us irremediably affected, ever-different and differing.

Deleuze thereby re-invokes the virtually excessive and imperceptible – the sonorous, singular, sensually shocking and beautiful *thisnesses* and haecceities that Marker and Resnais' cinemas encounter at the limit of the actual lived body 'beyond the organism', that 'intense and intensive' body without organs 'traversed by a wave that traces levels or thresholds in the body', a body freed from compromising hierarchical organisations of 'organs', sounds and qualities that are no longer attached to or representative of a body, human or otherwise (FB: 39).

For the body without organs is, like the force of bodies in Bacon's art, 'finally defined by the *temporary and provisional presence* of determinate organs', which, Deleuze continues, is 'one way of introducing time into the painting', *time itself*, that something invisible or imperceptible made visible and perceptible through revelations of the internal dynamisms of our actual, material bodies and states of affairs. 'To put time inside the Figure – this is the force of bodies in Bacon' (FB: 42). Through his examinations of the ways 'the body escapes from itself' in Bacon's art (FB: 43), Deleuze discerns that virtual excess, force or breeze that communicates an excessive, interminable presence through the 'insistence of the smile beyond the face and beneath the face', as well as the 'insistence of a scream that survives the mouth, the insistence of a body that survives the organism' (FB: 43–4).

With graffiti and actual Cats populating the film's screen, resonances of their grins linger affectively beyond their fleeting flashes on film, investing Deleuze's thoughts pertaining to the incorporeal body, scream and smile with new resonance: 'Bacon suggests that beyond the scream there is the smile . . . he has painted smiles that are among the most beautiful in painting, and which fulfill the strangest function, namely, that of securing the disappearance of the body. Bacon[, Marker] and Lewis Carroll meet on this single point: the smile of a cat' (FB: 25).

ॐ

At that moment they [the Cats] were just signs, but comforting ones. And how we did need comforting signs in those days. So somebody, at night, was risking his neck just to have a smile floating over the city. (CP)

Signs imply ways of living, possibilities of existence, they're the symptoms of life gushing forth or draining away. (N: 143)

A philosophy of the surface and of the event is always caught in a struggle with violent and destructive mixtures of bodies; it is always trying to give sense to a life of violent shocks, invasions and punctures. (Williams 2008a: 84)

'Où sont les Chats? où sont les Chats? où sont les Chats?' *Chats Perchés* demands. The Cats reappear, this time triumphantly with majestic fanfare and banner upon which reads the film's vital affirmation – 'FAITES DES CHATS PAS LA GUERRE!!!©' – the film's most explicit assertion of the creative, revolutionary potential embodied by the Cats and engendered through our productive, life-empowering encounters and becomings. The film freeze-frames once again to capture the image, now in black and white, of the revolutionary movement and 'creative war-machine' made perceptible, its declamatory banner flanked by two yellow graffiti Cats and born by Parisian street protestors.

And then, the flash of a woman's smile. Then another. Then another. The camera captures the final woman in slow motion as she bemusedly glances towards the lens while her puzzlement rapidly dissolves into a broad smile. The camera, seemingly equally amused and entranced, follows her gait, lingering upon the nape of her neck and spiral chignon as the most affecting images captured by Marker's lens, the ever-new sonorous beauty and *thisnesses* of a woman, resurface in the mind's eye ... And then, silence, as the woman strolls away. '1er juin': the date flashes upon a black title screen following which appears a still shot of a crowd gathered at the base of the Eiffel Tower. Suspended across the tower's base a large projection screen reads in French: 'Un compteur géant pour rappeler la réalité des chiffres des victimes du sida' (A *'die-in'* for the victims of AIDS).

Deleuze writes: 'There's a profound link between signs, events, life, and vitalism ... It's organisms that die, not life. Any work of art points a way through for life, finds a way through the cracks' (N: 143). The projection screen, consumed by giant red numbers tallying the deceased, flickers by moment as the fatal figure increases. *Chats Perchés* erratically jump cuts amongst the moments marking the deaths as it jerkily films members of the crowd, its takes edited in languid, reverent motion and its shots taken from distances further and yet further away.

The film cuts suddenly to a series of close shots capturing the demonstrators' faces and their multiple bodies sprawled across the ground so that their limbs appear intertwined and entirely en masse. Sanguinely evocative of life, blood, *Hiroshima mon amour*'s own plaintive beauty and the 'depths and ashes' of all films this book has encountered, the superimposed images flow, increasingly slowly upon one another. Silence, and then *Hiroshima mon amour*'s haunting refrain. The images, stilled and somewhat blurred, appear otherworldly as the young foretellers' bodies occupy a time already past and yet to come upon a ground of enduring wounds and pain. What then is a body and what are its relations to the very real wounds of experience and memory?

'The surface', writes Williams, 'is a real effect between actual causes (depth) and ideal propositions (elevation). It could be imagined as an opaque and unstable surface between a liquid and a gas' (2008a: 80). Redolent of this endlessly mutating surface that lines the depths of our actual sufferings, the affective intensive aura of the protestors' bodies rises, disembodied, imperceptible and invisible. And yet, if we might begin to perceive the imperceptible through such new becomings that grasp at the potential to extend the crack between life's virtual surface and actual depths, and so 'triumph over this hardened and faded present which alone subsists and signifies death' (LS: 160), might we truly embrace a future?

The ways through which we counteract our actual events via transitory *thisnesses*, affects and sensations that exceed fixed states speak to the liberative, excessive presence of a Cat's grin that soars high above a cityscape. Such life-affirming renewal and reinvention that doubles the actualisation with a counter-actualisation 'give[s] to the crack the chance of flying over its own incorporeal surface area, without stopping at the bursting within each body; it is, finally, ... the chance to go farther than we would have believed possible' (LS: 161).

'What is the Cat up to by now? After his triumph in the demos, he

14 *Depths and ashes,* Chats Perchés *(Marker 2004)*

seems just bound to relax, or fly. But his reputation keeps growing. He is sighted everywhere' (CP). The Cats are everywhere, omnipresent yet transient signs of the immanent potential within us to move beyond the depths of our present wounds. And yet, 'in his essence', writes Deleuze, 'the [Cheshire] cat is he who withdraws and diverts himself' (LS: 235). 'In short, it is a question of choosing between depth and height' (LS: 235), between the pain and resentment of *what happens to us*, or its embrace and love via a splendid affirmation *inside* what occurs, *Amor fati.* 'The event is not what occurs ... it is rather inside what occurs, the purely expressed' (LS: 149). The 'something *in* that which occurs, something yet to come', is the power to become worthy of what happens to us, to will and release the event and thereby be reborn (LS: 149).

The flowing, superimposed images of bodies lose colour and become black and white as the film distances itself a final time from their formations via a long shot. This overwhelmingly beautiful and haunting encounter of death with life bodily, tangibly, emotively incarnates Deleuze's most profound expressions of life for 'this is the point at which death turns against death' (LS: 153), the point where the 'splendour and the magnificence of the event is sense' (LS: 149), a virtual surface of sense[5] through which we encounter the brightness that doubles misfortune present in all events.

Yet, once again, how are we to embody this brilliance of misfortune; how might we embrace this virtual, immaterial, imperceptible surface at which we might counter our wounds already past and yet to come? We should look to the Cats. Our fatal compromises are, as Deleuze reflects, an endless threat; 'how any group will turn out, how it will fall back into history, presents a constant "concern"' (N: 173). Fearful of the Cats' disappearance, *Chats Perchés* retorts, 'And you wonder why the Cats abandon us?' Alas no, there 'comes a sign. The same unknown hand has painted circles of Cats on the sidewalk, to watch over our sleep' (CP).

Indeed, we must search for the signs, and so recall Deleuze and Guattari's assertion: 'Signs are not signs of a thing; they are signs of deterritorialization and reterritorialization, they mark a certain threshold crossed in the course of these movements, and it is for this reason that the word should be retained (as we have seen, this applies even to animal "signs")' (ATP: 67–8). At the threshold of the crack, that surface between the depths of our scars and their *'vital conquest'*, we must keep looking for the Cats.

Notes

1. 'Other than simply illustration of the object', Francis Bacon asks, 'Isn't it that one wants a thing to be as factual as possible and at the same time as deeply suggestive or ... unlocking of areas of sensation'? (Sylvester 1993: 56). See also Hammer and Calvocoressi 2005: 25.
2. See also Keith Ansell Pearson 2002: 168–70.
3. See Deleuze and Guattari's description: 'When the face becomes a haecceity' (ATP: 262).
4. Marker further confesses: 'A new toy allowed me to try it: the Casio wrist camera. You ostensibly check the time, and the person in front of you is caught. That small apparatus immediately triggered the title I would give to the experiment: *What time is she?* (I've got an unfashionable tendency to prefer women in my lens)' (Marker 2008: 30).
5. Williams' thoughts upon 'free creation alongside the fact' are particularly poignant and useful (see Williams 2008a, Chapter 4, 'Morals and events').

Conclusion

Inasmuch as the works of Marker, Resnais and Deleuze repeatedly encounter certain limits of film, thought and self as they revisit wounds and replay events of a recent past, this study has confronted limits of its own. Moved by tracking shots that persist along barbed-wire camp enclosures, and along the streets and river banks of Hiroshima-Nevers; captivated by 'freeze' frames of staring women on the islands of Cape Verde, and by glances within the under-grounds of the Métro; haunted by images of a pre-war Paris, and those of a post-annihilated Paris; and entranced by a heartbeat that resounds through the madness, haecceities or love between one body, face, city, time and another, these pages have embraced an experiential method to think beyond impasses of mimetic representation and authoritative history. Nevertheless, even a focus upon the material and tangible, ever in relation to transient yet lingering sensations of suffering and loss, cannot discharge the power and force of the films.

This book has attempted, however, to assess and evoke Marker, Resnais and Deleuze's own interrogative methods that thoroughly explore, in the manner of a revelatory 'schizoanalysis' or empiricism, molecular and variable operations beneath our 'molar' structures and organisations. As their respective schizoanalyses consider what exists *between* relations, their works in effect undercut the 'great molar organization that sustains us', 'the binary machines that give us a well-defined status', the 'values, morals, fatherlands, religions and private certitudes [of] our vanity and self-complacency' (ATP: 227). Brian Massumi notes that 'nomad thought goes by many names': 'Spinoza called it "ethics". Nietzsche called it the "gay science". Artaud called it "crowned anarchy". To Maurice Blanchot, it is the "space of literature". To Foucault, "outside thought"' (Massumi 1987: xiii). Does this book then, in its turn, offer a schizo-analysis of life through its materialist cine-philosophical examinations? As it reveals forces, effects and affects of a world mentality stubbornly entrenched in fatal systems of servitude and control that will provide an appointed people's salvation, or so religions and nations proclaim and maintain through genocidal, suicidal means, this book indeed attempts to posit an always-new resistance through art, cinema and thought.

But again, how to negotiate and effect the new, to release *affect* through this undertaking? These pages have thus turned to the flashes, piercings, punctuations and most touching reverberations of our selected films to glimpse, sense and think through how the films affect and are affected by life and time in its banality, joyousness or wretchedness. Relations between spectator, character, screen and world have been re-opened by these pages but in fundamental relation to an interconnected whole or world of relations wherein all 'images', memories, sensations, things and bodies are equally real, though not unified. Again, all forever newly repeats within this one being or life of *difference*. As these pages have then primarily focused upon collisions of self and screen with the inexpressible, imperceptible, unthinkable and invisible that yet can only be perceived, thought and seen, the preceding chapters have confronted and challenged dichotomies of external and internal. For, as this book has explored a self, screen and world's enfolding through a process that produces one within the other, which externalises a self's becoming-other as it at once internalises the subject as the self is enfolded into a larger fold, this book has confronted various conceptualisations and re-workings of a *limit*.

In a footnote to her synopsis of *Hiroshima mon amour*, Duras writes: 'Note: Certain spectators of the film thought she "ended up" by staying at Hiroshima. It's possible. I have no opinion. *Having taken her to the limit of her refusal to stay at Hiroshima*, we haven't been concerned to know whether – once the film was finished – she succeeded in reversing her refusal' (1961: 13; italics mine). 'At the limit', writes Deleuze,

> the imaginary is a virtual image that is interfused with the real object, and vice versa, thereby constituting a crystal of the unconscious ... It [the real object] must disengage *its own* virtual image at the same time that the latter ... makes its entry into the real, following a circuit where each of the two terms pursues the other, is interchanged with the other. 'Vision' is the product of this doubling or splitting in two, this coalescence. (ECC: 63)

As this book has accessed and assessed passages between actual and virtual, the 'inevitable passage from the physical to ideal, and from the ideal to the physical' (Williams 2008a: 182), it has variously confronted dimensions of depth and height through an event's inscription in the flesh and body. The 'identity of world and brain', to repeat Deleuze, form 'a limit, a membrane which puts an outside and an inside in contact, makes them present to each other, confronts them or makes them clash . . . The two forces of death which embrace, are ultimately exchanged and become ultimately indiscernible' (C2: 206).

The limit is then that which Marker and Resnais' cinemas approach as they push towards the very limits of the medium's potential to expose the intolerable in thought and invisible in sight. The violence, once more, corresponds to relations between the times of Chronos and Aion, the actualisation of an incorporeal crack in the depths of a body and the two aspects of personal and impersonal death that Deleuze's philosophy and Marker and Resnais' films repeatedly express. But 'above all', Deleuze insists, 'it's not a question of speaking for the unhappy, of speaking in the name of victims, of the tortured and the oppressed, but of producing a living line' (D: 28), a 'line of becoming' that 'has neither beginning nor end, departure nor arrival, origin nor destination' (ATP: 293).

As Marker, Resnais and Deleuze's works encounter that membrane between inside and outside through the foldings and doublings of self, time and memory that engender subjectivities beyond the human, the expression of such minor, variable relations effect movement within static forms of dominance and suppression. Marker and Resnais' commitments, ever attuned to each other, discover various means of resistance to systems of domination that define modern existence. By scrutinising these orders and constants that command and stratify life, by grasping the universal in the personal and the personal in the universal through performative embodiments of Deleuze's perceptions, their cinemas expose the impersonal and pre-individual singularities that give rise to actualisations and tendencies that may either empower or destroy life.

If 'all life', as Deleuze reflects by way of F. Scott Fitzgerald, 'is a process of breaking down' (LS: 154), then Deleuze's own philosophical process is, again, one of 'conceptual stuttering' (Bogue 2004: 22). This is a matter or style of incessantly 'cracking open the opinions and reaching regions without memories, when the self must be destroyed', while pushing towards a limit that might make language 'so *strained* that it starts to stutter, or to murmur or stammer' as it '*reaches the limit* that marks its outside and makes it confront silence' (ECC: 113). As Deleuze's writings strive towards this limit, crack or break, concepts continually reappear anew. Bogue elaborates:

Concepts Deleuze develops in one book reappear in another, enter into new combinations, then dissolve and form further alliances and interconnections in a third. In each work, the concepts undergo a slight metamorphosis, as if each repetition of a concept were a mere approximation, an effort once again to give it a name, but also a discovery of something new in the concept that only emerges with its restatement in a different context . . . What we meet are themes in constant variation, or variations without themes, a ruminative, meditative differential repetition, halting, stammering, stuttering from work to work . . . [the] clearest instances of stuttering in Deleuze appear in those aerial passages when he strains to describe the ineffable. (Bogue 2004: 22–3)

Clearly, as the process demands a shattering of certainty and self, this book itself repeatedly falters alongside the films and texts it reads as it strives to think and express endlessly mutating, living sensations from chapter to chapter. But while it moves towards expressing an immanent temporal awareness through overwhelming experiences of the human and self, as it reasserts art's resistance to 'death, slavery, infamy, shame' (N: 174), it at once reiterates that the dialogue pertaining to affect, sensation and violence in relation to a transcendental philosophy of the event must persist. 'How is a people created, through what terrible suffering?' 'When a people's created, it's through its own resources, but in a way that links up with something in art . . . or links up art to what it lacked' (N: 174). With regard to film studies and the increasingly popular domain of film-philosophy, it is necessary to continue to think through the events of our lives in relation to the events of art, film and philosophy. Once more, this is to encounter sense and duration through a violence and rupture, or event, which opens to virtual potentials and new ways of thinking. In this sense, as Williams suggests, 'there can be no limited and clearly defined actual thing whose existence does not presuppose a set of past and future catastrophic changes' (1997: 235).

To become-other through love, death, joy and sadness is to connect endlessly, to produce infinite series of relations and creations that give rise to a 'people' and art. To repeat: 'How any group will turn out, how it will fall back into history, presents a constant "concern"' (N: 173). If the production of art and philosophy in the face of human shame and 'vulgarization' is then what makes 'all philosophy' and some art 'political' (N: 172), it remains film-philosophy's task to continuously encounter, perceive and effect new relations between bodies of works and images. Film-philosophy must pursue its sensitive interrogations of affect and the means by which films effect intensity and imply meaning. If a work of art lives only through its encounters, and life only through art, film-philosophy must continue to connect not only to actual things and beings but also to their virtual sensations and intensities. Life, art and the infinite process of thinking the two through each other demands, in other words, a perception of the actual and virtual conditions and molar and molecular entities and vibrations that engender our sufferings and joys.

'Movement always happens behind the thinker's back, or in the moment when he blinks', Deleuze states. 'The aim is not to answer questions' (D: 1) but to invent problems, 'new forces or new weapons' (D: 5), to perceive becomings and coexistent multiplicities that do not convey definitive messages or meanings but that construct new affective assemblages and open-ended relations between all actual-virtual images and things. Deleuze's description of his experience of working with Guattari suggests ways through which Marker and Resnais' own collaborations may be thought:

> We were only two, but what was important for us was less our working together than this strange fact of working between the two of us. We stopped being 'author'. And these 'between-the-twos' referred back to other people ... The desert expanded, but in so doing became more populous. (D: 17)

In between the encounters of Marker and Resnais, Deleuze and Guattari, and all cine-philosophical encounters to come, are new problems, new disruptions, responses and movements that demand not solutions but new concepts, stutterings and affects that will continually discover ever-new unfoldings, expressions and styles of thought.

With regard to this process of learning through affects, signs and problems, Williams proposes that to 'learn is to learn how to be sensitive to and respond creatively to signs and problems, as things that necessarily go beyond what is known or what can be done in a given situation. This sensitivity and creativity are linked – no sensitivity without creation' (Williams 2003: 135–6). If the practices of film and film-philosophy are to push towards and beyond their limits, they must then move beyond memory and recognition towards new connections, productive forgettings and expressions of difference beyond the limits of any 'knowledge'. This process of thinking the works of Marker and Resnais through each other has thus revealed multiple 'lines of becomings', cracks, ruptures, stutterings and creative repetitions that will persist through many pages to come.

'Affects aren't feelings', Deleuze insists, 'they're becomings that spill over beyond whoever lives through them (thereby becoming someone else)' (N: 137). Perhaps this futurity, *difference*, becoming or 'living through' is, again, the audible, perceptible heartbeat of Marker and Resnais' cinemas, and the love which Duras describes: 'Love serves life by making dying easier' (Duras 1961: 92). If then, above all, it is not a question of speaking in the name of victims, or of addressing a people, it is a matter of a 'double becoming' of filmmaker, character and even viewer, of affect, affirmation, and a love that might reveal 'life beneath the ashes' (C2: 222; 256).

References

Works by Chris Marker

Marker, Chris (dir.) and Alain Resnais. 1953. *Les Statues meurent aussi*, Chris Marker (conception and text), Jean Negroni (voice), Alain Resnais (editing), Ghislain Cloquet (photography), Guy Bernard (music), Studios Marignan (sound). Présence Africaine/Tadié-Cinéma.
— 1962. *La Jetée*, Jean Ravel (editing), Trevor Duncan; Choirs of the Russian Cathedral in Paris (music), Mix Antoine Bonfanti (sound). Argos Films. [The Criterion Collection (DVD) with *Sans Soleil*, 2007.]
— 1977. *Le Fond de l'air est rouge* (*A Grin without a Cat*), Chris Marker (sound and montage). ISKRA.
— 1983. *Sans Soleil*, Chris Marker (conception and editing), Sandor Krasna/Chris Marker (camera). Argos Films. [The Criterion Collection (DVD) with *La Jetée*, 2007.]
— and Yannick Bellon. 2001. *Le Souvenir d'un Avenir*, Denise Bellon (photographs), Alexandra Stewart (voice). Les Films de l'Équinoxe (France)/ARTE France. [Icarus Films (DVD), 2001.]
— 2004. *Chats Perchés*, Chris Marker (video), Michel Krasna (soundtrack). Arte France/Les Films du Jeudi. [ARTE Vidéo (DVD), 2004.]
— 2007. *Staring Back*, an accompanying publication to the exhibition, *Staring Back*. Columbus: Wexner Center for the Arts, The Ohio State University.
— 2008. *A Farewell to Movies/Abschied vom Kino*. Zürich: Museum für Gestaltung Zürich.

Works by Alain Resnais

Resnais, Alain (dir.). 1955. *Nuit et Brouillard*, Jean Cayrol (text), Hanns Eisler (music). Argos Films/Como Films/Cocinor. [The Criterion Collection (DVD), 2003.]
Resnais, Alain (dir.) with 'Chris and Magic Marker' et al. 1956. *Toute la mémoire du monde*, Remi Forlano (text), Alain Resnais, Anne Sarraute, Claudine Merlin (editing), Ghislain Cloquet, assisted by Pierre Goupil (photography), Maurice Jarre, directed by Georges Delerue (music). Les Films de la Pléiade. [StudioCanal Image-Argos Films-Cineriz (Rome)/Optimum Releasing Ltd. (DVD), 2005.]

References

1959. *Hiroshima mon amour*, Marguerite Duras (text), Georges Delerue and Giovanni Fusco (music). Argos Films/Como Films (Paris)/Daiei (Tokyo)/Pathe Overseas. [The Criterion Collection (DVD), 2003.]

Works by Gilles Deleuze

Deleuze, Gilles. 1971. 'Cours Vincennes – 14/12/1971: The Nature of Flows', *Les Cours de Gilles Deleuze*, Karen Isabel Ocana (trans.), <http://www.webdeleuze.com/php/texte.php?cle=119&groupe=Anti%20Oedipe%20et%20Mille%20Plateaux&langue=2> (accessed 19 June 2007).

1978a. 'Cours Vincennes – 24/01/1978: Transcripts on Spinoza's Concept of Affect', *Les Cours de Gilles Deleuze*, Timothy S. Murphy (trans.), <http://www.webdeleuze.com/php/texte.php?cle=14&groupe=Spinoza&langue=2> (accessed 1 August 2007).

1978b. 'Cours Vincennes – 14/03/1978: Deleuze/Kant, Synthesis and Time', *Les Cours de Gilles Deleuze*, Melissa McMahon (trans.), <http://www.webdeleuze.com/php/texte.php?cle=66&groupe=Kant&langue=2> (accessed 15 January 2008).

1983. *Nietzsche and Philosophy*, Hugh Tomlinson (trans.). New York: Columbia University Press. [*Nietzsche et la philosophie* (Paris: Presses universitaires de France, 1962).]

and Félix Guattari. 1983. *Anti-Oedipus: Capitalism and Schizophrenia*, Robert Hurley, Mark Seem and Helen R. Lane (trans.). Minneapolis: University of Minnesota Press. [*L'Anti-Oedipe: Capitalisme et schizophrénie I* (Paris: Minuit, 1972).]

and Félix Guattari. 1986. *Kafka: Toward a Minor Literature*, Dana Polan (trans). Minneapolis: University of Minnesota Press. [*Kafka: Pour une littérature mineure* (Paris: Minuit, 1975).]

and Félix Guattari. 1987. *A Thousand Plateaus: Capitalism and Schizophrenia II*, Brian Massumi (trans.). Minneapolis: University of Minnesota Press. [*Mille plateaux: Capitalisme et schizophrénie II* (Paris: Minuit, 1980).]

1988a. *Bergsonism*, Hugh Tomlinson and Barbara Habberjam (trans.). New York: Zone Books. [*Le Bergsonisme* (Paris: Presses universitaires de France, 1966).]

1988b. *Spinoza: Practical Philosophy*, Robert Hurley (trans.). San Francisco: City Light Books. [*Spinoza: Philosophie pratique* (Paris: Presses universitaires de France, 1970).]

1989. *Cinema 2: The Time-Image*, Hugh Tomlinson and Robert Galeta (trans.). Minneapolis: The University of Minnesota Press. [*Cinéma 2, L'image-temps* (Paris: Minuit, 1985).]

1990a. *Expressionism in Philosophy: Spinoza*, Martin Joughin (trans.). New York: Zone Books. [*Spinoza et le problème de l'expression* (Paris: Minuit, 1968).]

1990b. *The Logic of Sense*, Mark Lester with Charles Stivale (trans.), Constantin V. Boundas (ed.). New York: Columbia University Press. [*Logique du sens* (Paris: Minuit, 1969).]

1993. *The Fold: Leibniz and the Baroque*, Tom Conley (trans.). Minneapolis: University of Minnesota Press. [*Le Pli. Leibniz et le baroque* (Paris: Minuit, 1988).]

1994. *Difference and Repetition*, Paul Patton (trans.). New York: Columbia University Press. [*Différence et répétition* (Paris: Presses universitaires de France, 1968).]

and Félix Guattari. 1994. *What is Philosophy?*, Hugh Tomlinson and Graham Burchell (trans.). New York: Columbia University Press. [*Qu'est-ce que la philosophie?* (Paris: Minuit, 1991).]

1995. *Negotiations, 1972–1990*, Martin Joughin (trans.). New York: Columbia University Press. [*Pourparlers 1972–1990* (Paris: Minuit, 1990).]

and Claire Parnet. 1996. *L'Abécédaire de Gilles Deleuze, avec Claire Parnet*, Pierre-André Boutang (dir.). Video Editions Montparnasse. Summary, <http://www.langlab.wayne.edu/CStivale/D-G/ABC1.html> (accessed 1 November 2005).

1997. *Essays Critical and Clinical*, Daniel W. Smith and Michael A. Greco (trans.). Minneapolis: University of Minnesota Press. [*Critique et clinique* (Paris: Minuit, 1993).]

1998a. 'Boulez, Proust and Time: "Occupying without Counting"', in *Angelaki: Journal of the Theoretical Humanities*, Timothy S. Murphy (trans.), 3(2): 69–74.

1998b. 'Having an Idea in Cinema (On the Cinema of Straub-Huillet)', in *Deleuze and Guattari: New Mappings in Politics and Philosophy*, Eleanor Kaufman (trans.), Eleanor Kaufman and Kevin Jon Heller (eds), 14–19. Minneapolis: University of Minnesota Press.

2000. *Proust and Signs*, Richard Howard (trans.). Minneapolis: University of Minnesota Press. [*Proust et les signes* (Paris: Presses universitaires de France, 1964).]

2001. *Pure Immanence: Essays on a Life*, Anne Boyman (trans.). New York: Zone Books.

2002. 'The actual and the virtual', in *Dialogues II*, Eliot Ross Albert (trans.), 148–52. New York: Columbia University Press.

and Claire Parnet. 2002. *Dialogues II*, Hugh Tomlinson and Barbara Habberjam (trans.). New York: Columbia University Press. [*Dialogues* (Paris: Flammarion, 1977).]

2003. *Francis Bacon: The Logic of Sensation*, Daniel W. Smith (trans.). Minneapolis: University of Minnesota Press. [*Francis Bacon: Logique de la sensation* (Paris: Editions de la difference, 1981).]

2004. *Desert Islands and Other Texts, 1953–1974*, Michael Taormina (trans.), David Lapoujade (ed.). New York: Semiotext(e). [*L'Ile déserte et autres textes* (Paris: Minuit, 2002).]

2006. *Two Regimes of Madness: Texts and Interviews, 1975–1995*, Ames Hodges and Michael Taormina (trans.), David Lapoujade (ed.). New York: Semiotext(e). [*Deux régimes de fous: textes et entretiens, 1975–1995* (Paris: Minuit, 2003).]

Other Works

Agamben, Giorgio. 1999. *Remnants of Auschwitz: The Witness and the Archive*, Daniel Heller-Roazen (trans.). New York: Zone Books.

Alter, Nora M. 2006. *Chris Marker*. Urbana and Chicago: University of Illinois Press.

Andrew, Dudley. 1997. 'André Bazin's "Evolution"', in *Defining Cinema*, Peter Lehman (ed.), 73–96. New Brunswick: Rutgers University Press.

Ansell Pearson, Keith. 2002. *Philosophy and the Adventure of the Virtual: Bergson and the time of life*. London: Routledge.

Barthes, Roland. 1977. 'The Photographic Message', in *Image, Music, Text*, Stephen Heath (trans.), 15–31. New York: Hill and Wang.

1981. *Camera Lucida: Reflections of Photography*, Richard Howard (trans.). New York: Hill and Wang.

Bazin, André. 1983. 'Chris Marker, *Lettre de Sibérie*', in *Le Cinéma français de la Libération à la Nouvelle Vague (1945–1958)*, 179–81. Paris: Cahiers du Cinéma.

Bergson, Henri. 1991. *Matter and Memory*, N. M. Paul and W. S. Palmer (trans.). New York: Zone Books.

Blanchot, Maurice. 1982. *The Space of Literature*, Ann Smock (trans.). Lincoln: University of Nebraska Press.

Bogue, Ronald. 1994. 'Foucault, Deleuze, and the Playful Fold of the Self', in *The Play of the Self*, Ronald Bogue and Mihai I. Spariosu (eds), 3–21. Albany: State University of New York Press.

1996. 'Gilles Deleuze: The Aesthetics of Force', in *Deleuze: A Critical Reader*, Paul Patton (ed.), 257–69. Oxford: Blackwell Publishers.

2003a. *Deleuze on Cinema*. New York: Routledge.

2003b. *Deleuze on Music, Painting, and the Arts*. New York: Routledge.

2004. *Deleuze's Wake: Tributes and Tributaries*. Albany: State University of New York Press.

2007. *Deleuze's Way: Essays in Transverse Ethics and Aesthetics*. Aldershot: Ashgate Publishing Limited.

Boundas, Constantin V. 1996. 'Transgressive Theorizing: A Report to Deleuze', *Man and World*, 29: 327–41.

Braidotti, Rosi. 2006. 'The Ethics of Becoming-Imperceptible', in *Deleuze and Philosophy*, Constantin V. Boundas (ed.), 133–59. Edinburgh: Edinburgh University Press.

Buchanan, Ian. 2000. *Deleuzism: A Metacommentary*. Durham: Duke University Press.

Cantor, Jay. 1996. 'Death and the Image', in *Beyond Document: Essays on Nonfiction Film*, Charles Warren (ed.), 23–49. Middletown: Wesleyan University Press.

Caruth, Cathy. 1995. *Trauma: Explorations in Memory*. Baltimore: The Johns Hopkins University Press.

    1996. *Unclaimed Experience: Trauma, Narrative, and History*. Baltimore: The Johns Hopkins University Press.

Conley, Tom. 1993. 'Translator's Foreword: A Plea for Leibniz', in *The Fold: Leibniz and the Baroque* by Gilles Deleuze, Tom Conley (trans.), ix–xx. Minneapolis: University of Minnesota Press.

    2005. 'The Desert Island', in *Deleuze and Space*, Ian Buchanan and Gregg Lambert (eds), 207–19. Edinburgh: Edinburgh University Press.

Cooper, Sarah. 2008. *Chris Marker*. Manchester: Manchester University Press.

Derrida, Jacques and Christie V. McDonald. 1982. 'Choreographies', *Diacritics*, 12(2): 66–76.

Duras, Marguerite. 1961. *Hiroshima mon amour*, Richard Seaver (trans.). New York: Grove Press, Inc.

Evenson, Brian. 1994. 'Brian Evenson Reviews Gilles Deleuze, "L'Épuisé"', *Journal of Beckett Studies*, Special Issue: 'Beckett in France', Thomas Cousineau (guest ed.), 4(1): 169–78, <http://mail.architexturez.net/+/Deleuze-Guattari-L/archive/msg20937.shtml> (accessed 22 October 2009).

Ferlinghetti, Lawrence. 2001. *San Francisco Poems*. San Francisco: City Lights Foundation.

Frichot, Hélène. 2005. 'Stealing into Gilles Deleuze's Baroque House', in *Deleuze and Space*, Ian Buchanan and Gregg Lambert (eds), 61–79. Edinburgh: Edinburgh University Press.

Fynsk, Christopher. 1991. 'Foreword', in *The Inoperative Community* by Jean Luc Nancy, Peter Connor (ed.), Peter Connor, Lisa Garbus, Michael Holland and Simona Sawhney (trans.), vii–xxxv. Minneapolis: University of Minnesota Press.

Hammer, Martin and Richard Calvocoressi. 2005. *Francis Bacon: Portraits and Heads*. Edinburgh: National Galleries of Scotland.

Holland, Eugene W. 1999. *Deleuze and Guattari's* Anti-Oedipus: *Introduction to Schizoanalysis*. London: Routledge.

    2005. 'Desire', in *Gilles Deleuze: Key Concepts*, Charles J. Stivale (ed.), 53–62. Chesham: Acumen Publishing Limited.

Houle, Karen and Paul Steenhuisen. 2006. 'Close (Vision) is (How We) Here', *Angelaki: Journal of the Theoretical Humanities*, Special Issue: 'Creative Philosophy: Theory and Praxis', Felicity Colman and Charles J. Stivale (eds), 11(1): 15–24.

Kear, Jon. 1999. *Sunless/Sans soleil*. Trowbridge: Flicks.

Laing, R.D. 1967. *The Politics of Experience*. New York: Ballantine.

Lambert, Gregg. 2002. *The Non-Philosophy of Gilles Deleuze*. New York: Continuum.

Lanzmann, Claude. 1985. *Shoah, An Oral History of the Holocaust: The Complete Text of the Film*. New York: Pantheon Books.

Levi, Primo. 1986. *Survival in Auschwitz and the Reawakening: Two Memoirs*, Stuart Wolf (trans.). New York: Summit.

Lupton, Catherine. 2005. *Chris Marker: Memories of the Future*. London: Reaktion Books.

MacCormack, Patricia. 2000. 'Faciality: Stamping in Anti-Corporeality', conference paper, 4th European Feminist Research Conference in Bologna on 'Body, Gender, Subjectivity: Crossing Disciplinary and Institutional Borders', <http://orlando.women.it/cyberarchive/files/mac-cormack.htm> (accessed 17 November 2008).

McMahon, Melissa. 2002. 'Beauty: Machinic Repetition in the Age of Art', in *A Shock to Thought: Expression After Deleuze and Guattari*, Brian Massumi (ed.), 3–8. London: Routledge.

Massumi, Brian. 1987. 'Translator's Foreword: Pleasures of Philosophy', in *A Thousand Plateaus: Capitalism and Schizophrenia II* by Gilles Deleuze and Félix Guattari, Brian Massumi (trans.), ix–xv. Minneapolis: University of Minnesota Press.

1996. 'The Autonomy of Affect', in *Deleuze: A Critical Reader*, Paul Patton (ed.), 217–39. Oxford: Blackwell Publishers Ltd.

2002a. 'Introduction: Like a Thought', in *A Shock to Thought: Expression After Deleuze and Guattari*, Brian Massumi (ed.), xiii–xxxix. London: Routledge.

2002b. *Parables for the Virtual: Movement, Affect, Sensation*. Durham: Duke University Press.

May, Todd. 2005. *Gilles Deleuze: An Introduction*. Cambridge: Cambridge University Press.

Nietzsche, Friedrich. 1997. *Untimely Meditations*, R. J. Hollingdale (trans.), Daniel Breazeale (ed.). Cambridge: Cambridge University Press.

Norden, N. Lindsay. 1919. 'A Brief Study of the Russian Liturgy and its Music', *The Musical Quarterly*, 5(3): 426–50.

Olkowski, Dorothea. 1994. 'Nietzsche's Dice Throw: Tragedy, Nihilism, and the Body Without Organs', in *Deleuze and the Theatre of Philosophy*, Constantin V. Boundas and Dorothea Olkowski (eds), 119–40. New York: Routledge.

Parr, Adrian. 2008. *Deleuze and Memorial Culture*. Edinburgh: Edinburgh University Press.

Rancière, Jacques. 2004. *The Politics of Aesthetics*, Gabriel Rockhill (trans.). London: Continuum.

Raskin, Richard. 1987. Nuit et Brouillard *by Alain Resnais: On the*

Making, Reception and Functions of a Major Documentary Film. Aarhus: Aarhus University Press.

Rhodes, Richard. 1986. *The Making of the Atomic Bomb.* London: Penguin Books Ltd.

Rodowick, D. N. 1997. *Gilles Deleuze's Time Machine.* Durham: Duke University Press.

Shaviro, Steven. 2002. 'Beauty Lies in the Eye', in *A Shock to Thought: Expression After Deleuze and Guattari,* Brian Massumi (ed.), 9–19. London: Routledge.

Silverman, Max. 2006. 'Horror and the Everyday in Post-Holocaust France: *Nuit et Brouillard* and Concentrationary Art', *French Cultural Studies,* 17(1): 5–18.

Smith, Daniel W. 1996. 'Deleuze's Theory of Sensation: Overcoming the Kantian Duality', in *Deleuze: A Critical Reader,* Paul Patton (ed.), 29–56. Oxford: Blackwell Publishers Ltd.

    1997. 'Introduction: "A Life of Pure Immanence": Deleuze's "Critique et Clinique" Project', in *Essays Critical and Clinical* by Gilles Deleuze, Daniel W. Smith and Michael A. Greco (trans.), xi–liii. Minneapolis: University of Minnesota Press.

    2003. 'Translator's Introduction: Deleuze on Bacon: Three Conceptual Trajectories in *The Logic of Sensation*', in *Francis Bacon: The Logic of Sensation* by Gilles Deleuze, Daniel W. Smith (trans.), vii–xxvii. Minneapolis: University of Minnesota Press.

    2006. 'Deleuze, Kant, and the Theory of Immanent Ideas', in *Deleuze and Philosophy,* Constantin V. Boundas (ed.), 43–61. Edinburgh: Edinburgh University Press.

    2007. 'Deleuze and the Question of Desire: Toward an Immanent Theory of Ethics', *Parrhesia,* 2: 66–78.

    and John Protevi. 2008. 'Gilles Deleuze', in Stanford Encyclopedia of Philosophy, <http://plato.stanford.edu/entries/deleuze/> (accessed 1 June 2008).

Stivale, Charles J. 1998. *The Two-Fold Thought of Gilles Deleuze and Felix Guattari: Intersections and Animations.* New York: The Guilford Press.

Sylvester, David. 1993. *The Brutality of Fact: Interviews with Francis Bacon, 1962–1979.* New York: Thames & Hudson Ltd.

Virilio, Paul. 1989. *War and Cinema: The Logistics of Perception,* Patrick Camiller (trans.). London: Verso.

Walker, James. 1981. 'Mussorgsky's *Sunless* Cycle in Russian Criticism: Focus of Controversy', *The Musical Quarterly,* 67(3): 382–91. Oxford University Press.

Williams, James. 1997. 'Deleuze on J. M. W. Turner', in *Deleuze and Philosophy: The Difference Engineer,* Keith Ansell Pearson (ed.), 233–46. London: Routledge.

References

2003. *Gilles Deleuze's* Difference and Repetition. Edinburgh: Edinburgh University Press.

2005. *The Transversal Thought of Gilles Deleuze: Encounters and Influences*. Manchester: Clinamen Press.

2008a. *Gilles Deleuze's* Logic of Sense. Edinburgh: Edinburgh University Press.

2008b. 'Why Deleuze Doesn't Blow the Actual on Virtual Priority. A Rejoinder to Jack Reynolds', *Deleuze Studies*, 2(1): 97–100.

Wilson, Emma. 2005. 'Material Remains: *Night and Fog*', *October*, 112: 89–110.

2006. *Alain Resnais*. Manchester: Manchester University Press.

Zourabichvili, François. 1996. 'Six Notes on the Percept (On the Relation Between the Critical and Clinical)', Iain Hamilton Grant (trans.), in *Deleuze: A Critical Reader*, Paul Patton (ed.), 188–216. Oxford: Blackwell Publishers Ltd.

Index